CONTENTS

CHAPTER ONE   The Parts of Speech   1
Lesson   1   The Noun   1
         2   The Pronoun   3
         3   The Adjective   5
         4   Review of Nouns, Pronouns, and Adjectives   7
         5   The Verb   9
         6   The Helping Verb   11
         7   The Adverb   13
         8   Adverbs Modify Adjectives and Other Adverbs   15
         9   The Preposition   17
        10   The Conjunction and the Interjection   19
        11   Chapter Review   21
        12   Usage: *Bring* and *Take, Good* and *Well*   23
        13   Spelling: The Unstressed Vowel Sound Called the "Schwa"   25
        14   Building Vocabulary: Choosing the Right Meaning   27

CHAPTER TWO   The Sentence Base: Verb and Subject   29
Lesson 15   Subject and Predicate   29
        16   The Verb   31
        17   The Simple Subject   33
        18   Finding the Subject   35
        19   Practice in Finding the Verb and Its Subject   37
        20   A Sentence Has a Verb and a Subject   39
        21   Sentence Completeness   41
        22   Chapter Review   43
        23   Cumulative Review   44
        24   Spelling: "Bringing Out" the Schwa Sound   45
        25   Building Vocabulary: Words to Learn   47

CHAPTER THREE   The Sentence Base: Complements   49
Lesson 26   The Subject Complement   49
        27   The Direct Object   51
        28   The Indirect Object   53
        29   Chapter Review   55
        30   Cumulative Review   57
        31   Spelling: Does It End in *-ar, -er,* or *-or*?   59
        32   Building Vocabulary: Choosing the Right Word   61

CHAPTER FOUR   Phrases and Clauses   63
Lesson 33   The Phrase   63
        34   The Adjective Phrase   65
        35   The Adverb Phrase   67
        36   The Clause   69
        37   The Adjective Clause   71

	38	The Adverb Clause	73
	39	The Noun Clause	75
	40	Chapter Review	77
	41	Cumulative Review	79
	42	Spelling: Three Ways of Spelling /-əl/	81
	43	Building Vocabulary: Words to Learn	83

CHAPTER FIVE Completeness in the Sentence — 85

Lesson	44	Phrase Fragments	85
	45	Subordinate Clause Fragments	87
	46	Correcting Fragments	89
	47	More Practice in Correcting Fragments	91
	48	Using End Marks	93
	49	Correcting the Run-on Sentence	95
	50	Chapter Review	97
	51	Cumulative Review	99
	52	Spelling: Using -ent and -ence	101
	53	Building Vocabulary: Analysing Words	103

CHAPTER SIX Capital Letters — 105

Lesson	54	Capitals for Geographical Names	105
	55	Capitals for Special Groups and Events	107
	56	Capitals for Titles	109
	57	Practice with Capital Letters	111
	58	Chapter Review	113
	59	Cumulative Review	115
	60	Spelling: Using -ant and -ance	117
	61	Building Vocabulary: Words to Learn	119

CHAPTER SEVEN Punctuation — 121

Lesson	62	The Comma: In Series	121
	63	The Comma: Appositives	123
	64	The Comma: Direct Address; Introductory Words	125
	65	The Comma: Parenthetical Expressions; Dates and Addresses	127
	66	The Comma: Compound Sentences	129
	67	The Comma: Introductory Phrases and Clauses	131
	68	Quotation Marks	133
	69	The Apostrophe to Show Ownership	135
	70	The Apostrophe in Pronouns and Contractions	137
	71	Chapter Review	139
	72	Cumulative Review	141
	73	Usage: Avoiding "Is when," "Being as," and "Had ought"	143
	74	Spelling: The Four Forms of in-	145
	75	Building Vocabulary: How Words Are Defined	147

CHAPTER EIGHT   Making Words Agree   149
Lesson 76   Agreement of Subject and Verb   149
        77   Subjects Followed by a Phrase   151
        78   The Compound Subject   153
        79   Subjects That Follow Verbs; Collective Nouns   155
        80   Reviewing Agreement of Verb and Subject   157
        81   Agreement of Pronoun and Antecedent   159
        82   Chapter Review   161
        83   Cumulative Review   163
        84   Spelling: The Many Forms of *ad-* and *sub-*   165
        85   Building Vocabulary: Words to Learn   167

CHAPTER NINE   Using Verbs Correctly   169
Lesson 86   Regular and Irregular Verbs   169
        87   More Irregular Verbs   171
        88   The Irregular Verbs *Lie* and *Lay*   173
        89   More Practice with *Lie* and *Lay*   175
        90   The Irregular Verbs *Sit* and *Set*   177
        91   The Verbs *Rise* and *Raise*   179
        92   Consistency of Tense   181
        93   Chapter Review   183
        94   Cumulative Review   185
        95   Spelling: How to Spell the /k/ Sound   187
        96   Building Vocabulary: The Total Context   189

CHAPTER TEN   Using Pronouns Correctly   191
Lesson 97   Uses of the Nominative Case: Subject   191
        98   Uses of the Nominative Case: Subject Complement   193
        99   Uses of the Objective Case: Object of the Verb   194
       100   Uses of the Objective Case: Object of a Preposition   195
       101   Pronoun Practice   197
       102   Pronouns After *Than* and *As*   199
       103   Chapter Review   201
       104   Cumulative Review   203
       105   Usage: Unnecessary Words and Letters   205
       106   Spelling: Always Write *u* after *q*   207
       107   Building Vocabulary: Words to Learn   209

CHAPTER ELEVEN   Sentence Combining   211
Lesson 108   Combining Sentences with Adjectives, Adverbs,
             and Prepositional Phrases   211
       109   Combining Sentences Through Co-ordination   213
       110   Combining with Appositive Phrases and Participial Phrases   215
       111   Combining Sentences with Adjective Clauses   217
       112   Combining Sentences with Adverb Clauses   219
       113   Combining Sentences with Noun Clauses   221

114 Review of Sentence Combining   223
115 Review of Sentence Combining, Continued   225

CHAPTER TWELVE Composition   227

Lesson 116 Choosing Effective Nouns and Verbs   227
117 Using Comparisons   231
118 What Is a Paragraph?   235
119 Writing the Paragraph: The Topic Sentence   237
120 Strong Topic Sentences   240
121 Writing the Paragraph: Sticking to the Topic   242
122 Writing the Paragraph: Developing the Topic Sentence   245
123 Arranging Ideas in a Paragraph   251
124 Using Transitional Devices   253
125 Writing a Narrative Paragraph   255
126 Writing a Descriptive Paragraph   257
127 Writing an Expository Paragraph That Gives Information   259
128 Writing an Expository Paragraph That Explains   261
129 Paragraphing and Outlining a Composition   263
130 Letter Writing: The Form of the Friendly Letter   270
131 Letter Writing: The Contents of the Friendly Letter   272
132 Letter Writing: Social Notes   274
133 Letter Writing: The Form of the Business Letter   276
134 Letter Writing: The Contents of the Business Letter   278

Index   279
Index of Vocabulary Words   280
A Note on Spelling   281
Consonant Sounds and Their Common Spellings   282
Vowel Sounds and Their Common Spellings   283

CHAPTER ONE

The Parts of Speech

Although there are over 600 000 words in the English language, you need to learn only eight terms, or *parts of speech,* to classify the ways these words can function in a sentence. The eight parts of speech are *noun, pronoun, adjective, verb, adverb, preposition, conjunction,* and *interjection.*

As you study the parts of speech, try to expand your knowledge and understanding of the work they do. Mastering the terms used in language study will help you to talk intelligently about your language and to express your ideas correctly and effectively.

LESSON 1

The Noun

A noun is a word used to name a person, place, thing, or idea.

EXAMPLES friend, manager, territory, neighbourhood, drama, belief, justice

Nouns like *belief* and *justice* name things which cannot be seen or touched. They name ideas. Similarly, *devotion, wisdom,* and *duty* are nouns; they name something we can talk about, though not see.

A proper noun names a particular person, place, or thing.

EXAMPLES Sarah Boone, Terra Nova National Park, *Great Expectations*

A proper noun begins with a capital letter.

EXERCISE A   Underline each noun, including proper nouns, in this passage. If a noun appears more than once, underline it each time it appears. Words like *we, his, I, they, me, my,* and *them* are not nouns; they merely refer to nouns. (Add 5 points for each correct answer.)

1   During a recent game, as I sat in the stadium and listened to the shouts

2   of the fans, I remembered the words of my teacher who said that it is

3   always easy to be brave at a distance. In the second quarter, the Argos

4   had, luckily, recovered a fumble, but they could not find a hole in the tight

5   defensive line of the Lions. As I watched the struggling teams, I thought,

6   "Am I ever glad I'm out for track instead of football!" But, rising to my

7   feet, I caught the spirit of the crowd and shouted, "Hit 'em hard! Fight,

8   team! Fight!"

EXERCISE B   Underline each noun, including proper nouns, in the following paragraphs. (Add 2 points for each correct answer.)

1   The formation of an island is a remarkable event. This process occurs

2   over millions of years. Erupting volcanoes build mountains on the floor

3   of the sea. Each eruption adds more lava to the pile of volcanic rock,

4   until after many years the volcanic mountain comes within reach of the

5   waves. The potential island may remain as a shoal for ages. When the

6   island finally emerges from under the waves, the cone is pushed up into

7   the air and a rampart of hardened lava is formed, protecting the new

8   island from attacking waves.

9   Plants and animals come to the island, either blown in on the wind or

10 washed in with the current. Some forms of life travel to the land on

11 natural rafts of uprooted trees and matted vegetation. Other forms are

12 carried by the birds that come to the island from other lands. In an

13 experiment Charles Darwin was able to raise eighty-two plants belonging

14 to five different species from the seeds found in a mud ball.

The Pronoun

A <u>pronoun</u> is a word used in place of one or more nouns.

Read the two sentences below. Notice how much better the second sentence sounds than the first. The second sentence contains pronouns.

EXAMPLES   Now that Paul has thoroughly cleaned *Paul's* motorcycle, *Paul* is ready to paint the *motorcycle* bright red.
Now that Paul has thoroughly cleaned **his** motorcycle, **he** is ready to paint **it** bright red.

By itself a pronoun conveys no clear meaning. Its meaning becomes clear and specific only when you know what noun it stands for. For this reason, this example needs the first "Paul" to make the meaning of *his* and *he* clear.

The following words are pronouns:

I	me	myself	my, mine	who	someone
you	him	yourself	your, yours	whom	anyone
he	her	himself	his	whose	everyone
she	us	herself	her, hers	whoever	none
it	them	itself	its	whomever	somebody
we		ourselves	our, ours		anybody
they		yourselves	their, theirs		everybody
		themselves			nobody

EXERCISE A   Fill the blanks in the following sentences with pronouns which may be used in place of the italicized nouns. (Add 10 points for each correct answer.)

1   *Edith Cavell* was a British nurse .... served in Belgium

2   during World War I. In 1907 *Dr. Antoine Depage* had asked Miss Cavell

3   to come to Brussels. .... wanted .... *hospital*

4   modernized according to the principles of Florence Nightingale. With

5   the outbreak of the war in 1914, ... became a Red Cross

6   hospital. The Germans marched into *Belgium* although ....

7   was a neutral country. The hospital was filled with many casualties of the

8   war. Edith Cavell joined an underground *group*. .... gave aid

9   to Belgians of military age and to escaped Allied prisoners. The *Germans*

10   discovered the group and in 1915 .... arrested Edith Cavell

11   and thirty-four other members. *Edith Cavell,* because of ....

12   religious convictions, refused to lie, even in order to protect

3

13 . . . . was sentenced to death and executed

14 by a firing squad on October 12, 1915.

The following words may be used as pronouns. They may take the place of nouns. (They may also be used as adjectives, as you will see later.)

which	these	neither	few	most	other
what	those	all	many	several	another
this	each	any	much	some	
that	either	both	more	one	

EXAMPLES The journalism students work together beautifully. Many report the news. Several do the typing. A few edit the copy and send it to the printer. (The pronouns *many, several,* and *few* take the place of the noun *students.*)

Mark showed me a white sweater and a green sweater. "Which do you think is appropriate?" he asked. "Either is," I replied. (*Which* and *either* are pronouns used in place of the noun *sweater.*)

EXERCISE B List in order in the spaces below the ten pronouns in the following story; after each pronoun write the word or words it stands for. (Add 5 points for each correct answer.)

Last Saturday at the teachers' convention we students worked hard. A few of us stood at the main door to distribute programs. Some wrote out name tags. Several served as ushers.

Beverly and Randall listened in during a discussion period. They were surprised by the comments of two teachers. One argued for tougher grading standards. Another protested that grades do not represent the true ability of the student. Neither seemed to win the argument. Each, however, took a firm stand.

1. . . . .   6. . . . .

2. . . . .   7. . . . .

3. . . . .   8. . . . .

4. . . . .   9. . . . .

5. . . . .   10. . . . .

The Adjective

An adjective is a word used to modify a noun or a pronoun.

To modify means *to limit*. An adjective limits the number of things or ideas to which a word can refer, making the meaning more definite. Notice how the adjectives below make more definite the meaning of the words they modify. Notice, too, that some of the words listed as pronouns in Lesson 2 are adjectives when they modify a noun or pronoun.

a big joke, a good joke, a new joke   all cars, both cars, one car
a tall tree, a scrubby tree, an oak tree   each one, another one

An adjective may answer one of three questions about the word it modifies. It may tell *which one, what kind,* or *how many.*

WHICH ONE?   this puppy, that room, the short one
WHAT KIND?   black ink, a rough street, delicious pudding
HOW MANY?   fifty cents, several signs, a few pages, one hit

The commonest adjectives are *a, an,* and *the*. They are sometimes called *articles*. Unless otherwise advised, ignore the articles when adjectives are required for exercises.

EXERCISE A Circle each adjective in the following paragraph and draw an arrow from the adjective to the word it modifies. (Add 5 points for each adjective and 5 points for each modified word.)

1   Many writers of fiction have predicted the use of holograms. A light
2   would go on, a beam would be shot into the darkened room, and a
3   three-dimensional image would form in the air. Holograms are now in use.
4   Actually, holograms are photographs of the light waves that reflect from
5   an object that is illuminated with laser light. The visual information is
6   stored on film. To project the hologram, coloured light is shone through
7   the hologram and reshaped into the wave forms of the light waves of
8   the original object.

An adjective does not always stand next to the noun or pronoun it modifies. Sometimes other words separate an adjective from the noun or pronoun modified.

My uncle is tall

We might have been late

Everyone on the rink looked cold

EXERCISE B Draw a circle around each of the twenty-five adjectives in the following story. Treat hyphenated compound words like *spine-tingling* as one word. Remember that an adjective modifies a noun or pronoun. (Add 4 points for each correct answer.)

BEWARE OF THE BEAR!

1   On hot summer nights, Julio and the other boys sleep out in the yard.

2   They put up a tent in a dark corner, where the trees and bushes are thick.

3   That way the boys can easily imagine they are in wild, uninhabited

4   country.

5   One evening Mike suggested that they tell ghost stories or tales of bear

6   hunts. After a particularly spine-tingling story, Mike couldn't sleep; he

7   was too nervous.

8   About midnight he saw something move in the shadows. "Yeow!" he

9   cried out. "There is a black bear! It is really big!"

10   In the ensuing confusion, the tent collapsed on top of the boys; each

11   one seemed eager to go in a different direction. Anxious parents ran

12   down from the house. They found a coal-black dog. Like a bear, this

13   animal was very curious. It was sniffing at the writhing, yelling tangle of

14   arms, legs, and bodies under the tent.

Review of Nouns, Pronouns, and Adjectives

EXERCISE A   Each of the following sentences contains two pronouns. In the first column at the right, write the first pronoun in the sentence and the noun it stands for. In the second column, write the second pronoun and the noun it stands for. Words like *my, our, his, her, its, their* should be considered possessive pronouns, not adjectives. (Add 5 points for each correct answer.)

1. Laura passed the ball to Ann, who caught it neatly.

2. Otis called his sister, but she didn't answer.

3. Asked about the game, Mike said, "I didn't see it."

4. Since Gabriella found the money, it belongs to her unless claimed.

5. The children like the new bus driver who takes them to school.

6. Although Elliot studied French in school, he didn't feel comfortable speaking it.

7. Denise brought sandwiches with her on the hike and carried them in a knapsack.

8. "You," Jerry said to Lee, "surprised me."

9. Because Sheila enjoyed musical comedies, she tried to see them as often as possible.

10. Paula enjoyed volleyball so much that she played it every day after school.

EXERCISE B   Write in order in the spaces at the right the part of speech of the italicized words in each line. Use these abbreviations: *n.* (noun), *pron.* (pronoun), *adj.* (adjective). (Add 5 points for each correct answer.)

1   *Ernest, who* is invited nearly everywhere by

2 friends, has his *favourite definition* of "life   . . . .

3 of the party." *He* believes that a *person* can   . . . .

4 be in the *limelight* merely by being a *good*   . . . .

5 listener. *"People* at a *party,"* he says, ...

6 "welcome a *chance* to make a *big* impression. If   . . . .

7 you are *quiet,* listening attentively, *you* give   . . . .

8 them an opportunity to make a *grand display* of   . . . .

9 their *talents.* If you let *other* people impress   . . . .

10 you, *they* will be impressed by your *graciousness."*   . . . .

EXERCISE C   Underline every adjective in the following passage and draw an arrow from it to the word it modifies. Ignore *a, an,* and *the.* Then draw a circle around every pronoun, including possessive pronouns. (Add 10 points for each correctly marked sentence.)

A. Magic tricks have great fascination for me.

1. Many tricks are uninteresting.

2. This stunt, however, is different.

3. Four people, who use only their forefingers, can lift a heavy boy.

4. He doesn't jump up; they actually lift him.

5. Two people stand on each side of the boy, who is seated in a chair.

6. First, they slap their hands on his head, with one hand on top of the other, in the order you would use to grasp the handle of a baseball bat in deciding which team bats first.

7. Then, quick forefingers shoot under the knees and armpits of the boy and easily lift him.

8. Everyone has a particular version of the explanation.

9. Some say the body becomes stiff; many claim breath control is the key.

10. Apparently, though, nobody knows the true solution to the mystery.

The Verb

A <u>verb</u> is a word that expresses action or helps to make a statement.

Action verbs express either physical action or mental action. The verb *think,* which expresses mental action, is just as truly an action verb as the verb *kick,* which expresses physical action.

EXAMPLES   Father works for the government.
Nicole threw the ball over my head.
She always imagines the worst.

EXERCISE A   Underline each verb in the following paragraph. There are twenty-five of them, and all are action verbs. There may be several verbs in a sentence. (Add 4 points for each correct answer.)

1   Mark, Louisa, and Lynn formed an art group. Since they needed a
2   clubhouse, they planned the construction of a small geodesic dome. The
3   group financed the structure through the sale of some of its work. Louisa
4   sold a portrait and an abstract painting. Mark constructed a Tiffany
5   lamp, and the Posnicks quickly bought it. They wanted the lamp for the
6   living room in their renovated brownstone apartment. Lynn sketched
7   several local scenes, fashioned the sketches into linoleum blocks, made
8   greeting cards with the blocks, and sold the cards through a local novelty
9   store. The group carefully studied *The Whole Earth Catalog* for instruc-
10 tions. Louisa, Mark, and Lynn decided on a 3.2 × 2.5 m building.
11 Louisa, the math whiz, performed the necessary mathematical calcu-
12 lations. Mark, an expert bargain finder, shopped for the materials. With
13 the group's earnings, he purchased wood struts, spoke hubs, and plastic
14 covering. The group asked Mark's parents for the use of part of their
15 backyard. They started the construction work on Monday. Louisa cut the
16 wood to the necessary dimensions. Mark formed the cut wood into
17 triangles, and Lynn fastened the triangles together in the shape of a
18 dome. They finished the skeletal structure on Friday. On Saturday they
19 attached the plastic covering. That evening the group celebrated its
20 success with a pizza and cokes.

A few verbs *link* a noun with a noun or a noun with an adjective. These verbs are called *linking verbs*.

LINKING VERBS   am, is, are, was, were, (will) be, (has) been, become, get (when it means *become*), seem, appear, look, feel, smell, taste, remain, sound

EXAMPLES   Mother **is** a good cyclist.   (mother = cyclist)
This room **has been** empty all day.   (empty room)
George **will be** our leader.   (George = leader)
The witness **remained** silent.   (silent witness)
The dog **seems** friendly.   (friendly dog)

Note: If you can put *is, are, was,* or *were* in place of a verb without greatly changing the meaning of the sentence, you may be sure the verb is a linking verb.

EXAMPLES   The bell **sounds** loud. The bell **is** loud.   (*Sounds* is a linking verb.)
The muffins **taste** good. The muffins **are** good.   (*Taste* is a linking verb.)

EXERCISE B   In the left column below are nouns modified by adjectives. By supplying verbs to link the nouns and adjectives, write sentences in the space at the right. Use five different linking verbs. (Add 10 points for each correct sentence.)

A. the stormy weather   A. *The weather looks stormy.*

1. the dull knife   1. ....

2. the haunted house   2. ....

3. the shy child   3. ....

4. the calm lake   4. ....

5. the bitter medicine   5. ....

In the left column below are groups of two nouns, both naming the *same* person or thing. By using various linking verbs to connect the paired nouns, write sentences in the space at the right.

B. Nero—an emperor   B. *Nero was an emperor.*

6. Marita—treasurer   6. ....

7. Kate—an actress   7. ....

8. the lighthouse—
   our guide   8. ....

9. mongrels—watchdogs   9. ....

10. the movie—Western   10. ....

The Helping Verb

Very often we use verbs which consist of more than one word.

EXAMPLES   He <u>may</u> help us.

I <u>should have</u> asked the teacher.

The criminal <u>must have been</u> planning an escape.

A verb of more than one word is called a *verb phrase*. A verb phrase is made up of a main verb preceded by one or more helping verbs. The helping verbs actually help to make the meaning of the main verb more exact.

EXAMPLES   I <u>will</u> sleep.   I <u>did</u> sleep.

I <u>would</u> sleep.   I <u>was</u> sleeping.

I <u>must</u> sleep.   I <u>may be</u> sleeping.

The helping verbs may be separated from the main verb, or parts of the helping verb may be separated from each other.

EXAMPLES   <u>Do</u> you believe them?   <u>Has</u> one ever <u>been</u> caught?

The common helping verbs are:

be (am, is, are—was, were—been); shall, will; have (has, had); do (does, did); can, could; should, would; may, must; might; ought (to)

EXERCISE A   Complete the verbs in the following sentences by writing suitable helping verbs in the spaces provided. Then underline the entire verb phrase. The word *not* is not part of the verb. (Add 10 points for each correct sentence.)

1. Someone . . . . broken into the house.

2. His car . . . . going too fast for safety.

3. I . . . . waiting for Helen.

4. . . . . you met my mother?

5. It . . . . be later than you think.

6. . . . . you help me?

7. . . . . you have a good time?

8. There . . . . been serious consequences.

9. Mr. Prinz . . . . not . . . . persuaded to change.

10. If he . . . . read better, he . . . . learn more.

EXERCISE B   Each line below contains a verb phrase. First find the verb phrase and underline it. Then, in the first column to the right, copy the helping verb (or

verbs). In the second column, copy the main verb. The word *not* is not part of the verb.
(Add 4 points for each correct line.)

	Helping verbs	Main verbs
A. Must you always see something with	*must*	*see*
1 your eyes before you will believe it?		
2 Since the Greeks could not see the		
3 air, they did not consider it real.		
4 Anaxagoras, however, would not agree		
5 with the crowd. He had discovered		
6 that air must be something real.		
7 Anaxagoras had had a revealing		
8 experience. One day he was carrying a		
9 goatskin which had been filled with		
10 air. (This goatskin may be compared		
11 to a football.) While he was walking		
12 on the beach, he must have stumbled		
13 over a rock. He did not get hurt		
14 because the goatskin had hit the ground		
15 first and the air inside had acted as		
16 a cushion. *Something*, air, had broken		
17 what could have been a very hard fall.		
18 Like Anaxagoras, we must admit that		
19 the air does contain something real.		
20 We could not even breathe if the air		
21 did not contain oxygen. Scientists		
22 have also found nitrogen in the air.		
23 Other elements have been found.		
24 We may discover new facts about air		
25 now that we are probing outer space.		

The Adverb

An <u>adverb</u> is a word used to modify a verb, an adjective, or another adverb.

As its name suggests, an ad*verb* usually tells something about a verb. It may tell (1) *how,* (2) *when,* (3) *where,* or (4) *how much* or *how often* the action of the verb occurs.

HOW	Watch closely. (*Closely* modifies *watch.*)
WHEN	We won recently. (*Recently* modifies *won.*)
WHERE	Hang the picture there. (*There* modifies *hang.*)
HOW OFTEN	Carl usually walks to school. (*Usually* modifies *walks.*)

EXERCISE A   Circle the adverb in each sentence. Draw an arrow to the verb it modifies. In the space at the right state what the adverb tells: *how, when, where, how much* or *how often.* (Add 10 points for each correctly marked sentence.)

A. The big drawing (always) attracts a crowd at the county fair.   *how often*

1. For weeks merchants cheerfully give numbered tickets with purchases.   . . . .

2. My cousin Lorraine and I finally collected forty tickets.   . . . .

3. "If we're lucky," I often told Lorraine, "we will win a beautiful new car!"   . . . .

4. Saturday came, and we merrily waded through the crowd at the fair.   . . . .

5. Rules stated that the holders of winning tickets must be there.   . . . .

6. At midnight, they promptly started the drawing.   . . . .

7. "The winner of the new Ford is 608–1313!" barked the announcer. "Will the holder of number 608–1313 come here?"   . . . .

8. Lorraine then surprised everybody.   . . . .

9. She walked slowly to the platform for her prize.   . . . .

10. She exclaimed cheerfully, "This is the first prize I have won!"   . . . .

13

EXERCISE B
Fill in each blank below with an appropriate adverb modifying a verb. Choose varied, interesting adverbs. (Add 5 points for each correct answer.)

TRYOUT

1   Rena . . . . wanted to get a part in her school's production of

2   *The Diary of Anne Frank.* She was . . . . nervous about audi-

3   tioning, and she . . . . awaited the day for tryouts. To prepare

4   herself, she . . . . scanned the play over the weekend.

5   . . . . she went back and . . . . studied the role of

6   Anne. . . . . she began to understand how it must have felt to

7   live in hiding for so long. She wondered if she could . . . .

8   portray the girl who had . . . . written the diary.

9   Rena arrived in the auditorium . . . . she

10 looked, she saw other students . . . . thumbing through scripts.

11 She . . . . watched the first group of students read a scene

12 . . . . her turn came. She . . . .

13 hoped that her understanding of the character would come through in

14 her reading. As she began to read the part, she . . . . relaxed.

15 She . . . . enjoyed bringing the play to life.

16   After her turn, she returned to her seat. She sat . . . . waiting

17 to hear the drama teacher's decision. She smiled . . . . when

18 she heard the teacher say, "The role of Anne Frank—Rena Ross."

Adverbs Modify Adjectives and Other Adverbs

Most adverbs modify verbs, but a few are commonly used to modify an adjective.

EXAMPLE   We saw a very good movie.

In this sentence you can spot *good* as an adjective modifying *movie*. The adverb *very* modifies the adjective *good*, telling *how* good. Other adverbs commonly used to modify adjectives are *so, too, rather, fairly, somewhat, quite, almost, extremely,* and *unusually.*

An adverb may also modify another adverb.

EXAMPLE   They talk too fast.

Fast is an adverb telling how they *talk; too* is an adverb modifying *fast,* telling *how* fast.

EXERCISE A   In each of the following sentences an adverb is italicized. Draw an arrow from this adverb to the word it modifies. In the space at the right tell whether the modified word is a verb, an adjective, or an adverb. (Add 2½ points for each correct answer.)

1. She plays tennis *well*.　　　　　　　　. . . . .

2. The price seems *very* reasonable.　　. . . . .

3. Melba *seldom* loses her head.　　　　. . . . .

4. Herbert seemed *unusually* happy.　　. . . . .

5. The *dangerously* narrow bridge scared me.　. . . . .

6. Bill cried out, "Don't run *so* fast!"　　. . . . .

7. He *almost* never writes a letter.　　　. . . . .

8. A *rather* fat clown was juggling oranges.　. . . . .

9. "I'm *too* drowsy for words," Annette yawned.　. . . . .

10. Sue works *unusually* hard on Saturdays.　. . . . .

11. Fran answered *somewhat* sarcastically.　. . . . .

12. They play an *extremely* fast game.　　. . . . .

13. Does hay *actually* cause hay fever?　　. . . . .

14. We will play a doubleheader *tomorrow*.　. . . . .

15. At a formal party, Jake speaks *properly*.　. . . . .

15

16. May we go to the wrestling match *now*?   . . . .

17. Florence *never* eats parsley.   . . . .

18. The second speech was *less* interesting.   . . . .

19. He was *fully* aware of his plight.   . . . .

20. Can you *really* capture chiggers alive?   . . . .

EXERCISE B Underline the adverbs in the following sentences. In the spaces at the right tell which word or words the adverb modifies and what it tells: *how, when, where, how much* or *how often*. If there are two adverbs in the sentence, list the words they modify and what they tell in order. (Add 5 points for each correctly marked line.)

A. Shall we leave <u>now</u>?   *shall leave   when*

 1. Come quickly.   . . . .

 2. I can run faster than you.   . . . .

 3. Sheila seems very sure of herself.   . . . .

 4. Later I believed him.   . . . .

 5. Our team was too slow.   . . . .

 6. Is he always tardy?   . . . .

 7. Your new books are here.   . . . .

 8. Did you work hard?   . . . .

 9. Marina has been there.   . . . .

10. This problem is especially hard.   . . . .

11. The boys work slowly.   . . . .

12. What shall we do now?   . . . .

13. These were expertly made.   . . . .

14. She will never believe you.   . . . .

15. I will be there.   . . . .

16. Karen danced gracefully.   . . . .

17. Joshua left yesterday for school.   . . . .

18. She won easily.   . . . .

19. Carla often goes to concerts.   . . . .

20. The troupe rehearsed diligently.   . . . .

The Preposition

A word used to show the relationship of a noun or a pronoun to another word in the sentence is called a preposition.

In the following sentences the prepositions, printed in red, tell how the underlined words are related.

EXAMPLES   The trail through the ravine is closed now.

Here is a box of fudge.

A gray squirrel ran around the barn.

Our dog sleeps under the couch.

The following words may be used as prepositions. Some may also be used as adverbs or conjunctions.

about	before	by	like	to
above	behind	concerning	near	toward
across	below	down	of	under
after	beneath	during	off	underneath
against	beside	except	on	until
along	between	for	over	up
among	beyond	from	past	upon
around	but (meaning	in	since	with
at	*except*)	into	through	without

A group of words beginning with a preposition and ending with a noun or a pronoun is called a prepositional phrase.

EXAMPLES   through the ravine   beside the lake

around the red barn   for you

before breakfast   between you and me

Note that the noun in the prepositional phrase may be modified.

EXERCISE A   Each of the following sentences contains two prepositional phrases. Draw a line under the phrases. (Add 5 points for each correct answer.)

A. The books of poetry are on the top shelf.

1. Do your work in study hall or do it at home.

2. After the dance we went to Gerry's house.

3. Gordon Lightfoot's concerts at Massey Hall were praised by critics.

4. Behind the fence I found my bicycle with a flat tire.

5. Since September she has been principal of our school.

17

6. As I walked from the building, I met the principal on the steps.

7. For social studies I read a book about Kateri Tekakwitha.

8. Margaret lives in an apartment building on Sheridan Avenue.

9. Beyond the valley the mountains were black against the sky.

10. During vacation I kept busy working around the house.

Many words commonly used as prepositions may also be used as adverbs. If you will remember that *a preposition always begins a phrase, but an adverb does not begin a phrase,* you will be able to tell whether a word is a preposition or an adverb.

EXAMPLES   I jumped **across** the deep ditch. (*Across* is a preposition beginning the prepositional phrase *across the deep ditch.*)

I jumped **across**. (*Across* is an adverb modifying *jumped* and telling where I jumped.)

He stayed **under** the water for a long time. (*Under* is a preposition beginning the prepositional phrase *under the water.*)

He stayed **under** for a long time. (*Under* is an adverb modifying *stayed* and telling where he stayed.)

EXERCISE B   In the space at the right, classify the italicized word as a preposition or as an adverb. Use these abbreviations: *prep.* (preposition), *adv.* (adverb). (Add 10 points for each correct answer.)

1. Time passes *on*. . . . .

2. I put my trophy *on* the coffee table. . . . .

3. "Have you seen him *since*?" she asked. . . . .

4. "I haven't seen him *since* the party," I replied. . . . .

5. *Behind* me stood Coach Davis. . . . .

6. He soon fell *behind* in his algebra class. . . . .

Write short sentences using these words as directed.

7. *up* as a preposition . . . .

8. *up* as an adverb . . . .

9. *down* as a preposition . . . .

10. *down* as an adverb . . . .

The Conjunction and the Interjection

A conjunction is a word that connects words or groups of words.

Only the conjunctions *and, but,* and *or* will be considered in this lesson. These three conjunctions join sentence parts which are alike.

EXAMPLES   Prejudice **and** ignorance go hand in hand. (*And* joins two nouns.)
Grandma is cranky **but** lovable. (*But* joins adjectives.)
During spare moments the students ice-skate **or** ski. (*Or* joins verbs.)
She speaks French clearly **and** fluently. (*And* joins adverbs.)
Go up the hill **and** past the pond. (*And* joins prepositional phrases.)
I told a good joke, **but** nobody laughed. (*But* joins two statements.)

EXERCISE A   Circle the conjunction or conjunctions in each sentence and underline the words or word groups which are connected by each conjunction. (Add 10 points for each correct answer.)

A.   I recognized you (but) not your brother.

1   Harriet and Judy had a short but interesting conversation about the
2   relationship between laughter and intelligence.
3   Harriet speculated: "A good sense of humour and real brainpower go
4   together. Of course, a child or a simpleton might laugh at slapstick
5   comedy. Only an intelligent person, however, laughs at subtle puns or at
6   ironic comments. It takes a good mind—one that can see into things and
7   grasp hidden meanings—to appreciate higher types of humour."
8   "Oh," Judy interrupted, "everybody in this class laughs at all kinds of
9   jokes, but I don't think we are especially smart."
10   "Maybe we're smart but not well-bred," Harriet replied. "I believe
11   Chesterfield said that well-bred people often smile but seldom laugh."

An interjection is an exclamation that expresses emotion. It has no grammatical relation to the rest of the sentence.

EXAMPLES   **Whew!** I'm glad that's over.
Hey! Stop that!
Oh, never mind.

Spotting the Parts of Speech   The work that a word does in a sentence determines what part of speech it is in that sentence. The same word may be

19

used as several different parts of speech. Notice how the words printed in red in the following sentences are used as different parts of speech.

EXAMPLES   We often study geography together. (verb expressing action)
            She has a large desk in her study. (noun naming a type of room)
            We finished our work in study hall. (adjective modifying *hall*)

            He drew a picture of the sea. (noun naming a thing)
            Can you picture me as an acrobat? (verb expressing mental action)
            Our picture window is cracked. (adjective modifying *window*)

EXERCISE B   In the space at the right of each sentence, write the part of speech of the italicized word. In making your decision, ask yourself what work the word does in the sentence. (Add 5 points for each correct answer.)

1. We took an express *train.*   . . . .

2. A *train* whistle sounded in the distance.   . . . .

3. I will *train* your dog.   . . . .

4. *Cross* the street on a green light.   . . . .

5. Turn right at the next *cross* street.   . . . .

6. She was wearing a gold *cross.*   . . . .

7. The boss will *fire* me.   . . . .

8. The *fire* department is always ready.   . . . .

9. We saw a large *fire* in the distance.   . . . .

10. He has a bald *head.*   . . . .

11. Who is the *head* usher?   . . . .

12. She will *head* the grade ten class.   . . . .

13. He can *field* a ball faster than any other player.   . . . .

14. The new athletic *field* is ready for use.   . . . .

15. A *field* mouse scampered by.   . . . .

16. Everyone *left* the building in a hurry.   . . . .

17. I sat on the *left* side of the room.   . . . .

18. Turn *left* at the next corner.   . . . .

19. Let's walk *around.*   . . . .

20. They walked *around* the block.   . . . .

Chapter Review

EXERCISE A Write in the spaces at the right the part of speech described. (Add 10 points for each correct answer.)

1. modifies a noun . . . .
2. joins together two words or word groups . . . .
3. modifies an adverb . . . .
4. names a person, place, thing, or idea . . . .
5. expresses action . . . .
6. shows the relationship between a following noun or pronoun and some other word . . . .
7. takes the place of a noun . . . .
8. modifies a pronoun . . . .
9. expresses sudden emotion . . . .
10. modifies a verb . . . .

EXERCISE B Write complete sentences using the italicized words as directed. (Add 5 points for each correct sentence.)

1. *play* as a verb . . . .
2. *play* as a noun . . . .
3. *scratch* as a verb . . . .
4. *scratch* as a noun . . . .
5. *light* as a noun . . . .
6. *light* as an adjective . . . .
7. *light* as a verb . . . .
8. *bus* as a noun . . . .
9. *bus* as an adjective . . . .
10. *Sunday* as a noun . . . .
11. *Sunday* as an adjective . . . .
12. *each* as a pronoun . . . .
13. *each* as an adjective . . . .
14. *pepper* as an adjective . . . .

15. *pepper* as a verb . . . .

16. *pepper* as a noun . . . .

17. *bicycle* as a noun . . . .

18. *bicycle* as an adjective . . . .

19. *mushroom* as a noun . . . .

20. *mushroom* as a verb . . . .

EXERCISE C   In the space to the right of each line, write the part of speech of the italicized word. Use these abbreviations: *n.* (noun), *pron.* (pronoun), *adj.* (adjective), *v.* (verb), *adv.* (adverb), *prep.* (preposition), *conj.* (conjunction). Study the way the word is used before making up your mind. (Add 5 points for each correct answer.)

1   The destructive *force* of the atom is familiar to all of   . . . .

2   us, but we know *considerably* less about its constructive uses.   . . . .

3   Materials *like* sulphur, zinc, and iodine can be made radio-   . . . .

4   active for *scientific* purposes. The atoms of such materials   . . . .

5   are said to be "tagged" with radioactivity. *Their* movements

6   can be *traced* with a Geiger counter.   . . . .

7   By injecting the tagged elements into *living* organisms, ...

8   *Canadian* scientists are learning much about the growth and   . . . .

9   *structure* of cells. Botanists using tagged atoms may at last   . . . .

10   discover how green leaves *manufacture* starch. Surgeons   . . . .

11   equipped with a *Geiger* counter can find the exact location of a   . . . .

12   brain tumour by tracing a dye mixed *with* radioactive material.   . . . .

13   Doctors have learned to treat diseases like anemia *or* cancer   . . . .

14   of the thyroid with radioactive *iron* or iodine.   . . . .

15   Industry too has found uses for tagged atoms. *They* help   . . . .

16   geologists to map underground oil deposits. They *can* also be   . . . .

17   a means of measuring the thickness of glass and *plastic,* and of   . . . .

18   finding flaws in metal *castings,* impurities in steel, and leaks

19   in water pipe. *Undoubtedly,* the uses for tagged atoms will   . . . .

20   continue to grow, making possible *future* miracles of science.   . . . .

Usage: BRING and TAKE, GOOD and WELL

bring, take Use *bring* when the meaning is to convey something *to* the person speaking. Use *take* when the meaning is to convey something *away from* the person speaking. It's all a matter of direction. *Bring* corresponds with *come, take* with *go*.

STANDARD When you *come* to see me, **bring** your new camera.
STANDARD Please *go* to the library and **take** this book with you.
STANDARD After the dog had **brought** me the newspaper, it grabbed my socks and **took** them into Mom and Dad's room.

good, well *Good* is always an adjective. Do not use *good* to modify a verb, that is, to describe an action. People do not perform actions good; they always do them *well.* Use the adverb *well* to modify a verb.

NONSTANDARD She spoke *good* in the debate.
STANDARD She spoke **well** in the debate. (adverb modifying the verb *spoke*)
STANDARD Her arguments were **good**. (adjective modifying the noun *arguments*)

Well, however, may be used as an adjective, too, when it has certain special meanings.

1. To appear well dressed or well groomed.

EXAMPLE She looks **well** in blue. (modifies *she*)

2. To be in good health

EXAMPLES Since his vacation, he looks **well**. (modifies *he*)
Aren't you feeling **well** today? (modifies *you*)

EXERCISE Select the correct one of the two words in parentheses and copy it in the space at the right. (Add 5 points for each correct answer.)

1. When I go to Manning Park, I always (bring, take) my skis along. . . . .

2. Perhaps someday I will drive a truck as (good, well) as you do. . . . .

3. Why don't you (bring, take) Rosalie when you come back? . . . .

4. Everyone agrees that she plays first base unusually (good, well). . . . .

5. "Come here this instant!" Mother called to Doug. "And (bring, take) those matches with you!" . . . .

6. If your parents give you permission, we will (bring, take) you with us on our vacation. . . . .

7. Not one of the meals at camp tasted (good, well). . . . .

8. If you will trust me with that much money, I will (bring, take) it to the bank for you. . . . .

9. Now that he is leaving, isn't he going to (bring, take) these tennis racquets with him? . . . .

10. Dennis did not trim the hedge as (good, well) as usual. . . . .

11. Come to the dance tonight, and (bring, take) your sister with you. . . . .

12. A big breakfast always looks (good, well) to Aunt Harriet. . . . .

13. When she goes for a walk, she always (brings, takes) her German shepherd with her. . . . .

14. You can (bring, take) a guest when you come to the party. . . . .

15. We did the job as (good, well) as we could. . . . .

16. When the country doctor went to see Grandmother, he often (brought, took) a box of aspirin and a small sack of stick candy. . . . .

17. The outfield did (good, well) to make only two errors this afternoon. . . . .

18. Does that musk aftershave lotion smell (good, well), or is it too strong? . . . .

19. Did she remember to (bring, take) her sunglasses when she left for the beach? . . . .

20. We should (bring, take) our jackets when we go to the stadium tonight. . . . .

Before you begin this first spelling lesson, read the section "A Note on Spelling," on page 251, and become familiar with the two charts that follow it. These charts will be referred to in many of the spelling lessons in this book. You should find them useful in learning to spell the *majority* of English words.

Remember: When a letter appears between a pair of slanted lines, it is the *sound* that is being referred to; a letter alone refers to that *letter* itself.

Spelling: The Unstressed Vowel Sound Called the "Schwa"

A great many of the spelling problems in English are in words that contain an indistinct vowel sound. Pronounce each of the following words. Identify the vowel sound in the *accented* syllable in each word. Can you do the same for the vowel sound in the unstressed (unaccented) syllable?

1	*2*	*3*
ác tor	tráv el	e ráse
lín en	tó tal	co coón
cél lar	cív il	a whíle

As you can hear, the vowel sounds in the unstressed syllables in these words all sound very much alike. You cannot tell whether the vowel is *a, e, i, o,* or *u.* The stressed syllables, however, have a distinct and identifiable sound. In the word *tráv el* (list 2), the vowel *a* in the stressed syllable has the sound /a/. What is the sound of the *o* in *tó tal* and of the first *i* in *cív il*? Because the vowel sounds in the stressed syllables can usually be identified, they seldom cause spelling problems.

It is the unstressed vowel sound that causes trouble. This sound, which is extremely common in our language, is called a *schwa*, and is shown by the symbol /ə/, a sort of upside-down *e.*

In the next five spelling lessons (which come near the end of each of the next five chapters), you will be given some rules and aids to help you spell words containing this difficult sound. Where no rules or aids apply, you simply have to memorize the spelling of the words.

EXERCISE A Identify the sounds of the italicized vowels in the following words by writing *long, short,* or *schwa* in the blanks. If you wish, use the chart "Vowel Sounds and Their Common Spellings" on the inside back cover of this book. (Add 5 points for each correct answer.)

EXAMPLE ba sin ....*long*.... *schwa*.

1. les son ....
2. lev el ....
3. fo cus ....
4. help ful ....
5. an gel ....

6. ex ter nal ....
7. hu man ....
8. pro fes sor ....
9. pyr a mid ....
10. gold en ....

EXERCISE B Circle any syllable in the words below that contains the vowel sound /ə/. Remember, this sound occurs in unstressed syllables, so it may be helpful to say each word softly to yourself first. (Add 10 points for each correct answer.)

1. pen cil
2. beg gar
3. fall en
4. ta ble
5. stim u lus

6. fa tal
7. cre a tor
8. stee ple
9. clar i fy
10. a way

EXERCISE C Make a class list of twenty spelling demons that are demons because they contain a schwa sound. (Use words that were not taught in this lesson.) Your teacher will write the words on the board. (Before you suggest a word for the demon list, check in a dictionary to make sure the spelling problem in the word is caused by a schwa sound.) After all the words have been written on the board, narrow the list to the twenty most troublesome. Then copy the twenty words in a section of your notebook. When they have been copied, they should be erased from the board. Now study the twenty words, and be ready to write them from dictation in the blanks below. (Add 5 points for each correctly spelled word.)

1. ....
2. ....
3. ....
4. ....
5. ....
6. ....
7. ....
8. ....
9. ....
10. ....

11. ....
12. ....
13. ....
14. ....
15. ....
16. ....
17. ....
18. ....
19. ....
20. ....

Building Vocabulary: Choosing the Right Meaning

At the end of each chapter in ENGLISH WORKSHOP, you will find a lesson called "Building Vocabulary." In some of these lessons, you will study some useful methods of enlarging your vocabulary. In other lessons, you will study lists of words and meanings which you should try to add to your vocabulary. In this first vocabulary lesson, you will review some ideas about *context,* one of the basic means of building vocabulary and of using correctly the words you already know.

The context of a word is the *situation* in which it is used. The situation means both the *surrounding words* in a sentence or paragraph (the *verbal* context) and the *whole subject* of the sentence or paragraph.

The context in which a word is used shows what it means in that instance.

Many English words have several different though related meanings. In reading, we can usually tell from the context which meaning the writer intends. Often, too, we can form a good idea of the meaning of an unfamiliar word, if we know how to interpret context clues.

EXAMPLES   Mr. Seeley was a **contemporary** of my mother at **school.**
Our house is furnished entirely in the **contemporary** style.

Notice how much these two contexts tell you about the word *contemporary.* In the first sentence, it is used as a noun, in the second as an adjective. The first sentence means that Mother and Mr. Seeley were at school together. *Contemporary* must mean "one who lives at the same time." As an adjective it can mean "happening at the same time," but is that the meaning in the second sentence? Here, *contemporary* means "contemporary with us—happening in the present time." Often *contemporary* is used as an adjective and means "modern."

Think of other contexts in which you might use the word *contemporary* in these two different meanings. Then, in preparation for the exercise that follows, study the meanings and examples given for the following words.

contemporary /kən tém pə rér ē/   1. *adj.* Living or happening at the same time. —*n.* A person living at the same time as another. 2. *adj.* Like something in the present time; modern.

deliberate /di líb ər it/ *adj.*   1. Carefully thought out, done on purpose: *a deliberate lie.* 2. Slow, unhurried: *a deliberate movement.*

equilibrium /ē kwə líb rē əm/ *n.*   1. The condition of an object which is acted on by opposing forces in such a way that it does not move: *The diving bell sank halfway down and stopped, in a state of equilibrium.*

The tightrope walker used a long pole to maintain equilibrium. 2. A calm, well-balanced state of mind: *Herman's bad mark has upset his equilibrium.*

grapple /gráp əl/ *v.*   1. To hold tightly, as with a hook designed for the purpose: *The cruiser grappled the captured submarine to its side.* 2. To fight at close quarters: *The guard grappled with the bank robber.*

inconsistent /ín kən sís tənt/ *adj.*   1. Not in agreement or harmony with something: *a statement inconsistent with the facts.* 2. Changeable, unreliable: *inconsistent behaviour.*

inertia /in úr shə/ *n.* 1. In science, the tendency of an object to keep moving or remain standing still until some force acts on it: *When the rocket engines cut out, the ship's inertia will carry it to the moon.* 2. Of persons, sluggishness, unwillingness to make an effort: *Dale failed the course through sheer inertia.*

liability /lī ə bíl ə tē/ *n.* 1. In law, the state of being responsible for a debt, penalty, or expense: *A person who causes an accident has a liability for the damage.* 2. A debt (often used in the plural); anything that lessens the worth or effectiveness of a person or thing: *Although Christopher is sometimes quite witty, his sharp tongue is more a liability than an asset.*

Note: The pronunciation charts for the vocabulary lessons will be found on page 252 and the inside back cover of this book.

EXERCISE In the blank space in each sentence, write the word from the lesson that makes the best sense in the context. Then, in the parentheses after the blank, write the number of the meaning of the word that applies in the context. (Add 5 points for each correct answer.)

1. Art's behaviour has been rather . . . . (   ), but I think his

   failure to improve has been due simply to . . . . (   ).

2. The court established Mr. Chutney's . . . . (   ) for his son's

   debts.

3. Lester Pearson was a(n) . . . . (   ) of John Diefenbaker.

4. Dad likes classical music, but Mother prefers . . . . (   )

   music.

5. Martha . . . . (   ) with the problem for over an hour but still

   could not find the answer.

6. The incoming waves and the outgoing tide held the boat in a state of

   . . . . (   ).

7. On the moon, an automobile would have about one sixth of the force of

   gravity it has on earth, but its . . . . (   ) would be exactly

   the same.

8. Max's very . . . . (   ) way of speaking is a(n) . . . .

   (   ) to any group that wants to reach a quick decision.

CHAPTER TWO

The Sentence Base: Verb and Subject

The eight parts of speech are of little use until they are organized into sentences to express thoughts. You can better understand what a sentence is and how its parts work together if you learn to recognize the "sentence base." This knowledge will help you to understand the grammar of your language and to write your own ideas in clear, complete sentences.

LESSON 15

Subject and Predicate

A sentence consists of two parts: the subject and the predicate. The subject of the sentence is that part about which something is being said. The predicate is that part which says something about the subject.

SUBJECT	PREDICATE
A heavy rain	had spoiled our plans.

PREDICATE	SUBJECT
In the distance were	low-lying black clouds.

EXERCISE A Underline the subject once and the predicate twice. The predicate may come before the subject. (Add 10 points for each correctly marked sentence.)

A. Alice plays the clarinet.

B. In the doorway stood my father.

1. I frequently daydream about the future.

2. The achievements of scientists will change our lives.

3. Education will undoubtedly benefit from scientific progress.

4. Teaching machines may someday replace classroom lectures.

5. Tape recordings have already taught important facts to students.

6. Hypnotism could revolutionize teaching procedures.

7. More interesting are other speculations.

8. We may freeze a person alive one day.

9. This person might be revived after decades of the deep-freeze treatment.

10. Today's fantastic science fiction often becomes tomorrow's reality.

29

EXERCISE B The groups of words below are not sentences. In some of them the subject is missing; in others the predicate is missing. Make up the missing part for each and write it in the space given. Include some modifiers for each added subject or predicate. Underline the subject once, the predicate twice. (Add 10 points for each correct sentence.)

1. . . . .

   decided to have an international luncheon in honour of United Nations Day.

2. . . . .

   decorated their classroom with flags from other countries.

3. In the centre of the room was . . . .

   . . . .

4. Many friends and relatives . . . .

   . . . .

5. Calzone from Italy . . . .

   . . . .

6. . . . .

   brought some fried banana chips.

7. Souvlaki and feta cheese from Greece . . . .

   . . . .

8. . . . .

   ate too many Viennese pastries.

9. Delightful little marzipan animals . . . .

   . . . .

10. After two hours at the luncheon table we . . . .

    . . . .

The Verb

The verb is the principal word or group of words in the complete predicate.

The words underlined twice in the examples below make up the *complete predicate*. The words in red are the *simple predicate*, usually referred to as the *verb*.

EXAMPLE   Ralph **bought** a new typewriter.

verb: *bought*

When helping verbs are used, the verb in a sentence is a group of words.

EXAMPLE   Helen **has revealed** the secret.

verb: *has revealed*

In a verb of more than one word (a verb phrase), the words may be separated.

EXAMPLES   Ralph **will** probably **sell** his old machine.
Has Helen already **revealed** the secret?

In questions the parts of the verb are often separated. You can easily find all the words that make up the verb by changing the question into a statement. Even though the statement will not always make much sense, the parts of the verb will come together.

QUESTION   What **is** that dog **barking** at?
STATEMENT   That dog **is barking** at what.

EXERCISE A   Draw a line under the complete predicate and a circle around the verb in each of the following sentences. If the parts of a verb are separated, be sure to circle each part. In your mind, change questions into statements. The word *not* is not part of the verb. It is an adverb. (Add 10 points for each correctly marked sentence.)

A. The moon ⟨will⟩ then ⟨pass⟩ between the earth and the sun.

1. The FIDO system disperses fog on airport runways.

2. Your help has always been valuable to me.

3. Worst of all is the multiple-choice spelling test.

4. Sea urchins have scores of movable spines.

5. The rusty hatchet looks dull.

6. Did the burglar have a key to the store?

7. The surgeon did not recommend an immediate operation.

8. Is the pilot light of the furnace still burning?

9. Have you ever heard of a "devil's tattoo"?

10. A diet limited to proteins and fats will actually starve a rat to death.

EXERCISE B Underline the verb in each sentence. Be sure to include all parts of a verb of more than one word. (Add 5 points for each correctly marked verb.)

1. Tellers of folk tales and legends have peopled the world with imaginary creatures.

2. Many of these creatures are composed of parts of various real animals.

3. According to legend, the cockatrice could kill a person with its deadly glance.

4. It was supposedly hatched from the egg of a cock by a serpent.

5. This strange creature had the body of a serpent and the head, tail, and wings of a cock.

6. A glance at the Gorgon could also be an unpleasant occurrence.

7. With a woman's body and face, the Gorgon grew snakes from her head as hair.

8. One look into the Gorgon's eyes would turn the unfortunate viewer into stone.

9. The Griffin was formed from the head and wings of an eagle and the body of a lion.

10. With the temperament of both of these animals, the Griffin was also known for its predatory habits.

11. Have you read the story of the labours of Hercules?

12. The king had assigned to Hercules the task of killing the Hydra.

13. Why was the task considered impossible?

14. The Hydra had the body of a dog with nine snake heads on long necks.

15. One snake head could be cut off.

16. Two more heads would immediately grow in its place.

17. The ingenious Hercules cauterized each neck.

18. Because of this action, the heads could not grow back.

19. The Chimera is commonly pictured with the head of a lion, the body of a goat, and the tail of a serpent.

20. Bellerophon slew the Chimera from the safe distance of winged Pegasus' back.

The Simple Subject

The simple subject is the main word or group of words in the complete subject.

The complete subject is built around the simple subject just as the complete predicate is built around the verb. In the examples below, the complete subject is underlined; the simple subject is in red.

EXAMPLES   The neighbours' children play mostly in our yard.

          simple subject: *children*

          Into the ring stepped the unpopular champion.

          simple subject: *champion*

In this book the term *subject* will be used to mean the simple subject. To find the subject in a sentence, first find the verb. Then ask yourself *who?* or *what?* in front of the verb.

EXAMPLES   The characters in **Mordecai Richler's** novel are realistic.
          1. verb: *are*
          2. Who are? *characters* are
          3. subject: *characters*

          This new spaceship has been designed for the earth-moon run.
          1. verb: *has been designed*
          2. What has been designed? *spaceship* has been designed
          3. subject: *spaceship*

The words *there* and *here* are not subjects although they may seem to be when they come at the beginning of a sentence. If you find the verb first and then answer the question *who?* or *what?* about the verb, you will never make the mistake of selecting *there* or *here* as subjects.

EXAMPLE   There will be a dance after the basketball game.
          1. verb: *will be*
          2. What will be? *dance* will be
          3. subject: *dance*

Sometimes you will find the subject in a question more easily if you change the question into a statement. *Where did you find the lost wallet?* becomes the statement *You did find the lost wallet where.* Changing the question to a statement puts the subject in its more usual position before the verb.

EXAMPLE   Where did you find the lost wallet?
          1. verb: *did find*
          2. Who did find? *you* did find
          3. subject: *you*

EXERCISE Find the verb in each of the following sentences and write it in the verb column. Then ask *who?* or *what?* before the verb and write the subject in the subject column. Watch out for sentences beginning with *there* or *here*. (Add 5 points for each correct answer.)

	Subject	Verb
A. A new bridge across the Chilcotin River was built last summer.	*bridge*	*was built*
1. The water main was in the way of the new bridge.		
2. What solution did the town adopt?		
3. There was a good place for a new pipe along the underside of the bridge.		
4. Last night brought the coldest weather in ten years.		
5. At three o'clock in the morning the town was awakened by the fire siren.		
6. A big house in the centre of town was blazing.		
7. The five hoses were useless.		
8. The water had frozen in the exposed main under the bridge.		
9. The owner of the house was the construction engineer on the new bridge.		
10. The poor man's mistake had come home to roost.		

Finding the Subject

In command or request sentences, the subject <u>you</u> is understood even though the word <u>you</u> does not appear in the sentence.

EXAMPLES Open the window.   Leave the room!
1. verb: *open*   1. verb: *leave*
2. Who opens? (*you*) open 2. Who leaves? (*you*) leave
3. subject: *you*   3. subject: *you*

When the subject consists of two or more connected words that have the same verb, it is called a <u>compound subject</u>. The usual connecting words are <u>and</u>, <u>or</u>, and <u>nor</u>.

EXAMPLES Seniors and juniors may take this course.
1. verb: *may take*
2. Who may take? *seniors* and *juniors* may take
3. compound subject: *seniors . . . juniors*

Books, stationery, and other school supplies are sold here.
1. verb: *are sold*
2. What are sold? *books, stationery,* and *supplies* are sold
3. compound subject: *books, stationery, . . . supplies*

A <u>compound verb</u> consists of two or more connected verbs that have the same subject. The usual connecting words are <u>and</u>, <u>but</u>, <u>or</u>, and <u>nor</u>.

EXAMPLE I took your advice and went to the special help class.
compound verb: *took . . . went*

The subject of a sentence is never in a prepositional phrase.

EXAMPLE Two of your answers are correct.
1. verb: *are*   2. What are? *two* are   3. subject: *two*

In this example, the subject cannot be *answers* because the sentence does not say, "Your answers are correct"; it says, "Two . . . are correct." *Answers* is part of the prepositional phrase *of your answers*. An easy way to avoid choosing the incorrect word as subject in sentences like this is to draw a line through all prepositional phrases in the sentence.

EXERCISE Draw a line through all prepositional phrases in each of the following sentences. Select the verb and the subject from each sentence and write them in the spaces at the right. An understood subject should be placed in parentheses (*you*). Be sure to include all parts of a compound subject or a compound verb. (Add 5 points for each correct sentence.)

		Subject	Verb
A.	Each of the men will help.	*Each*	*will help*

1. Do you and Maria like humorous fiction?
....

2. Read James Thurber's stories.
....

3. His funny stories are full of peculiar people and animals.
....

4. Can such demented relatives and dogs actually exist?
....

5. Sit down and listen to me.
....

6. Here are three particularly odd characters.
....

7. Have you ever been afraid of burglars during the night?
....

8. One of Thurber's aunts has such a phobia.
....

9. Why is she always throwing shoes?
....

10. The point of this action is her fear of imaginary burglars.
....

11. That is the only reason!
....

12. A cousin in this story is also odd.
....

13. How does he act at night?
....

14. Every hour he wakes up breathless and grabs spirits of camphor.
....

15. One sniff from the bottle will revive the sinking invalid.
....

16. Otherwise there is the danger of suffocation!
....

17. How peculiar relatives are!
....

18. What are Thurber's dogs doing?
....

19. One of his dogs growls and bites at the air near panic-stricken guests.
....

20. Other dogs and relatives are even more delightfully insane.
....

36

Practice in Finding the Verb and Its Subject

EXERCISE A Write the verb and subject in each of the following sentences; put understood subjects in parentheses. Remember to (1) cross out prepositional phrases; (2) find the verb first, then ask *who?* or *what?;* and (3) include all parts of a compound subject, a compound verb, and a verb of more than one word. (Add 10 points for each correct sentence.)

	Subject	*Verb*
1. The tilt of the earth is one reason for changes in daylight hours.		
2. Do earthquakes cause tidal waves?		
3. Skin the catfish.		
4. How does a hibernating animal avoid starvation?		
5. I have never played shadow tag.		
6. Sir Henry Pellatt built beautiful Casa Loma.		
7. Then there followed a violent struggle for life.		
8. There are many differences between an alligator and a crocodile.		
9. Trees and telephone wires were severely damaged by the storm.		
10. In her purse were several dollars and some valuable papers.		

EXERCISE B Follow the directions for Exercise A. (Add 5 points for each correct sentence.)

	Subject	*Verb*
1. With a touch of its horn, a unicorn could purify a poisoned stream.		
2. Do plants and animals thrive in the Arctic?		
3. Parasol ants raise their own crop of mushrooms and eat nothing else.		
4. What does this signal mean to an airplane pilot?		

5. Hurry home and tell your parents. . . . .

6. Among the modern poets are Miriam Waddington and Margaret Atwood. . . . .

7. Have the fire fighters and the police been notified yet? . . . .

8. Did you or she write and send this note? . . . .

9. A flashy new sports car rounded the corner and pulled up beside us. . . . .

10. Open the box and look inside. . . . .

11. Boys and girls busily washed the dishes and cleaned the house. . . . .

12. Neither of my cousins has ever been here. . . . .

13. There are both sopranos and tenors in the choir. . . . .

14. Brett and Mary will probably win the election. . . . .

15. By how much did the committee underestimate our expenses? . . . .

16. At last came her long-awaited opportunity. . . . .

17. Study the alphabet and observe its weaknesses in representing sounds. . . . .

18. Three well-known Canadian actresses are Barbara Hamilton, Kate Reid and Martha Henry. . . . .

19. Philip wrote the music and choreographed the dances for the show. . . . .

20. Several treasures from King Tutankhamen's tomb were exhibited at the Art Gallery of Ontario. . . . .

A Sentence Has a Verb and a Subject

The two essential parts of a *sentence base* are the verb and its subject. If a group of words does not contain these two elements, it is not a sentence. It is important to be able to identify the verb and its subject so that you can be sure that you have written *sentences* in your own writing. A common error of some students results from their belief that a present participle (a verb form ending in *-ing*, like *going, seeing,* or *running*) can be used alone as the verb of a sentence.

Present participles are verbs only when they have a helper.

The helping verbs used with the present participle are the forms of the verb *to be: am, is, are—was, were;* and verbs of more than one word ending with *be* or *been: will be, has been, might have been,* and so on. Notice how these "nonsentences," built around the present participle, can be changed to sentences by the addition of an appropriate helping verb.

NONSENTENCES	SENTENCES
Linda *going* home	Linda was going home.
Cheryl *playing* the piccolo	Cheryl has been playing the piccolo.
Horses *drinking* from the trough	Horses were drinking from the trough.

Sentence Fragments A group of words which does not contain both a verb and its subject is not a sentence. It is merely a *fragment* of a sentence.

EXAMPLES At the end of a long dusty road
The girl in the green sweater
Running with a hose to put out the fire
Carla, my friend from Calgary
The girls in 4B
Himself winning third prize

EXERCISE Apply the verb-and-subject test to each of the following items. If the group of words has a verb and its subject, draw two lines under the verb and one line under the subject, and write *S* for *sentence* in the space provided. (Watch for "understood" subjects.) If it does not have a verb and its subject, write *F* for *fragment* of a sentence. (Add 4 points for each correctly marked item.)

1. Acting like a mischievous chimpanzee. . . . .

2. Acting like a mischievous chimpanzee, Joe bounced across the stage. . . . .

3. His arms hanging limp, dangling almost to the floor. . . . .

4. His arms, hanging limp, were dangling almost to the floor. . . . .

39

5. His arms were hanging limp, dangling almost to the floor. . . . .

6. The audience laughing at his comic appearance. . . . .

7. Mrs. Henderson, the director of this slapstick comedy. . . . .

8. Near the end of the first act. . . . .

9. Charlene was playing the part of Lady Macbeth. . . . .

10. Walking aimlessly about and rubbing her hands. . . . .

11. At the final curtain came a loud burst of applause. . . . .

12. The actors staying in character during five curtain calls. . . . .

13. The most successful performance of the season. . . . .

14. What is the director planning next? . . . .

15. In the spring she will direct Federico García Lorca's
    Blood Wedding. . . . .

16. Is that a comedy or a tragedy? . . . .

17. Are you interested in Spanish drama? . . . .

18. Hoping for the role of Leonardo. . . . .

19. Practise the part now and memorize the lines in time for
    the audition. . . . .

20. Who will play the heroine? . . . .

21. A production of the play on CBC Television. . . . .

22. The necessity of a good translation. . . . .

23. In *Blood Wedding* death is represented as an old beggar. . . . .

24. The actors must say the lines of poetry in the rhythms of
    normal speech. . . . .

25. A very difficult and trying task for inexperienced actors. . . . .

Sentence Completeness

A sentence is a group of words containing a verb and its subject and expressing a complete thought.

A group of words may have a verb and its subject, but it is not a sentence unless the thought is complete.

EXAMPLES *When you have finished your homework* (Although it contains a verb and its subject, this is not a sentence because it is not a complete thought. It is a fragment of a sentence.)
When you have finished your homework, you may watch television. (This is a sentence because the thought is complete.)

If there is enough snow (This is not a sentence because the thought is not complete.)
If there is enough snow, we will go skiing. (This is a sentence. The thought is complete.)

EXERCISE A In the space at the right of each group of words, write *S* if the group is a sentence, *F* if it is a fragment of a sentence. Ask yourself whether the thought in each group is complete. If it is not, the group of words is only a fragment. Reading aloud may help you to decide. A question is a sentence if it contains a verb and its subject. A command is a sentence because the subject is understood. (Add 4 points for each correct answer.)

1. Taking a canoe trip in Jasper.

2. Sufficient food for a week's journey.   . . . .

3. Others had camped there before us.   . . . .

4. Ashes indicated the place.   . . . .

5. Where their fire had been.   . . . .

6. How clearly was the trail marked?   . . . .

7. A Blackfoot village at the end of the trail.   . . . .

8. The group spent the morning together.   . . . .

9. Talking over plans for the afternoon.   . . . .

10. As we rounded a bend in the river.   . . . .

11. Could you hear the noise of the waterfall?   . . . .

12. Before you could see it.   . . . .

13. We could not paddle against the wind unless the guide helped us.   . . . .

41

14. The wind blowing spray over us. ....

15. Drenched to the skin. ....

16. The rapids in the river were occasional hazards. ....

17. The excitement of shooting the rapids. ....

18. We steered and balanced carefully. ....

19. Around boulders in the stream. ....

20. Deciding whether to go through the rapids or portage the canoe around them. ....

21. On our knees in the canoe, we became painfully cramped. ....

22. There was no chance, however, to stretch our legs. ....

23. From the beginning of the rapids to the end. ....

24. Grazing the side of the canoe on rounded boulders. ....

25. After we had taken a swim in the calm water beyond the rapids. ....

EXERCISE B By adding words to make the thought complete, make each of the following fragments a sentence. (Add 10 points for each correct sentence.)

1. While you rest . . . .

2. . . . . as he had often promised to do.

3. When I was a child . . . .

4. . . . . until the rain stops.

5. If you are ill . . . .

6. . . . . since I had already heard the story twice.

7. . . . . where we camped.

8. The girls sleeping in the tent near us . . . .

. . . .

9. Holding to the stern of the boat with one hand and groping for the sinking minnow bucket with the other . . . .

. . . .

10. . . . . talking over our plans.

42

Chapter Review

EXERCISE In the spaces at the right copy the verb and its subject in each of the following sentences. Your answers will be more accurate if you draw a line through prepositional phrases, mentally change questions into statements, and select the verb first, asking *who?* or *what?* before it. Be sure to copy all parts of a verb of more than one word and all parts of a compound subject or verb. (Add 5 points for each correct sentence.)

	Subject	Verb
A. Are all of the boys working?	*all*	*are working*
1. Pam and she made the popcorn.		
2. Did any of the cups break?		
3. There is a hat in the closet.		
4. Do not tell me the answer yet.		
5. Here is a copy of the play.		
6. None of the food was edible.		
7. What could he have been doing?		
8. Under the bridge was quicksand.		
9. Has either of you seen Elena?		
10. I read Irving Layton's poem and then wrote my term paper.		
11. Both of the twins are talented.		
12. You and she are the favourites.		
13. Has the bell rung?		
14. I mailed the letter on Monday and received a reply on Wednesday.		
15. When are you leaving?		
16. Beyond the lake are mountains.		
17. I washed and dried the dishes.		
18. Read three more pages.		
19. How beautiful the sunset is!		
20. How did you like the play?		

Cumulative Review

A Above each italicized word write what part of speech it is. Use these abbreviations: *n.* for *noun*, *pron.* for *pronoun*, *adj.* for *adjective*, *v.* for *verb*, *prep.* for *preposition*, *adv.* for *adverb*, *conj.* for *conjunction*, *int.* for *interjection*. (Add 5 points for each correct answer.)

1   When *Hurricane*, my *pet* dog, does not get his way, *he* pouts. If ex-

2   tremely *angry*, Hurricane *hides under* the sofa and sulks. Then, many kind

3   words *or* even *choice* morsels do not please him. *We* usually cope with his

4   rude *behaviour* by arousing his curiosity. The curious dog *always* inves-

5   tigates the *cause of* any excitement. We *sometimes* dash to the window

6   *and* exclaim, "*Oh*, here comes Aunt Kate!" Hurricane *immediately*

7   comes out of hiding, barks his way *to* the window, and *peers* out to see

8   where Aunt Kate *is*.

B Draw a line under each adjective in the following sentences. Draw a circle around each adverb. Draw an arrow from each adjective or adverb to the word it modifies. Do not mark the articles *a, an,* and *the.* (Add 20 points for each correctly marked sentence.)

A. In contrast to the solid landmass of the Antarctic, the Arctic is completely fluid.

1. The ice pack that covers the Arctic is not a totally solid layer of ice, as people generally imagine.

2. It consists of huge chunks and floes that vary greatly in size and thickness.

3. In fact, it contains many quite large open stretches.

4. Now the atomic submarine has enabled explorers to travel under the frozen sea to the Pole.

5. In August, 1958, the *Nautilus* became the first submarine to reach the Pole under the ice.

Spelling: "Bringing out" the Schwa Sound

In many instances, you can help yourself to spell an unstressed vowel sound (a schwa) by changing the form of the word so that the unstressed vowel will have to be stressed. Doing this will enable you to hear the indefinite and troublesome vowel more clearly and so to write it correctly. This "trick" does not, of course, work with all words having schwa sounds, but it is helpful in quite a few common words. Pronounce each pair of words below, listening for the change in the italicized vowel sounds:

ló c*a*l	loc*á*l ity
mó m*e*nt	mom*é*nt um
cív *i*l	civ*í*l ian
át *o*m	at*ó*m ic

The italicized vowels in the left-hand list all occur in unstressed syllables and have the schwa /ə/ sound. You cannot tell from the sound whether to spell the vowel *a, e, i,* or *o.* Now look at the italicized vowels in the right-hand list. By changing each word in the left-hand column to a related word, the stress or accent falls on a different syllable. The vowel that had the indistinct schwa sound no longer occurs in an unstressed syllable. It is now in a stressed syllable, and therefore has a definite vowel sound that you can hear and identify. You cannot "hear" the *a* in *local,* but you can identify it as an /a/ sound in *locality.* The same is true of the *e* in *momentum,* the second *i* in *civilian,* and the *o* in *atomic.* Thus, you can often "bring out" the characteristic sound of an unstressed vowel by adding a suffix that shifts the stress or accent.

EXERCISE A   By filling in the stressed, easily identified vowel in each word in list *1* below, you can correctly spell the unstressed, indistinct vowel (the schwa) in the related word in list *2.* First fill in the "easy" vowel in list *1,* and then write the same vowel for the schwa sound in the paired word in list *2.* (Add 10 points for each pair of correct vowels.)

EXAMPLE: brut . *a* lity   brut . *a* l

1	*2*
1. spect . . . . tor	spect . . . . cle
2. form . . . . lity	form l
3. ess . . . . ntial	ess . . . . nce
4. cel . . . brity	cel . . . . brate
5. hum . . . . nity	hum . . . . n
6. gramm . . . . tical	gramm . . . . r
7. influ . . . . ntial	influ . . . . nce

8. or....ginal   or....gin
9. gener....lity   gener....l
10. narr....tion   narr....tive

EXERCISE B The blank in each of the ten words at the left below is a schwa /ə/ in an unstressed syllable. You cannot "hear" a clear vowel, and so you cannot be sure whether to write an *a, e, i,* or *o.* In the long blank at the right, write a related word in which the stress falls on a different syllable, thereby "bringing out" the vowel sound of the original word containing the schwa. Then write the same letter in the original word. Circle the vowel that has been "brought out" in the related word. (The definition of the related word is given in parentheses.) (Add 10 points for each pair of correct vowels.)

EXAMPLE vit.*a*.l ... *vit(a)lity* . (great energy)

1. liber....l   .... (to set free)

2. pers....n   .... (to represent or regard a nonhuman thing as having human qualities)

3. ang....l   .... (pure, innocent, heavenly)

4. org....n   .... (produced by animals or plants)

5. rel....tive   .... (to give an account of; to tell)

6. acad....my   .... (having to do with scholarly matters)

7. emph....sis   .... (energetic, forceful)

8. popul....r   .... (quality of being liked)

9. invent....r   .... (a collection and list of articles; stock)

10. frug....l   .... (thrift; avoidance of waste)

REVIEW EXERCISE Circle the unstressed vowel sound (the schwa) in each word below. (Add 10 points for each correct answer.)

1. cellar   6. linen

2. angel   7. creator

3. stimulus   8. external

4. pyramid   9. clarify

5. golden   10. beggar

Building Vocabulary: Words to Learn

degenerate /di jén ə rāt/ v. To become worse; to sink down to a lower level of conduct, physical condition, activity: *The hockey game degenerated into a free-for-all.* — **degenerate** /di jén ər it/ n. One who has degenerated, especially morally; a person whose inner nature is evil.

depict /di píkt/ v. To show in a picture; hence, to describe vividly in words: *He depicted the life of London's poor with deep sympathy.*

diminutive /di mín yə tiv/ adj. Very small and delicate: *The child's tools were diminutive copies of an adult's.*

ensue /en sū/ v. To follow something in time, often as a result: *In its last game, the football team clinched the championship, and an enthusiastic celebration ensued.*

fragile /fráj əl/ adj. Easily broken; hence, delicately made: *The ancient vase was so fragile that the explorers who found it were afraid to move it.*

inference /ín fər əns/ n. A conclusion reached by any process of reasoning from known facts or from general principles: *From the dents in Mr. Walmsby's fenders, it was a natural inference that he is not a skilful driver.* — **infer** /in fúr/ v.

omen /ṓ mən/ n. Any thing or event taken as a sign of something to come: *Breaking a mirror is often considered a bad omen.*

profound /prə foúnd/ adj. Deep, thorough, or intense: *A profound respect for all living things caused her to become a veterinarian.*

prudent /prūd nt/ adj. Careful and sensible in conduct; not rash; of actions, cautious and sensible: *A prudent executive would not have put the company's money in such a risky undertaking.*

rebate /rḗ bāt/ n. A deduction from or payment back of a part of an amount already charged or paid: *As a result of their heavy medical expenses last year, my parents received a rebate on their income taxes.*

EXERCISE Fill each blank with the word from this lesson that makes the best sense in the context. (Add 10 points for each correct answer.)

1. The defence lawyer . . . . her client's character and home life in glowing terms.

2. Gregory had a quick, wide-ranging mind, but he was not as . . . . a thinker as his friend Mildred.

3. Mable's Department Store gives a ten percent . . . . to any customer who spends more than a certain amount per month.

4. The quality of our club meetings has . . . . considerably since the lively discussions we had at the beginning of the year.

5. That Gary Schimmel's mother is a well-educated person is a reasonable . . . . from her large vocabulary and constant reading.

6. When Mimo found a dollar bill on the street, he took it as a good . . . . of his future financial success.

7. That ship model is very handsome, but it is much too . . . . for a small child to play with.

8. General Tom Thumb, a circus midget, was probably the most
   .... person ever to achieve world-wide fame.

9. Finally, the children grew tired of playing the piano, and a delightful
   period of silence ....

10. It is hardly .... to use gasoline to help start a fire.

REVIEW EXERCISE Fill each blank with the word from the list below that
makes the best sense in the context. Some words appear twice, with different meanings. (Add 10 points for each correct answer.)

contemporary   equilibrium   inconsistent   liability
deliberate   grapple   inertia

1. Mrs. Luciano did not mind Ann's arriving late, but her ....
   refusal to apologize infuriated her.

2. The rocket .... itself to the space station and opened its
   airlock.

3. If you continue to walk at so .... a pace, we'll be late.

4. The witness' testimony was .... with the report given by the
   police.

5. Any player who does not come out for practice is a .... to the
   whole team.

6. For a few moments, the two men .... on the floor, and then
   the detective got the upper hand.

7. The poet Joy Kogawa is a less well-known .... of Anne
   Hébert.

8. At first, Henderson refused to pay, but the court later established his
   .... under the law.

9. The pendulum gradually stopped swinging and returned to its original
   state of ....

10. Next spring the company is moving from its present shabby office to a
    new, ...-looking building.

You have studied two parts of a sentence base: the verb and its subject. In this chapter you will study sentence bases that have three parts. The third part completes the meaning begun by the subject and verb. It is called a *complement,* which means "completer."

LESSON 26

The Subject Complement

As you read the following sentences, notice how the complement *completes* the meaning of the verb and its subject.

		COMPLEMENT
1.	You are	the **winner** .
2.	That must have been	a **surprise** .
3.	He is	a **captain** .
4.	Rosa looks	**pretty** .

In these sentences the complements refer to the subjects. In the first three sentences the complements are nouns that explain the subjects by naming the same persons or things as the subjects. In sentence 4, the complement *pretty* is an adjective. It describes the subject *Rosa.*

A complement that describes or explains the subject is called a subject complement.[1]

Subject complements follow linking verbs only. The verb *to be* (*am, is, are—was, were—been*) may be followed by a noun, a pronoun, or an adjective. Other linking verbs are usually followed only by adjectives: *become, seem, appear, look, feel, smell, taste, remain, sound.*

A subject complement may be compound; that is, it may have two or more parts.

EXAMPLES His favourite Canadian playwrights are **Erica Ritter** and **Michel Tremblay**.
The script was **short** but **powerful**.

[1] When a noun or a pronoun is a subject complement, it is sometimes called a *predicate nominative.* When an adjective is a subject complement, it is sometimes called a *predicate adjective.* These terms are not used in this book.

To find the subject complement in a question, rearrange the sentence so that it becomes a statement.

EXAMPLE   Was it the teacher?

It was the teacher.

Like the subject, the subject complement is never found in a prepositional phrase.

EXAMPLE   The winner was one of my brothers.

EXERCISE   Draw a circle around the complements in the following sentences. First, find the verb and its subject. (Crossing out prepositional phrases will help you.) Then draw an arrow from the complement to the subject to which it refers. Three of the sentences do not have complements. (Add 10 points for each correctly marked sentence.)

A. Vicky is my best friend.

B. Her comments seem pointless to most people.

1. According to my other friends, facts should be useful.

2. For Vicky, however, the discovery of useless facts is fun.

3. Her discoveries often become the topics of our conversations.

4. Here is a list of Vicky's favourite questions and comments.

5. Is a pumpkin a fruit or a vegetable?

6. Must a flying mare remain earthbound?

7. Why are the volcanoes on Mars active?

8. There are no alligators in Canada.

9. Among the early bicycles, what was the difference between a *walk-along* and a *boneshaker*?

10. Vicky's odd type of knowledge goes beyond the narrow limits of mere practicality.

The Direct Object

Study the following sentences.

SUBJECT	VERB	COMPLEMENT
They	brought	the **children**.
I	remember	the **route** very well.
Marcia	built	her own **boat**.

You can easily see that these complements do not refer to the subject. They are not subject complements. They are, however, related to the verb. They name something that is affected by the action of the verb. The *children* are what were *brought;* the *route* is what was *remembered;* the *boat* is what was *built.* A complement which is affected by the action of the verb is called a direct object. The direct object may be a noun or pronoun.

A direct object receives the action of the verb or names the result of this action.

Only action verbs have direct objects. The verb's action may be either physical or mental.

EXAMPLES   Roy knocked the ball into the stands.   (physical action)

You can imagine the result.   (mental action)

Usually the direct object comes after the verb, but it may come before it.

EXAMPLE   This I enjoy.

Like subjects and subject complements, direct objects are never found in a prepositional phrase.

EXAMPLE   She brought one of the new racquets.

Direct objects may be compound.

EXAMPLE   Jack has invited you and me to his party.

EXERCISE   The complement in each of the following sentences is a direct object. Underline the subject of each sentence once and the verb twice. Draw a line through any prepositional phrase. Then draw an arrow from the verb to the direct object (some objects are compound) and write the object(s) in the space to the right of each sentence. (Add 10 points for each correctly marked sentence.)

A. Louise misspelled ten words on the test.   *words*

B. Her failure she attributed to the teacher.   *failure*

51

1. I have already solved the first problem. ....
2. Last night's hail greatly damaged crops in this area. ....
3. How many of these have you made? ....
4. Four workers lifted the piano onto the stage. ....
5. The class elected two boys and two girls. ....
6. These things he left behind. ....
7. The huge crowd pushed Sean and me into the wrong bus. ....
8. Allen brought home three pheasants and a rabbit. ....
9. The outfielder quickly threw the ball to home plate. ....
10. Heavy armour protects the armadillo. ....

REVIEW EXERCISE Underline the subject of each sentence once and the verb twice. Circle each complement. Then write the complement in the first space at the right, and, in the second space, write *d.o.* if the complement is a *direct object* and *s.c.* if it is a *subject complement.* (Add 10 points for each correctly marked sentence.)

1. The grade nine class planned a craft fair. ....
2. All of the students would sell their own hand-crafted objects. ....
3. The class would donate the proceeds to a local charity for the holiday season. ....
4. Naomi asked several restaurant owners for empty wine bottles. ....
5. Her collection was an interesting assortment of bottles of many shapes, sizes, and colours. ....
6. Naomi carefully cut the tops off each of the bottles. ....
7. Then she sanded the rough edges. ....
8. The old bottles became beautiful drinking goblets. ....
9. One green bottle with a rounded bottom was especially attractive. ....
10. Naomi turned this bottle into a vase. ....

The Indirect Object

An indirect object is a complement that tells <u>to whom</u> or <u>for whom</u> (or <u>to what</u> or <u>for what</u>) the action of the verb is done.

The indirect object normally comes before the direct object.

d.o.

EXAMPLES   Lisa made me a <u>kite</u>.   (for me)

d.o.

Fred sent Doris a birthday <u>present</u>.   (to Doris)

In these sentences the words *me* and *Doris* are indirect objects. As shown by the phrases in parentheses, the words act as prepositional phrases. If the preposition appeared in the sentence, however, the words would be objects of the preposition, *not* indirect objects of the verb. It is the omission of the preposition that makes them indirect objects. *The indirect object is never found in a prepositional phrase.*

EXAMPLES   The plumber handed the bill to me.   (*Me* is the object of the preposition *to*.)

The plumber handed me the bill.   (*Me* is the indirect object of the verb *handed*.)

An indirect object may be compound.

EXAMPLE   She sold Jeff and me *tickets* for the rock concert.

EXERCISE   Draw a line through each prepositional phrase. Underline each direct and indirect object and write each one in the appropriate column at the right. You will not find an indirect object in every sentence. (Add 10 points for each correctly marked sentence.)

	Indirect object	Direct object
A. The event gave <u>Roger</u> an <u>inspiration</u> ~~for a story~~.	*Roger*	*inspiration*
1. He sold Alvin a red sweater.		
2. Bring me the book about ghosts.		
3. I'll give the receipt for the money to Helen.		
4. The caller left you this message.		
5. I threw Carmen the ball.		

6. Has he read his students these stories? ....

7. Someone must have criticized his methods. ....

8. Dr. Mabie is leaving the museum a valuable collection of old manuscripts. ....

9. Should I give the baby a bagel? ....

10. Shall I get it for you? ....

REVIEW EXERCISE In the space at the right of each sentence put the proper abbreviations, in order, identifying the italicized word or words: *s.c.* for subject complement; *d.o.* for direct object; *i.o.* for indirect object. Remember that subject complements follow linking verbs and direct objects follow action verbs. (Add 10 points for each correct sentence.)

A. Rosalie showed *me* her new *camera.* ..*i.o., d.o.*.

B. An egocentric person is a *bore.* ....*s.c.*...

1. Raccoons can easily outwit *dogs.* ....

2. The Governor in Council granted the *prisoner* his *freedom.* ....

3. I may become a *veterinarian.* ....

4. Healthy young lions rarely attack human *beings.* ....

5. Ilona wrote the *lyrics* to that song. ....

6. Mrs. Jacklitsh teaches *trigonometry* at the high school. ....

7. William Hutt was the *star* of the Stratford play. ....

8. The booby prize will be a useless measuring *tape.* ....

9. Marcy tossed *me* her fountain *pen.* ....

10. Are you *afraid* of high places? ....

Chapter Review

EXERCISE A Cross out all prepositional phrases. Then, in the space at the right, write each complement and its classification. Use one of these abbreviations: *s.c.* (subject complement), *d.o.* (direct object), *i.o.* (indirect object). Remember that subject complements follow linking verbs only; direct objects and indirect objects follow action verbs only. (Add 5 points for each correct line.)

A. Ants caused me trouble ~~in my backyard.~~   *me, i.o.–trouble, d.o.*

1. Solomon gave the sluggard good advice. ....

2. Have you ever watched ants at work? ....

3. Daily I watered the lawn after school. ....

4. This chore became interesting work for me. ....

5. I flooded a huge ant hill with water. ....

6. I thus declared war on the colony of ants. ....

7. Can ants ever have committee meetings? ....

8. Their subsequent action seemed sensible. ....

9. These ants were unusually crafty. ....

10. In fact, they eventually outwitted a human! ....

11. Soon the ants built four new strongholds. ....

12. These nests they built in various places. ....

13. I gave all of the ants another drenching. ....

14. Did defeat appear inevitable to the ants? ....

15. Quickly they showed me their ingenuity. ....

16. They perforated the lawn with tiny ant hills! ....

17. Again I mercilessly flooded their homes. ....

18. A change in strategy became necessary. ....

19. The ants made a united, orderly retreat. ....

20. Finally they found safety in one big happy
ant hill—in my next-door neighbour's yard! ....

EXERCISE B The complements in the following sentences are in italics. Over each complement write the proper one of the following abbreviations: *s.c.* for subject complement; *d.o.* for direct object; *i.o.* for indirect object. (Add 5 points for each correct answer.)

1. Tales of Sasquatch, or Bigfoot, haunted *me* throughout my childhood in British Columbia.

2. Several people travelled the mountain *trails* and brought *tales* back from their trips.

3. Some of these tales seemed *incredible*.

4. One camper told *me* a strange *story*.

5. While hiking in the backwoods, she saw large *footprints* on the trail ahead of her.

6. They appeared too *large* to belong to a human.

7. She made plaster *casts* of the footprints and gave an *anthropologist* the *casts*.

8. The unknown walker must be a large *creature*.

9. Probably 225 kg is its *mass* and 2.5 m its *height*.

10. It has a long, flatfooted *gait*.

11. The expert asked the *camper* this *question*.

12. Are the footprints a *hoax*?

13. Is the creature Bigfoot a *myth* or is it a *reality*?

EXERCISE C Write original sentences in the specified word order. Add modifiers when needed. Underline the required parts in your sentences. (Add 20 points for each correct sentence.)

A. Subject—verb—compound direct object.

The waiter then served my father and me.

1. Subject—verb—direct object.

....

2. Subject—verb—indirect object—direct object.

....

3. Subject—verb—subject complement.

....

4. Helping verb—subject—main verb—direct object.

....

5. Subject—verb—compound subject complement.

....

Cumulative Review

A Over each italicized word write what part of speech it is. Use these abbreviations: noun, *n.*; pronoun, *pron.*; adjective, *adj.*; verb, *v.*; adverb, *adv.*; preposition, *prep.*; conjunction, *conj.*; interjection, *int.* (Add 5 points for each correct answer.)

1 "*Wow!* Look *at* this *news* story," said Louise. "The *police* are *now* using

2 hypnosis to solve crimes."

3 "*They* are using what?" asked Sara *incredulously.*

4 "They're using hypnosis," *replied* Louise. "*Listen.* In order to find the

5 *culprit* in a hit-and-run accident, the department had the witness hypno-

6 tized *by* a doctor, *and* hypnosis *enabled* the witness to remember the licence

7 plate number *of* the *hit-and-run driver's* car. *With this* information, the

8 police were able to apprehend the *guilty* party *quickly.*"

B In the first space at the right, place an *S* if the group of words is a sentence, and an *F* if it is not a sentence. If you decide that it is not a sentence, give the reason for your decision by using the letter of the appropriate reason: *a*—lacks a verb and its subject, or *b*—has a verb and its subject but is not a complete thought. (Add 10 points for each correctly marked sentence.)

A. There are three types of matter.   *S.* ....

B. That have volume but no definite form.   *F.* *b*

1. A liquid is one of these types.   ....

2. A liquid, taking the shape of its container.   ....

3. Acting exactly as gases do.   ....

4. Which is called a fluid?   ....

5. Are liquids and gases both fluids?   ....

6. When a liquid reaches its boiling point.   ....

7. It becomes a gas.   ....

8. A liquid also becomes solid.   ....

9. At its freezing point, like water becoming ice.   ....

10. The melting process turns ice into water.   ....

C Cross out the prepositional phrases in the sentences below. Find the base of each sentence and write the parts of the base in the appropriate column below, after the number of the sentence. Be sure to include all parts of compound subjects, verbs, and complements. Not all of these sentences contain complements. (Add 2 points for each correct answer.)

A. Bill dropped his work and came with us.

	Subjects	Verbs	Complements
A.	*Bill*	*dropped, came*	*work*

1. The Sunday afternoon sunshine faded quickly. 2. Without much warning the peaceful summer day reached a premature end. 3. A storm moved in over the lake. 4. People ran from the lake to the shelter of their cabins. 5. Dark, wind-torn sheets of rain enveloped the landscape and swallowed up the happy brightness of the day. 6. Even the bushes and trees seemed fearful and forlorn. 7. They cowered in the strange green light and huddled closer together. 8. We stood inside our cabin and looked out the window. 9. A swirling funnel emerged from a black cloud and threatened destruction and death. 10. For a while the funnel played a game of harmless leapfrog and then, like the evil witches in *Macbeth*, vanished in the stormy air.

	Subjects	Verbs	Complements
1.			
2.			
3.			
4.			
5.			
6.			
7.			
8.			
9.			
10.			

Spelling: Does It End in *-ar, -er,* or *-or?*

Like many people, do you have trouble knowing whether certain common words end in *-ar, -er,* or *-or?* In referring to a physician, do you write *doct-,* and then try to decide whether the word ends in *-er* or *-or?* You have difficulty because the suffix in such words is an unstressed syllable. You say *dóc tor.* Therefore the vowel in the final syllable is reduced to the indistinct schwa sound /ə/ you learned about in Lessons 13 and 24. You cannot tell from the *sound* whether the vowel is *a, e,* or *o* in such endings.

Although you cannot use sound as a spelling clue, all is not hopeless. There are some guides that can help you decide. The suffix *-er* (and its variants *-or* and *-ar*) turns verbs into nouns. It means "one who." "One who *climbs*" is a *climber.* What is "one who *buys*"?

Here are some guides to the correct spelling of nouns meaning "one who":

● Only five common words in this category have the suffix spelled with *-ar.* If you can memorize these five, then you will know the important "one who" words ending in *-ar.*

> begg **ar**   li **ar**   schol **ar**   burgl **ar**   registr **ar**

● Verbs that end in *-ate* take the *-or* spelling when they are changed into nouns meaning "one who." You can therefore "test" the ending of a noun by turning it back into its verb form.

> oper*ate* → operat **or**   imit*ate* → imitat **or**

● The "one who" suffix is spelled *-or* in nouns of Latin origin. Generally, such words refer to positions of prestige, authority, or importance.

> govern **or**   profess **or**   edit **or**   act **or**

● The "one who" suffix is generally spelled *-er* in words that refer to trades or simply to situations.

> carpent **er**   plumb **er**   dream **er**   runn **er**

EXERCISE A Write the letter *e, a,* or *o* in the blank in each of the following words. Use the four guides to help you decide. (Add 10 points for each correct answer.)

1. farm . . . . r
2. burgl . . . . r
3. ambassad . . . . r
4. nominat . . . . r
5. help . . . . r
6. imitat . . . . r
7. wait . . . . r
8. bystand . . . . r
9. schol . . . . r
10. auth . . . . r

Add *e, a,* or *o* to the word containing a blank in each sentence below. Use the guides, as well as the clues in the sentences themselves. (Add 10 points for each correct answer.)

1. Being a garden....r sounds like a healthy trade.

2. A person who does not tell the truth is a li....r.

3. Lawy....rs did not always have the prestige they have today.

4. Kate will be one of the competing swimm....rs this afternoon.

5. Outside the building sat a pitiful begg....r.

6. A spons....r controls a TV program.

7. Who is the conduct....r of the orchestra?

8. Heather's grandfather was an airplane radio operat....r.

9. A pitch....r is only one member of a baseball team.

10. Dr. J. S. Plaskett was an astronom....r.

EXERCISE C   Be prepared to write from dictation all of the words taught in this lesson. (Add 2 points for each correctly spelled word.)

REVIEW EXERCISE   In the blank in each word below, write the vowel that correctly completes the word. Each vowel you write occurs in an unstressed syllable and will have the schwa /ə/ sound. Try to think of a "related" word to help you decide which vowel to use. (Add 10 points for each correct answer.)

1. rel....tive

2. form....l

3. popul....r

4. cel....brate

5. loc....l

6. invent....r

7. or....gin

8. emph....sis

9. civ....l

10. org....n

Building Vocabulary: Choosing the Right Word

English is amazingly rich in *synonyms*—words that have nearly, though never exactly, the same meaning. Often, we find one very general word like *big* surrounded by a whole cluster of words (*huge, gigantic, monstrous,* for example) that have more limited and specific meanings. For effective writing and speaking, we must sort out the specific meanings of such words and fit the right word to the right context.

EXAMPLES   That store has a **reputation** for low prices and good service.

Madame Benoit has achieved **renown** as a gourmet cook.

The film star achieved a certain **notoriety** through his wild parties.

The three words printed in red mean the opinion which people have of a person or thing. *Reputation* is the most general of the three—a reputation may be good or bad, important or insignificant. *Renown* means a *good* reputation for outstanding achievement. *Notoriety* is a *bad* reputation for something harmful and unimportant. It would be as wrong to speak of the movie star's *renown* as to speak of Madame Benoit's *notoriety*. In each case, the context shows which synonym fits.

A dictionary usually explains the differences between close synonyms. Under *big,* for example, you might find a reference to *large,* in which a list of synonyms and a discussion of their differences would be given.

EXERCISE A   Each sentence offers a choice of closely related words given in parentheses. Using a dictionary (be sure to consult lists of synonyms), decide which word fits the context best and write this word on the blank line below the sentence. After the word you have chosen, write the dictionary meaning that fits the context. (Add 10 points for each correct item.)

1. The Romans were (contemptuous, contemptible) of other nations, whom they called barbarians.

. . . .

2. A more (intelligent, intelligible) person would have understood the problem better.

. . . .

3. An argument that is (wise, sensible, rational) is based on logic and clear thinking rather than on an appeal to the emotions.

. . . .

4. The new circus lion is an extremely (gentle, docile, compliant) one, and Angela finds it very easy to train.

. . . .

5. Thornton's disposition is so (placid, sober, self-controlled) that neither happiness nor unhappiness has ever disturbed it.

. . . .

6. The accused man (stated, affirmed, alleged) that he had been in Brazil at the time of the crime, but the jury demanded proof.

. . . .

7. The toy's (breakable, frail, delicate) construction did not stand up under the hard use the children gave it.

. . . .

8. The illness was caused by a (deficiency, imperfection, lack) of the necessary vitamins and minerals in her diet.

. . . .

9. Mother Teresa, recipient of the Nobel Peace Prize in 1979, is known for her (mercy, tenderness, compassion) toward the destitute.

. . . .

10. The judge's wise sentence can only (intensify, enhance, increase) her reputation for honesty and integrity.

. . . .

EXERCISE B Write the letter of the best meaning to the left of each word. (Add 10 points for each correct answer.)

.... 1. allege, *v.*

.... 2. compassion, *n.*

.... 3. contemptuous, *adj.*

.... 4. deficiency, *n.*

.... 5. delicate, *adj.*

.... 6. docile, *adj.*

.... 7. enhance, *v.*

.... 8. intelligent, *adj.*

.... 9. placid, *adj.*

.... 10. rational, *adj.*

a. quick to understand

b. weakness due to lack

c. pity with desire to help

d. to raise still higher

e. easily taught, led

f. calm, untroubled

g. scornful

h. finely made and easily damaged

i. to state without proof

j. according to reason; logical

CHAPTER FOUR

Phrases and Clauses

You have learned that a sentence base consists of a subject, a verb, and (in some sentences) a complement. In addition to these three basic parts, a sentence usually contains words used as modifiers: adjectives and adverbs. A sentence may also contain groups of words which belong together and work together as modifiers. In this chapter you will learn more about two important word groups: phrases and clauses.

LESSON 33

The Phrase

A phrase is a group of related words used as a single part of speech that does not contain a verb and its subject.

EXAMPLES   He lives **in a brick house**. (phrase used as an adverb telling *where* he lives)

It is the house **with green shutters**. (phrase used as an adjective describing *house*)

A prepositional phrase is a group of words beginning with a preposition and ending with a noun or pronoun.

EXAMPLES   **at** *home*   **to** *me*   **by** *Virginia Hamilton*

Do not confuse an infinitive (*to* plus a *verb*) with a prepositional phrase. Phrases like *to go, to see,* and *to use* are the infinitive form of verbs. Prepositional phrases end with a noun or a pronoun, not a verb: *to town, to them.*

The following words may be used as prepositions. Some may also be used as adverbs or conjunctions.

aboard	before	by	near	to
about	behind	concerning	of	toward
above	below	down	off	under
across	beneath	during	on	underneath
after	beside	except	onto	unlike
against	besides	for	over	until
along	between	from	past	up
among	beyond	in	since	upon
around	but (meaning	into	through	with
at	*except*)	like	throughout	within
				without

Some prepositions consist of more than one word: *because of, in spite of, instead of, on account of.*

The noun or pronoun which ends the prepositional phrase is the object of the preposition which begins the phrase.

EXAMPLES   from my sister   because of him
              near Edmonton   for Gilles Bolvin

EXERCISE A In each blank in the first column below, write a preposition to introduce each prepositional phrase. Do not use any prepositions twice. In the second column, complete each prepositional phrase by adding an appropriate object or objects. Correct pronoun forms used as objects of prepositions are *me, you, her, him, it, them, us.* (Add 10 points for each correct numbered item.)

1. .... the soup   6. beyond the ....

2. .... a magic wand   7. except .... and ....

3. .... them   8. during a ....

4. .... my bobsled   9. concerning.....................

5. .... Janet and her   10. to .... and ....

EXERCISE B Draw a line under each prepositional phrase in the following paragraph. Circle the object of the preposition. There are twenty-three prepositional phrases. (Add 4 points for each correctly marked phrase.)

1   On Ferry Wharf of Halifax Harbour in the shadow of the Historic

2   Waterfront Development Project stands the Fisherman's Market,

3   perhaps the city's busiest. During the cold hours before dawn, the fish

4   market springs into action as people unload their boats and lay their

5   wares along Halifax's restored Granville Street. Buyers and sellers

6   conduct their business in a rising crescendo of noise, which by early

7   morning exceeds the noises coming from the heart of the city. Inside,

8   the market is jammed to the ceiling with crated fish from distant

9   places, iced and ready to be distributed through the city. The market

10   is no place for the squeamish. The smell is what you would expect;

11   the sounds are deafening. On the boats there are many "colourful

12   characters," dressed for the weather, their faces made swarthy by At-

13   lantic winds. Before noon the last fish has been sent on his way, the

14   the last deck has been hosed down. Fish for dinner, anyone?

The Adjective Phrase

An underlined adjective phrase is a prepositional phrase used as an adjective to modify a noun or a pronoun.

By comparing the sentences in the following example, you will see how a phrase acts as an adjective. The first sentence contains an adjective and the second contains an adjective phrase. Notice that the adjective phrase *follows* the word it modifies.

EXAMPLE   Our **Quebec** cousins are visiting us.

Our cousins **from Quebec** are visiting us.

A prepositional phrase may modify the object of another prepositional phrase.

EXAMPLE   Those stamps **at the front of the album** are valuable.

EXERCISE A   Add an adjective phrase to each of the following nouns and pronouns. Do not use the same preposition twice. (Add 10 points for each correct answer.)

A. a man ... *on a horse* ....

1. the highway ....

6. everyone ....

2. the one ....

7. the girl ....

3. a window ....

8. a necklace ....

4. letters ....

9. a school ....

5. a book ....

10. houses ....

EXERCISE B   Replace each adjective phrase in the following sentences with a single adjective that has the same meaning as the phrase. Underline the phrase. In the first space at the right, write the adjective which replaces the phrase. In the second space write the noun the adjective modifies. (Add 5 points for each correct sentence.)

	Adjective	Word modified
A. Tales about the West are popular.	*Western*	*tales*
1. I like stories with ghosts.	....	....
2. Winds in March often disturb me.	....	....
3. Finally I bought a box for tools.	....	....
4. Fins on fish can injure anglers.	....	....

65

5. He needed words of encouragement. ....

6. The gentleman from Victoria nodded. ....

7. I used a hammer with a claw. ....

8. A boat for racing had sunk. ....

9. Basketball is a game of action. ....

10. Storms during the spring are sudden. ....

11. This is a gem of value. ....

12. He drives a truck with a trailer. ....

13. Jeanne d'Arc is a heroine of France. ....

14. This dish contains food for the turtle. ....

15. The shops in Avon close early. ....

16. She is a girl from France. ....

17. Victoria was a queen of England. ....

18. Lena wants a career in science. ....

19. The store for hats was closed. ....

20. The house at the corner is empty. ....

EXERCISE C Circle each adjective phrase in the following sentences. Then draw an arrow to the word it modifies. There are twenty phrases to identify. (Add 5 points for each correct answer.)

1   A liquid like water normally takes the exact shape of its container.

2   When water reaches a level beyond a jar's capacity, the water at the top

3   spills out. This fact of liquids is one of the principal reasons for clogged

4   gas burners on kitchen stoves. A trick from a newspaper column cer-

5   tainly baffled the students in my science class. The water-filled glass on

6   the teacher's desk contained a number of pennies. The water above the

7   rim was not spilling! A classmate behind me exclaimed, "Wow! The

8   water in that glass must be supernatural!" Conversation between the

9   teacher and me soon gave everyone the right key to the mystery con-

10   cerning the water level. The pennies in the glass had been immersed

11   carefully, thus slowly raising the level of the water. The surface tension of

12   the water formed a meniscus and prevented its spilling.

The Adverb Phrase

An <u>adverb phrase</u> **is a prepositional phrase used as an adverb to modify a verb, an adjective, or an adverb.**

EXAMPLES   We searched **with great patience**. (phrase modifies a verb)

I am afraid **of high places**. (phrase modifies an adjective)

They scored early **in the game**. (phrase modifies an adverb)

Like an adverb, an adverb phrase may tell one of five things about the word it modifies. It may tell *how, when, where, why,* or *how much.*

EXAMPLES   She overcame evil **with kindness**. (tells *how*)
During the summer, rainfall is heavy. (tells *when*)
I jumped **into the swirling water**. (tells *where*)
We failed **because of excessive absences**. (tells *why*)
We played **for an hour**. (tells *how much*)

Adverb phrases may be separated by other words from the words they modify. This separation makes them a little more difficult to spot than adjective phrases, which usually come directly after the words they modify.

EXERCISE A   Each of the following sentences contains an adverb phrase. Circle each phrase and draw an arrow from the phrase to the word it modifies. In the space at the right, write what the phrase tells: *how, when, where, why,* or *how much.* (Add 5 points for each correct response in marking a phrase and in filling a blank.)

1. Many groups of primitive people explain unusual natu-

   ral phenomena through myths. . . . .

2. In the past the Australian aborigines told a clever tale

   about the mallee tree. . . . .

3. The mallee tree grows into a peculiar shape. . . . .

4. Toward the top, the trunk of the tree twists and turns. . . . .

5. For many years the tree grew straight. . . . .

6. Then, by a stroke of genius, Rat Man invented the

   boomerang. . . . .

7. With careful craftsmanship, he made a new weapon for

   hunting. . . . .

8. Because of its strange flight the boomerang fascinated

   the mallee. . . . .

9. The mallee followed the boomerang's flight by turning
its body. . . . .

10. Since that day all descendants of the first mallee tree
have had twisted trunks. . . . .

EXERCISE B Circle each adverb phrase in the following sentences. Then draw an arrow from the phrase to the word it modifies. (Add 10 points for each correctly marked sentence.)

1. Luis and I have watched reruns of *Star Trek* for many years.

2. We have viewed each show with avid interest.

3. I even know the dialogue for some of the shows by heart.

4. A cult of *Star Trek* fans has developed within the last few years.

5. Every year they hold a *Star Trek* convention in New York City.

6. Luis and I attended the convention out of curiosity.

7. A small replica of the spaceship stood near the centre of the room.

8. We approached the ship and looked inside the windows.

9. A miniature of James T. Kirk sat in the captain's chair.

10. Spock lay beneath the phaser bank, fixing the machinery.

EXERCISE C Circle the phrase in each sentence and draw an arrow from the phrase to the word it modifies. In the space at the right tell whether the phrase is being used as an adjective or an adverb. (Add 5 points for each correct response in marking a phrase and filling a blank.)

1. The dog with the long tail is mine. . . . .

2. Pam writes with her left hand. . . . .

3. From the north came a driving snowstorm. . . . .

4. The photographs by Michael Snow are inspiring. . . . .

5. My book report was not copied from the book jacket. . . . .

6. Teams from twenty schools entered the tournament. . . . .

7. Buy your school supplies at Zing's. . . . .

8. I want another book by Marian Engel. . . . .

9. Madame Curie's achievements in science were
remarkable. . . . .

10. You must come home before midnight. . . . .

The Clause

A group of words that contains a verb and its subject and is used as a part of a sentence is called a clause.

The principal difference between a clause and a phrase is that a clause has both a verb and a subject, whereas a phrase does not.

PHRASES   after school (no subject or verb)
           had been stolen (a verb without a subject)

CLAUSES   when school was out (subject: *school;* verb: *was*)
           which had been stolen (subject: *which;* verb: *had been stolen*)

There are two kinds of clauses: independent clauses and subordinate clauses.

An independent clause makes sense by itself; it expresses a complete thought.

When an independent clause stands by itself, it is called a sentence.

SENTENCES   Ms. Stamford is a good driver. She does not like to drive.

When these complete thoughts are combined into one sentence, they are called independent clauses, *parts* of a sentence.

           INDEPENDENT CLAUSE   INDEPENDENT CLAUSE
EXAMPLE   Ms. Stamford is a good driver, but she does not like to drive.

Independent clauses are usually joined by the conjunctions *and, but,* and *or.*

A subordinate clause by itself is only a fragment of a sentence. It must be connected with an independent clause to make its meaning complete.

SUBORDINATE CLAUSE   When L. M. Montgomery was young

           SUBORDINATE CLAUSE   INDEPENDENT CLAUSE
SENTENCE   When L. M. Montgomery was young, she began writing.

Such conjunctions as *after, although, as if, because, before, if, since, though, unless, until, when, where,* and *while* are subordinate clause signals. *What, who, whom, whose, which,* and *that* can also introduce subordinate clauses.

EXAMPLES   We were fishing when the sun rose.
           As the coach had feared, our team was defeated.
           This is the man who helped us.
           I realized that the teacher had been right.

EXERCISE A The subordinate clauses in the sentences below are italicized. Underline the subject of each subordinate clause once and the verb twice. Select the verb first; then find the subject by asking *who?* or *what?* (Add 25 points for each correctly marked sentence.)

1. *If failures do not quit,* they may eventually succeed, *as Churchill did.*

2. *When Janice was ill,* she read Gregory Clark's "Professional," *which you had recommended.*

3. *After I had overcome my stage fright,* I forgot *what my next line was!*

4. Mr. Habeeb, *who is a superb teacher,* answers questions *that the class should have asked.*

EXERCISE B Underline the subordinate clauses in the following paragraph. (Add 5 points for each correct answer.)

1   After we had studied various ecological systems, Mrs. Roth suggested
2   that we divide into groups. Each group would choose a project which
3   was of interest to them. The project that we chose was building a
4   woodland terrarium. Since our school is within walking distance of a
5   park with a woodland terrain, we would be able to gather the necessary
6   materials. After school was over for the day, we hiked to the park where
7   we hunted for materials. Sheila found several flowering plants such as
8   wintergreen, whose flowers are white and bell-shaped, and pipsissewa,
9   which has leaves that are used for medicinal purposes. She put the plants
10   in cut-off milk containers whose bottoms were filled with soil so that she
11   could carry them home. While I was looking for a moss-covered rock, I
12   found a salamander for the terrarium. Although it was quite fast, I
13   managed to catch it. We gathered our finds and went home before it got
14   dark. The next day we started work on our project. Mrs. Roth said that
15   we could use the aquarium tank from the science closet if another class
16   wasn't using it. We covered the base of the tank with gravel so that the
17   soil would have adequate drainage. Then we added a layer of woodland
18   soil. After we had placed the moss-covered rock in the terrarium, we
19   added my salamander. We planted small ferns, seedlings from spruce
20   trees, flowering plants, acorns, and beechnuts. When we had finished
21   planting, we placed the terrarium in a cool spot.

The Adjective Clause

Subordinate clauses, like phrases, are used as single parts of speech: adjective, adverb, and noun.

An adjective clause is a subordinate clause used as an adjective to modify a noun or a pronoun.

Study the following examples to see how a subordinate clause acts as an adjective.

ADJECTIVES	ADJECTIVE CLAUSES
We saw a **hilarious** movie.	We saw a movie **which was hilarious**.
He is an **entertaining** speaker.	He is a speaker **who entertains his audience**.
The **Baffin** expeditions explored the Canadian Arctic.	The expeditions **that Baffin led** explored the Canadian Arctic.

Adjective clauses are usually introduced by the relative pronouns *who, whom, whose, that,* and *which.*

EXAMPLES   Ask the woman **who** owns one.
Are those the boys **whom** you referred to?
No one had read the stories **which** were assigned.
This is the dress **that** I want.
This is the book from **which** I took my information.

Sometimes the relative pronoun is omitted.

EXAMPLES   This is the dress I want.
Are those the boys you referred to?

EXERCISE A   Circle each of the ten adjective clauses in the following sentences. Draw an arrow from the clause to the word it modifies. (Add 10 points for each correctly marked clause.)

A. The postal service in Quebec, which was established by the British, appointed Benjamin Franklin as the Deputy Postmaster General.

1. Do you know any people who have emigrated to Israel?

2. John Macoun was the Canadian botanist whose explorations resulted in the discovery of many plants.

3. Last summer Mona visited Moncton, which is her birthplace.

71

4. Satire, which is a kind of writing, makes fun of people who are absurd.

5. Opossums that are cornered have a unique method of self-defence.

6. Nutritionists advocate consumer awareness, which is essential for good health.

7. A person whom others call "lucky" is usually an intelligent hard worker who takes full advantage of opportunities.

8. The dog to which I gave the bone growled at me.

EXERCISE B Change the second sentence in each pair into an adjective clause and write the clause above the first sentence, using a caret (∧) to indicate where it should be inserted. In sentences 2, 4, 7, and 8, you should set off the adjective clause with commas. You will learn about this later. (Add 10 points for each correct sentence.)

A. Dale McLaren *, who is our best pitcher,* was named to the All-Star team.
   He is our best ∧ pitcher.

1. Tell Miss Juarez you want the book.
   I returned it.

2. Cynthia Watson will be the new dramatics coach.
   She was once a well-known actress.

3. Mr. Holden refused to pay us the money.
   We had earned the money.

4. The building is completely air-conditioned.
   It houses the cafeteria.

5. The seniors are dedicating their annual celebration to a teacher.
   They love and respect the teacher.   (Use *whom.*)

6. The eight detectives are working around the clock.
   They were assigned to this case.

7. Your box of chocolates tempted everyone in the room.
   It was lying open on the desk.

8. Frank Augustyn performs ballet around the world.
   He grew up in Hamilton.

9. The plan will receive Canadian support.
   England proposed the plan.

10. All of the seniors are going to the outing.
    I talked to several seniors.   (Use *whom.*)

The Adverb Clause

An **adverb clause** is a subordinate clause used as an adverb.

An adverb clause tells *how, when, where, why, how much,* or *under what conditions.*

EXAMPLES   Gerald behaved as though he were angry. (tells *how* Gerald behaved)
We came when we were called. (tells *when* we came)
I will go wherever you send me. (tells *where* I will go)
The team lost because the players were tired. (tells *why* the team lost)
The girls worked harder than the boys did. (tells *how much* harder the girls worked)
You will pass the course if you pass this test. (tells *under what conditions* you will pass)

Adverb clauses are introduced by subordinating conjunctions. The most frequently used subordinating conjunctions are the following:

after	as if	before	than	when	wherever
although	as though	if	unless	whenever	while
as	because	since	until	where	

EXERCISE A   Underline the adverb clause in each sentence. Circle the subordinating conjunction. In the space at the right, put the letter which shows what the clause tells. (Add 2½ points for each correctly marked clause and each correct letter.)

a. how   c. where   e. how much
b. when   d. why   f. under what conditions

A. (When) you are near a hot stove, notice the rising air.   *b*

1. The air above the stove wiggles because heat affects air.   ....

2. If air becomes hot, molecules in it quickly scatter.   ....

3. Since heat causes this expansion, the hot air moves.   ....

4. Hot air is lighter than cold air is.   ....

5. Because it is heavy, cold air hovers near the earth.   ....

6. Wherever hot and cold air come together, there is a breeze.   ....

7. Air above the sea is cooler than air is above the hot beach.   ....

8. When the warm air rises, the cool air rushes underneath.   ....

9. Because this movement occurs, sea breezes blow inland.   ....

10. Is there no wind unless the temperature of air varies?   ....

11. Before you answer, you must know about prevailing winds.   . . . .

12. Wherever the climate is hot, air rises rapidly.   . . . .

13. Air goes downward wherever the climate is cold.   . . . .

14. Tropical air travels toward the poles as the polar air moves toward the equator.   . . . .

15. Because this movement is constant, the winds prevail.   . . . .

16. We must not act as if this is the complete picture.   . . . .

17. Since the earth rotates, it affects wind direction.   . . . .

18. As the earth rotates toward the east, it causes westerly winds in the Northern Hemisphere.   . . . .

19. Although I have read about these changes, I still want to know more.   . . . .

20. My curiosity will not rest until I understand "doldrums."   . . . .

EXERCISE B The following sentences contain adverb and adjective clauses. Underline each clause and tell in the space at the right whether it is an adjective clause or an adverb clause. (Add 5 points for each correct underlining and identification.)

Kind of clause

A. There's a car that looks just like ours.   *adj*

 1. Sally's room looks as though a tornado had hit it.   . . . .

 2. The calendar which we use today was introduced in 1582.   . . . .

 3. It was Alec and Clara who put life into that party!   . . . .

 4. I shall write when I receive your new address.   . . . .

 5. If I hear any news, I will call you.   . . . .

 6. Although taxes are unpopular, they are necessary.   . . . .

 7. Take the road which follows the coast.   . . . .

 8. Don't volunteer unless you want to work.   . . . .

 9. I saved all the money that you gave me.   . . . .

10. His arm hurts where the pitched ball struck it.   . . . .

The Noun Clause

A noun clause is a subordinate clause used as a noun.

Like nouns, noun clauses may be used as subjects, subject complements, and objects.

	NOUNS	NOUN CLAUSES
SUBJECT	His speech alarmed us.	What he said alarmed us.
SUBJ. COMP.	This is our route.	This is where we are going.
DIRECT OBJECT	I know her mother.	I know who her mother is.
OBJ. OF PREP.	We will give it to the highest bidder.	We will give it to whoever bids the highest.

EXERCISE A Underline the noun clause in each of the following sentences. In the space at the right tell how the clause is used: *s.*(subject), *s.c.* (subject complement), *d.o.* (direct object), *o.p.* (object of preposition). (Add 5 points for each correct answer.)

A. Do you know why an architect uses a quirk?   *d.o.*

1. I now understand what a scratch hit is.   . . . .

2. That he was safe on second seemed obvious to me.   . . . .

3. Kathy Kreiner knows how important good skis are.   . . . .

4. I'll take whoever wants a ride.   . . . .

5. This is what she gave me.   . . . .

6. Whoever gets the job will have to work hard.   . . . .

7. A new athletic field is what we need most.   . . . .

8. I wrote about what I did last summer.   . . . .

9. Where Marian went remained a secret.   . . . .

10. Whoever finishes first is the winner.   . . . .

EXERCISE B Underline the subordinate clauses. In the first space at the right name the kind of clause, using the abbreviations *adj., adv., n.* Fill the second space as follows:

For adjective clauses, write the noun or pronoun modified.
For adverb clauses, write what the clause tells: *how, when, where, why, condition.*
For noun clauses, tell how the clause is used: *s., s.c., d.o., o.p.*
(Add 5 points for each correct sentence.)

A. The accounts that witnesses gave varied greatly. *adj. accounts*

B. Before you decide, consider all the facts. *adv. when*

C. He pretended that he did not know me. *n. d.o.*

75

1. Where tattooing began is a mystery. . . . .

2. Some women who live in New Guinea are tattooed. . . . .

3. Many men in Canada also have tattoos. . . . .

4. Wherever you go, you will find unusual customs. . . . .

5. Politicians who kiss babies may seem odd to someone from the Orient. . . . .

6. The custom of kissing, which is popular in North America and Europe, was never widely accepted in China. . . . .

7. If we were Samoans, we would sniff instead of kiss! . . . .

8. This book says that a dog's lick is its kiss. . . . .

9. Mrs. Bell, who teaches science, denies this fact. . . . .

10. Dogs lick us because they like our salty taste. . . . .

11. That is what Mrs. Bell says. . . . .

12. Mrs. Bell smiled, however, when she made the statement. . . . .

13. I think that kowtowing is an interesting custom. . . . .

14. It is a way of bowing that is often done in a servile manner. . . . .

15. The Chinese think that it indicates respect. . . . .

16. Do you know where nose-rubbing indicates friendship? . . . .

17. When Eskimos want to show affection, they rub noses. . . . .

18. Shaking hands is a Western custom whose origins are unusual. . . . .

19. By shaking hands, people could determine if someone were holding a weapon. . . . .

20. Do you know what the origin of toasting is? . . . .

Chapter Review

EXERCISE A   Circle each prepositional phrase. Draw an arrow from the phrase to the word it modifies. Tell what kind of phrase it is by writing above it *adj.* or *adv.* (Add 5 points for each correctly marked phrase.)

1   Beyond a doubt, the camel is one of the strangest domesticated
2   animals. Unlike the horse or the dog, the camel has never experienced
3   affection for human beings or from human beings. A camel with a
4   grievance will often spit its cud into its owner's face. This has not created
5   good will between humans and camels. If people were suddenly removed
6   from the earth, most domesticated animals would perish before long.
7   The camel would survive without difficulty. It has never become depend-
8   ent upon humans. The average camel can carry almost 180 kg on
9   its back without showing signs of tiring. Each camel has its own
10   limit. If the owner goes beyond the limit by even a minute amount,
11   the camel will suddenly collapse under the load from the strain and
12   perhaps die. This fact is the basis for the saying, "It was the straw that
13   broke the camel's back."

EXERCISE B   Each of the following sentences contains two subordinate clauses. Underline the clauses. In the spaces at the right name the clauses in order: *adjective, adverb,* or *noun.* (Add 2½ points for each correctly marked clause and correct identification.)

1. If you see Nancy, ask her about the books
   that I gave her.   . . . .

2. Since we have no practice room, we have
   dropped varsity wrestling, which has always
   been a popular sport.   . . . .

3. What I asked for was a book that had a
   poem by E. J. Pratt in it.   . . . .

4. The losses which they suffered in the stock
   market were losses which all brokers expect.   . . . .

5. When he opened the mail, he found the
   letter that he had been looking for.   . . . .

6. Wherever you go, you will find people who are interesting. . . . .

7. If you like to write, include a course in creative writing among those that you elect. . . . .

8. Although I spent two hours on my homework, I was unprepared when Mr. Horton called on me. . . . .

9. I was offered the job that I wanted, but my parents, who had other plans for me, would not let me accept it. . . . .

10. Don't repeat what she said, because she does not want to be quoted. . . . .

EXERCISE C On the lines provided, rewrite each of the following pairs of sentences, changing the italicized sentence into a subordinate clause as directed. (Add 20 points for each correct sentence.)

1. My pen pal collects stamps. *He lives in Nigeria.* (adjective clause)

. . . .

. . . .

2. Dad cannot start the fire. *The wood is wet.* (adverb clause telling why)

. . . .

. . . .

3. That girl ought to know something about first aid. *Her mother is a doctor.* (adjective clause introduced by *whose*)

. . . .

. . . .

4. *My dog ran away.* I'll never understand it. (noun clause introduced by *why* in place of the direct object *it*)

. . . .

. . . .

5. I remembered the answer. *It was too late.* (adverb clause telling when)

. . . .

. . . .

Cumulative Review

A Above each italicized word, write the part of speech. Use the following abbreviations: *n.* (noun); *pron.* (pronoun); *adj.* (adjective); *v.* (verb); *adv.* (adverb); *prep.* (preposition); *conj.* (conjunction); and *int.* (interjection). (Add 5 points for each correct answer.)

1   A few years ago, a *funny creature* called Ookpik *quickly captured*

2   the hearts *of* many. Ookpik was a sealskin *Arctic owl cleverly* designed

3   *by* Eskimo craftsmen of Fort Chimo, Quebec. It *had* a *round* head, a

4   round body, two round eyes *and* a big *carrot-like* nose. *When* the Cana-

5   dian *Department* of Trade and Commerce *featured* Ookpik *at* a trade

6   fair, *it instantly* won public acceptance. *Indeed,* Ookpik was so popular,

7   it was used as a symbol in the promotion of Eskimo crafts.

B Find the sentence base in each of the following sentences; underline the subject once, the verb twice, and circle the complement. Some sentences contain more than one complement. (Add 5 points for each correctly marked sentence.)

A. Did Willis ever lend you that book?

1. Everyone in the audience was enthusiastic.

2. The boat at the dock belongs to Mrs. Anderson.

3. She offered me a second chance.

4. Eric and Elena are going to the picnic together.

5. Diahann takes judo lessons after school.

6. The circumference of the earth at the equator is almost 40 225 km.

7. Dale expected a larger reward.

8. Students and teachers were critical of the plan.

9. Mac and she took Jean and him with them.

10. The mail carrier gave Eugenio both of the letters.

11. Celia dried the first plate and then stopped.

12. In the second term, we will take either speech or creative writing.

13. Duck hunting is a cold and dismal sport.

14. Mr. Dietz can probably give you the information.

15. During the rough weather nearly everyone on board became seasick.

16. Leave behind you the mistakes of the past.

17. Mother and Dad sent us apples from the Okanagan Valley.

18. There are several good reasons for his success.

19. In the new school Helen did not seem very happy.

20. Both the Ford and the Chevrolet need the attention of a mechanic.

C Underline the twenty complements in the following sentences. Above each complement write the proper identification: *d.o.*, *i.o.*, or *s.c.* Not every sentence has a complement. Remember also that a complement is never part of a prepositional phrase. (Add 5 points for each correctly marked complement.)

1. That is the best kind of bicycle.

2. Someone should have told him the truth.

3. The dog wants its dinner.

4. Where did you see my name?

5. Henry gave me half of his sandwich and kept the rest for himself.

6. She is more athletic than I.

7. Will you give the boy in the middle this information?

8. Is your father the famous musician from Quebec City?

9. I gave my little sister a book for her birthday.

10. In the morning, a glittering layer of ice was on all the trees.

11. Moderate exercise can be beneficial to persons of any age.

12. Geraldine still owes me a thank-you letter.

13. Cora had already written a short note to her uncle.

14. Here comes the committee from the anti-pollution society.

15. They were the ones with the best plans for our party.

16. Park your car in the lot behind the building.

Spelling: Three Ways of Spelling /-əl/

The sound /-əl/ is a very difficult one to spell. It appears in unstressed syllables at the end of many nouns, verbs, and adjectives. Therefore, you cannot tell by listening which vowel and consonant combination represents the sound in a particular word. The troublesome sound /-əl/ is most commonly spelled -al, -le, or -el. (It is also spelled -ile or -il, as in *hostile, fertile, evil,* and *pencil,* but since these spellings are relatively uncommon, they will not be treated here.)

How, then, do you know whether to use -le or -al or -el? There are no rules, but there are some guides that can help you decide. Try to memorize the guides below and the example words that illustrate them.

● The -le spelling is most generally used after the consonant letters *b, p, d, t,* hard *g, k, f,* and *z.*

sta**ble**	bri**dle**	an**gle**	ri**fle**
sta**ple**	brit**tle**	an**kle**	puz**zle**

● The spelling -al is a Latin suffix most commonly added to nouns to turn them into adjectives. The majority of such adjectives are made from words that can stand alone—without the suffix -al. Words ending in -le or -el can never stand alone when the -le or -el ending is removed. (As you read the words in the right-hand column below, notice that a final e is dropped and that a final y is changed to i in the base word when -al is added.)

origin	original	fate	fatal
accident	accidental	bride	bridal
profession	professional	bury	burial
music	musical	secretary	secretarial

Note: Some adjectives (and a few nouns) ending in -al have entered English directly from Latin or French, and thus have no separate noun form that can stand alone in English. Here are some of the more common of these words: Memorize them.

frug**al** leg**al** mor**al** rur**al** annu**al** dent**al** anim**al** hospit**al**

●The -el spelling is used in most other words to which the two guides above do not apply. Among these -el words are:

kenn**el** vess**el** quarr**el** parc**el** tunn**el** chann**el** barr**el** gav**el**

EXERCISE A Use the guides you have learned to spell correctly the /-əl/ sound omitted from each word or word part below. Write -le, -al, or -el in the short blank. Then write the complete word, correctly spelled, in the longer blank. Remember the rules about changing y to i, and dropping final e. The meaning of each word you are to write is given in parentheses. (Add 10 points for each correctly spelled word.)

EXAMPLE parent *al*. *parental*. (having to do with parents)

1. logic.... .... (according to the rules of logic)

2. simp.... .... (plain, unadorned)

3. matrimony.... .... (pertaining to marriage)

4. midd.... .... (halfway between)

5. pick.... .... (a cucumber aged in brine)

6. flann.... .... (a fabric much used in pajamas)

7. baff.... .... (to perplex)

8. caram.... .... (a chewy candy)

9. catt.... .... (cows, steers, bulls)

10. universe.... .... (pertaining to the universe)

EXERCISE B Study the guides and all of the words taught in this lesson, and be prepared to write the words from dictation. (Add 4 points for each correctly spelled word.)

REVIEW EXERCISE Write the letter *a*, *e*, or *o*, whichever is correct, in the blank in each word. (Add 10 points for each correct answer.)

1. bystand....r

2. profess....r

3. burgl....r

4. auth....r

5. begg....r

6. carpent....r

7. schol....r

8. lawy....r

9. govern....r

10. operat....r

Building Vocabulary: Words to Learn

administrator /ad mín is trā́ tər/ *n.* A person responsible for managing the affairs of a business, government body, or other organization: *An administrator does not always have a voice in deciding the policies that are carried out.*—**administer**, *v.*

agile /áj əl/ *adj.* Light, quick, and sure in movement: *A high-jumper must be extremely agile. An agile mind moves quickly from one idea to the next without making mistakes.* —**agility** /ə jíl ə tē/ *n.*

aspiration /ás pə rā́ shən/ *n.* A deep longing for something higher or better than one has or is: *The scientist's highest aspiration was to find a cure for cancer.*

faction /fák shən/ *n.* A group within a political party, legislature, or other organization, often used unfavourably: *A faction within the party is opposed to the bill and will stop at nothing to prevent its passage.*

glamorous /glám ər əs/ *adj.* Attractive and exciting but also deceptive, unreal, like magic: *Acting is considered a glamorous career, but teaching, which may be exciting*

and rewarding, is not usually thought of as glamorous.—**glamour**, *n.*

grotesque /grō tésk/ *adj.* Strange and fantastic in shape or appearance; absurdly misshapen: *The clowns wore grotesque costumes. Their sense of humour was grotesque.*

heedless /héd lis/ *adj.* Paying no attention; ignoring advice, a warning, etc.: *The sign said "Danger! Road Under Construction," but the heedless man drove on without even slowing down.*

sulk /sulk/ *v.* To be cross and ill-humoured, refusing to be cheered up: *When Sean could not have his own way, he sulked for an hour.*—**sulky**, *adj.*

supersede /sū́ pər sḗd/ *v.* To take the place of something because it is in some way better: *Beginning in the 1920's, talking pictures gradually superseded the old silent films.*

valid /vál id/ *adj.* Based on evidence that can be supported; true and significant: *Sickness is a valid reason for staying out of school.*—**validity** /və líd ə tē/ *n.*

EXERCISE Fill each blank with the word from this lesson that makes the best sense in the context. (Add 10 points for each correct answer.)

1. Many people considered the Twenties a .... decade when in reality several signs of impending economic disaster were evident.

2. A small .... within the club was determined to raise the dues, regardless of what the rest of us thought.

3. Automatic machines may one day .... handwork in most manufacturing operations.

4. With a(n) .... leap, the dog cleared the top of the fence and escaped.

5. At the party, the prize for the most .... costume went to the boy who came dressed as a gorilla.

6. A school principal must be an able .... as well as a trained educator.

7. A person's . . . . in life should reach higher than merely having a well-paying job and a comfortable home.

8. Aaron said over and over that he thought we were mistaken, but in fact he gave no . . . . reasons for his opinion.

9. I don't believe Coreen is the . . . . sort of person who would ignore such an obvious danger.

10. Even if you don't get your own way, you don't need to . . . . about it.

REVIEW EXERCISE In the space to the left of each sentence, write the letter of the word that could best fill the blank. (Add 10 points for each correct answer.)

a. deficiency   d. diminutive   g. fragile   j. placid
b. degenerate   e. enhance   h. inertia   k. rational
c. depict   f. ensue   i. inference   l. rebate

. . . . 1. He slammed on the brakes, but the car's ＿＿ carried it off the road.

. . . . 2. The novel ＿＿ life on a Western ranch a hundred years ago.

. . . . 3. The dishes are handsome, but they are too ＿＿ for everyday use.

. . . . 4. A scientist makes logical ＿＿ from known facts.

. . . . 5. Paula carried the ＿＿ dog around with her like a toy.

. . . . 6. Americans believed that the British had disregarded their rights, and the War of 1812——.

. . . . 7. This coupon entitles you to a 10 percent ＿＿ on your next purchase of our product.

. . . . 8. This movie is not likely to ＿＿ the star's reputation.

. . . . 9. The children's bickering would upset even the most ＿＿ disposition.

. . . . 10. The sickly lion cubs suffered from a vitamin ＿＿.

CHAPTER FIVE

Completeness in the Sentence

There are only two things that you need to know in order to make your sentences complete, but they are basic. You must know what a sentence is and you must know where it ends. If you know what a sentence is, you will never punctuate a piece of a sentence—a sentence fragment—as if it were a whole sentence. If you know where a sentence ends, you will always put a suitable end mark after it so that you do not string sentences together to make run-on sentences. With practice, you can learn to write complete, correctly punctuated sentences.

LESSON 44

Phrase Fragments

A **phrase** is a fragment of a sentence. It must not be written by itself as a sentence.

You know that a phrase is a group of words used as a single part of speech, and you should be able to recognize and avoid prepositional phrase fragments. You should also be on your guard against three other kinds of phrases from which careless writers make sentence fragments by treating them as if they were complete sentences.

The Participial Phrase A participle is a word formed from a verb and used as an adjective. A present participle, indicating present time, is formed by adding *-ing* to the verb. A past participle, indicating past time, is formed in various ways, but most often by adding *-ed* to the verb.

FRAGMENT Jody robbed a beehive. *Filled with honey.* (phrase fragment made from a past participle)
SENTENCE Jody robbed a beehive filled with honey.
FRAGMENT He plunged into a stream. *Thus avoiding the angry bees.* (phrase fragment built around a present participle)
SENTENCE He plunged into a stream, thus avoiding the angry bees.

The Appositive Phrase An appositive phrase is a group of words which explains or identifies the noun or pronoun it follows. It is set off by commas.

FRAGMENT I met Mr. Seton. *The owner of the beehive.* (phrase fragment made from an appositive)
SENTENCE I met Mr. Seton, the owner of the beehive.

85

The Infinitive Phrase An infinitive is made up of *to* plus a verb: *to strive, to seek, to find, to yield.* An infinitive phrase begins with an infinitive.

FRAGMENT   Mr. Seton told me. *To let his bees alone.* (phrase fragment made from an infinitive)
SENTENCE   Mr. Seton told me to let his bees alone.

EXERCISE   Some of the items in this exercise contain phrase fragments while others contain only complete sentences. In the space to the left of each item, write *S* for complete sentences. Identify each sentence fragment by writing in the space at the left one of the following abbreviations: *prep.* (prepositional phrase fragment); *part.* (participial phrase fragment); *app.* (appositive phrase fragment); *inf.* (infinitive phrase fragment). For all fragments, cross out the incorrect period and capital letter. You will not be marked for commas that may be needed. (Add 10 points for each correctly marked item.)

.... 1. The blizzard paralyzed the city. Causing the mayor to proclaim a state of emergency.

.... 2. We spent the night in Kenora. A city located in western Ontario.

.... 3. Mr. Mohan told me how hard the job would be. Then he offered it to me at $1.50 an hour.

.... 4. You will drive farther but reach home sooner if you take this route. Following side roads to avoid the crowded highways.

.... 5. Being uncertain about the results of his experiment, Mr. Cole sent us out of the laboratory. Eagerly expecting an explosion, we waited in the corridor.

.... 6. Barbara decided to go to the performance. To see Rudolf Nureyev dance with the National Ballet.

.... 7. Noreen wanted to try cross-country skiing. One of the fastest-growing winter sports in Canada.

.... 8. The entertainment committee scored its greatest success last night. With its skit on the faculty and an exhibition by the band.

.... 9. Nancy asked me to come to her house this evening. She wants me to help her with some back assignments in algebra.

.... 10. She lives in the town's oldest house. A beautiful Tudor-style home.

Subordinate Clause Fragments

A subordinate clause is a fragment of a sentence. It must not be written by itself as a sentence.

Like a phrase, a subordinate clause does not express a complete thought. It must always be attached to the sentence of which it is a part, rather than left by itself with a capital letter at the beginning and a period at the end.

FRAGMENT   The earthquake occurred because of a fault. *Which is a break in the crust of the earth.*

SENTENCE   The earthquake occurred because of a fault, which is a break in the crust of the earth.

FRAGMENT   Our government maintains scores of seismograph observatories. *Because seismographs record both the location and the intensity of an earthquake.*

SENTENCE   Our government maintains scores of seismograph observatories because seismographs record both the location and the intensity of an earthquake.

Subordinate clauses can usually be identified by the words with which they begin. The following words commonly begin subordinate clauses:

who (whose, whom)	although	because	than	whenever
which	as	before	unless	where
that	as if	if	until	wherever
after	as though	since	when	while

EXERCISE A   Some of the items below are sentence fragments. Others consist of a complete sentence and a sentence fragment. Rewrite the incorrect items, joining fragments to their sentences or supplying a new independent clause to go with a fragment. Do nothing with any item that is correct as it stands. (Add 20 points for each correctly treated item.)

1. Joe Clark, who was Canada's Prime Minister. . . . .

. . . .

2. If your car skids on ice, don't use the brakes. . . . .

. . . .

3. If you break a string in your tennis racquet. Get it re-strung without delay.

. . . .

. . . .

4. I would like to read a book. Which is written in basic English. . . . . . .

. . . .

. . . .

5. Larry drove off in the camp truck. Leaving the rest of us without food.

. . . .

. . . .

EXERCISE B   There are ten uncorrected sentence fragments in the paragraph below. Join each to a sentence by crossing out the unnecessary period and replacing the incorrect capital letter with a small letter. (Add 10 points for each corrected fragment.)

1   At our school, everyone looks forward to Clean-up Day. Even though

2   it means hard work for all of us. All ninth-grade classes are excused for

3   the afternoon on Clean-up Day. Which is observed every spring. Mem-

4   bers of the student council supervise the work. After they have met

5   previously to decide the area for which each class will be responsible.

6   Some students are equipped with rakes and spades. That are loaned by

7   trusting parents who are interested in the project. Trash baskets, wheel-

8   barrows, bushel baskets, hedge clippers, and even lawn mowers are

9   rushed into action. When the time for work arrives at the beginning of

10   the sixth period. After Clean-up Day ninth-graders are naturally inter-

11   ested in keeping the grounds neat. Because they have worked hard to get

12   them that way. They don't want to see them littered with paper. You

13   don't dare throw a gum wrapper or a lunch bag anywhere but in the

14   trash baskets. Unless you want to have trouble with ninth-graders.

15   Almost everyone enjoys Clean-up Day. Probably because most of us like

16   to get out of going to classes. There are always some loafers. Who are

17   more interested in getting out of work than in helping. Even the loafers,

18   however, get busy. When they see how seriously most of the students

19   take the work.

Correcting Fragments

EXERCISE Some of the following items are complete sentences. Others contain fragments of sentences. Write *S* before those which are complete sentences. Write *F* before those which contain fragments. Cross out punctuation and replace capital letters with small letters so that each fragment will be part of a sentence. You need not consider commas in this exercise. (Add 5 points for each correctly marked item.)

.... 1. As civilizations developed, people realized the need for systems of measurement. That would allow them to trade among themselves.

.... 2. Linear measurements are measurements of length. Measurements of the body provided the most convenient basis of linear measurements.

.... 3. Among the first groups to develop a system of measurement were the Egyptians. Who were using measuring devices as early as 3000 B.C.

.... 4. The Egyptian unit of measure for length was the cubit. Which equalled the length of the arm from the elbow to the fingertips.

.... 5. The need for a standard unit of measure was recognized. Since a cubit could differ from one person to another.

.... 6. Using the length of the pharaoh's forearm, a cubit stick was created and used. In much the same manner as a ruler is used today.

.... 7. The accuracy of the cubit stick can be judged by considering the dimensions of the pyramids. The sides of the Great Pyramid of Gizeh vary by no more than .05 percent.

.... 8. The Romans kept their standards for length and weight in the temple. By decree of law, people were required to use weights and measures exactly like the standards.

.... 9. As they were conquered by Rome, other lands were forced to adopt the Roman standards for weights and measures. To allow for convenient trade between the parts of the empire.

.... 10. The Roman unit of measure for length was the foot, which was divided into twelve *unciae*, or inches. Weight was measured in libras.

.... 11. Rome forced a period of unification on Western Europe. When Rome fell, much of the unity of Europe collapsed with it.

.... 12. Communication between the various parts of the empire broke down. Forcing the different groups within the empire to develop independently.

.... 13. Although medieval Europe retained the system of weights and measures inherited from the Romans. Many regional differences developed.

.... 14. At the beginning of the ninth century. Charlemagne tried to reunite parts of the former Roman Empire.

.... 15. One of his reforms was to try to impose standards of weights and measures. Since so many variations had crept into the old Roman system. In fact, almost every town had its own system.

.... 16. Though Charlemagne's efforts met with little success. Some degree of uniformity was imposed by the great trade fairs. Held during the twelfth and thirteenth centuries.

.... 17. Merchants had to conform to the standards of the fairs. In order to participate in them.

.... 18. As England grew as a separate nation, its rulers established an English system of measurement. And imposed it on the people throughout its realm.

.... 19. Recognizing the need for standard units. Henry I defined the yard as the distance from the point of his nose to the end of his thumb.

.... 20. An inch was defined as the length of three dry barleycorns placed end to end. While a pound was established as the weight of 7680 grains of wheat.

More Practice in Correcting Fragments

EXERCISE A The following paragraph contains several phrases and subordinate clauses incorrectly used as though they were complete sentences. By crossing out end marks and replacing capital letters with small letters, change the paragraphs so that there are no fragments. You will not be graded on your use of commas. (Add 10 points for each corrected fragment.)

1   In 1670 Gabriel Mouton made a radical suggestion. The adoption of a
2 totally new system of weights and measures for France. This new system
3 would use measurements of the earth as a basis for defining units. Rather
4 than measurements of the body. Which had provided the previous
5 standards. Each unit would be based on a multiple of 10. The prefixes
6 attached to the unit would indicate the multiple. Mouton's proposal was
7 argued about for 120 years. Before any concrete action was taken on it.
8 After the fall of the Bastille, the National Assembly attempted to
9 modernize the French government. It was a time of radical ideas, and
10 Talleyrand revived Mouton's radical proposal. Declaring the need for a
11 more efficient system that all people could easily learn.

12   In 1795 the metric system was officially adopted. Making the metre
13 the standard for length, the gram for mass, and the litre for volume.
14 Prefixes derived from Greek were added to the units to indicate larger
15 or smaller units. So that it was readily apparent that one *kilo*gram
16 equalled 1000 grams and one *centi*metre equalled one one-hundredth
17 of a metre. Certainly a system in which every unit is a multiple of 10 is
18 easier than the English system. Where 12 inches equal one foot, three
19 feet equal one yard, and 5280 feet equal one mile. As Napoleon con-
20 quered other nations, he forced them to adopt the metric system. Just
21 as the Romans had forced conquered nations to adopt their system.

22   Today the metric system is used in most of the major nations through-
23 out the world. Sometimes its adoption followed revolution. As in the
24 cases of France, the U.S.S.R., and China. Sometimes it followed political
25 reform and modernization. In any case, a system of measurement in

26 international use has aided trade of both goods and ideas throughout the
27 world.

EXERCISE B Follow the directions given for Exercise A. (Add 5 points for each corrected fragment.)

1   Every afternoon the playground is filled with boys and girls. Who are
2   getting rid of their stored-up energy. As soon as they get out of the
3   cafeteria. They head for the play areas. Which are behind the school
4   building. It isn't long before the children are playing a dozen differ-
5   ent games. Such as soccer, volleyball, handball, and basketball. There are
6   usually several softball games. Because there are three diamonds laid out
7   on the playground. Sometimes the three games get mixed. With the
8   outfielders running into each other. Occasionally one of our outfielders
9   will be surprised. When the ball from another game hits the player in the
10 back. Once I saw a leftfielder on one diamond stop a ball. Which had
11 been hit by a batter on another diamond. I watched to see what he did
12 with the ball. To my surprise Kevin looked over at the other game. Saw
13 the situation there. And threw the runner out at second base. This act
14 brought on an argument. Which was soon settled. When the umpire
15 declared the runner safe. As soon as everyone understood what had
16 happened. They applauded the umpire's decision. As I watched this
17 incident, I thought it would be fun to lay out three diamonds. So that
18 they would have the same outfield. An arrangement that would make life
19 exciting for the fielders. Who would have to play in three games at the
20 same time. In a professional game, the outfielders would have to get
21 three times their normal pay. Because they would do three times as much
22 work. Of course team owners would not like this arrangement. Unless the
23 games could draw three times as many fans. In such a layout there would
24 be many other exciting possibilities. Which you can easily imagine. If
25 you know anything about baseball.

Using End Marks

In preparation for your study of the run-on sentence, the second major error in writing complete sentences, you may need a review of the punctuation marks used at the end of a sentence. This lesson will give you a quick review of these end marks.

A sentence is followed by an appropriate end mark (period, question mark, exclamation point).

1. **A sentence that makes a statement is followed by a period.**

EXAMPLES   Marion Macpherson was High Commissioner to Sri Lanka.
She has also been Inspector-General of all Canadian missions abroad.

2. **A sentence that asks a question is followed by a question mark.**

EXAMPLES   What shall we do?
Where are you going?

3. **An indirect question that is part of a statement is not followed by a question mark.**

EXAMPLES   We asked the teacher what we should do.
I asked the girls where they were going.

4. **An exclamation is followed by an exclamation point.**

EXAMPLES   What good luck we had!
The roof is falling in!

5. **A sentence that expresses a request or a command may be followed by either a period or an exclamation point, depending upon the purpose of the sentence.**

EXAMPLES   Take this note to Miss Fredericks, please.
Look out, Jim!

EXERCISE A   Place the proper end mark after each of the following sentences. In this exercise when an end mark and quotation marks come together, place the end mark *inside* the quotation marks. (Add 10 points for each correct answer.)

1. What did I say in my note to Celia

2. I asked her what animal uses its nose for an arm

3. How quickly she wrote the answer, an elephant

4. Celia's note to me said, "Try to stump me again "

5. Imagine our surprise when we saw Mr. Baker behind us

6. Why do Celia and I always get caught

7. Mr. Baker said gruffly, "Tell me why tears come to your eyes when you are peeling an onion "

8. After a moment of silence, he asked, "What is the difference between an onion and an apple "

9. Stalling for time, Celia exclaimed, "An onion and an apple "

10. "Pay attention to today's lesson, and learn the answer to my riddle," Mr. Baker advised sternly

EXERCISE B Change each of the following sentences as directed and use appropriate end marks. Add or omit words when necessary. (Add 10 points for each correct sentence.)

The game starts at two o'clock.

A. *Direct question:* ..... *Does the game start at two o'clock?*

B. *Command:* ..... *Start the game at two o'clock!*

That fumble will cost us the game.

1. *Direct question:* ....

2. *Exclamation:* ....

Mario should leave at once.

3. *Direct question:* ....

4. *Command:* ....

Was that road dangerous?

5. *Statement:* ....

6. *Exclamation:* ....

You told him what I said.

7. *Direct question:* ....

8. *Exclamation:* ....

The rug should be cleaned right away.

9. *Direct question:* ....

10. *Command:* ....

94

Correcting the Run-on Sentence

Failure to use an end mark when you have completed a sentence is a serious error in writing. Another serious error is placing a comma at the end of a sentence. A comma is not an end mark. Sentences which are not followed by an end mark *run on* into the following sentence. They are therefore called run-on sentences.

RUN-ON   Virginia was busy campaigning for her favourite candidate she passed out pamphlets to all the people in her apartment building one day a week she worked at the candidate's office downtown. (No end marks are given. Each sentence runs on into the next.)

CORRECTED   Virginia was busy campaigning for her favourite candidate ▪ She passed out pamphlets to all the people in her building ▪ One day a week she worked at the candidate's office downtown.

RUN-ON   Ken liked shop best of all his classes, he was good at making things with his hands, last year he made some beautiful pieces of furniture for his room at home. (Commas have been used in place of end marks. Each sentence runs on into the next.)

CORRECTED   Ken liked shop best of all his classes ▪ He was good at making things with his hands ▪ Last year he made some beautiful pieces of furniture for his room at home.

EXERCISE Read the following groups of sentences. End marks have been omitted. Insert proper end marks in the right places and put a capital letter at the beginning of each sentence. (Add 4 points for each corrected run-on).

1. The guests pushed their chairs back from the table when they were through eating Helen's father set up his movie projector on the table and showed some pictures he had taken during his recent trip on the white wall of the dining room the pictures showed up very well.

2. Mr. Solomon had coached our town's football teams for twenty years in that time he had had five undefeated teams and ten championships when he retired, the whole town turned out to pay homage to him.

3. Jackie Barnes, who lives next door, has been taking cornet lessons every evening after supper she practises sitting in our living room, we struggle through every exercise with her our muscles grow tense and our nerves jump as Jackie slurs her way up to a high note will she make it will she muff it when she has either succeeded or failed, we relax until the next effort.

4. Do you know how to dance the limbo it's really quite easy two people hold a pole a metre from the ground the limbo dancers sway to the strong rhythm of the music as they bend their knees and go under the pole if the dancers touch the pole, they are out the pole is lowered bit by bit until only one dancer is left.

5. The ancient Chinese believed in an ultimate spirit, called the *Tao* this spirit was divided into two opposing forces. The yin was the negative force. It was receptive, absorbing, and passive the yang was the positive force it was penetrating, creative, and active although the yin and yang were opposites, the root of each was found in the other when they were in harmony, the world was at peace when they were in a state of imbalance, there was strife.

6. The period between 1860 and 1874 was a time of anarchy in the Canadian West the power of the Hudson's Bay Company had weakened and the North West Mounted Police had not yet been created the huge frontier was known as Whoop-Up Country it was ruled by an American frontiersman, Johnny Jerome Healey, who was a bootlegging gangster he tried to set up trading posts in Alberta and Saskatchewan all flying the Stars and Stripes Healey wanted to cheat the Indians with alcohol he called "Injun coffin varnish."

Chapter Review

EXERCISE A The following paragraph is composed of run-on sentences. Some of the commas have been incorrectly used as end marks. Decide where the sentences end and insert the proper end marks. Begin each sentence with a capital letter. Be careful not to create any fragments. (Add 10 points for each corrected run-on.)

1 A few years ago, we experienced a terrible hailstorm in this city it
2 caused a great deal of damage and several people were injured. I re-
3 member that it was a beautiful Sunday afternoon and the weather
4 forecasters had said there was a chance of an evening thunderstorm
5 even they didn't have much knowledge of what was really going to
6 happen. We had finished our backyard picnic and had gone inside to
7 listen to records when we left our friend's house at eight o'clock we
8 had no idea about the storm just 5 km away. Nancy and I drove
9 home along the side streets, wondering what all the white stuff was
10 piled up against the trees, at first we thought it was the white fluff that
11 floats off of the poplar. Tree branches were everywhere too. We ar-
12 rived at my apartment and mom stared at us when we asked if there
13 had been a storm, it seems a huge hailstone had even broken the dining
14 room window. Almost every window facing west in our section of the
15 city had been smashed, several homes had lost entire roofs. Mom said
16 the rain tunnelled down our street and she watched cars struggling, up
17 to their headlights in rushing water, trying to get up the hill. Since we
18 had a great accumulation of hail on the balcony, I decided to take
19 some pictures, my camera, however, was out of film. Of course, Mon-
20 day's paper was full of photos showing the results of the storm and I
21 saved every one, they would be a reminder of what the expression
22 "freak storm" really means!

EXERCISE B The following paragraphs are confusing because they contain fragments and run-on sentences. Make the paragraphs clear by changing the punctuation and capital letters so that there will be no fragments or run-on sentences. (Add 4 points for each correct fragment or run-on.)

1 Anne and some of her friends were interested in Canadian painting,
2 they formed a group to study it. They enjoyed examining all of the

3   available information on the pictures. Although they were not knowl-
4   edgable about art. Each week one of the members reported on an artist.
5   At the end of the month. They compared notes on what had been
6   discussed. One of the facts that they immediately noticed was that
7   many of the first important painters came from England. Most of the
8   group were unfamiliar with English art. They found it convenient to
9   make a study of English painting. For the purpose of comparison with
10   Canadian painting.

11   The painters in England, the landscapists and the pre-Raphaelites,
12   depicted nature and figures photographically, they were also influenced
13   by French art. Popular artists were Millais, Burne-Jones, Morris,
14   Courbet, and Bouguereau, and to some extent, the Impressionists. Art
15   Nouveau was popular. Which proved important. Although it was
16   difficult to remember the different influences, styles and approaches
17   and the different artists who had affected the development of Canadian
18   painting. The girls wanted to obtain as much background informa-
19   tion as possible for their understanding.

20   Anne was due to give her report that week, she was reporting on
21   Robert Harris, a nineteenth-century painter. He was from the Mari-
22   times. Anne found that he was popular. Because of his gift for catching
23   likenesses. As a result of this ability. He painted mainly portraits and
24   genre pictures. And he was commissioned to paint the Fathers of
25   Confederation. This was important to Harris, he made many sketches
26   of each man. He then assembled the figures in a well-balanced com-
27   position. Unfortunately, in 1916. The picture was burned in the fire
28   which destroyed the Parliament Buildings, by studying old photo-
29   graphs, however, it is possible to see what the painting looked like.
30   Anne also researched some of Harris' other paintings and drawings.
31   Including a small work called *Harmony*, which was exhibited at the
32   World Fair of 1893. This painting was lost until art historians dis-
33   covered it a few years ago, now it hangs in the National Gallery of
34   Canada.

Cumulative Review

A In the spaces to the right of each sentence name in order the part of speech of the italicized words in the sentence. Use abbreviations. (Add 5 points for each correct answer.)

1. *In* 1666, Jean Talon *took* the first census of New France.   . . . .

2. He *noticed* that men *sharply* outnumbered women.   . . . .

3. *He* sent for *groups* of young single women to be brides for the men.   . . . .

4. The *young* women were *often* orphans *and* were named the king's *daughters*.   . . . .

5. A *responsible, married* woman *chaperoned* the brides *during* the long voyage.   . . . .

6. *With* so many *marriages* taking place, couples were married *quickly* in groups of thirty.   . . . .

7. *Prudent* bachelors, desiring a *smart* and pretty wife, would *usually* build a home before the brides arrived, insuring themselves a better choice.   . . . .

B In the spaces to the right give the subject and verb in each sentence. Select the verb first and write it in the second column. Be sure to give all parts of the verb. (Add 5 points for each correct answer.)

	Subject	*Verb*
1. Has either of you ever bitten into a green persimmon?	. . . .	. . . .
2. Some of the fuses are not good.	. . . .	. . . .
3. Splashing among the rocks was a school of lively fish.	. . . .	. . . .
4. Can Sam or Clarissa cook quail?	. . . .	. . . .
5. Saturday I watered the lawn and spaded the flower beds.	. . . .	. . . .
6. There have been few objections to the new schedule.	. . . .	. . . .
7. To the pitcher went full credit for the victory.	. . . .	. . . .
8. Linda's collection of old comic books will be on display.	. . . .	. . . .
9. Where is your book report?	. . . .	. . . .
10. Do not waste your money.	. . . .	. . . .

C In the first space at the right copy the complement(s) in each sentence. In the second space name the kind of complement, using these abbreviations: subject complement, *s.c.;* direct object, *d.o.;* indirect object, *i.o.* (Add 5 points for each correct answer.)

	Complement	Kind
1. Some employees fear automation.	. . . .	. . . . . .
2. Define an obtuse angle.	. . . .	. . . . . .
3. What ancient people worshipped a bull?	. . . .	. . . . . .
4. Our sandwiches became soggy.	. . . .	. . . . . .
5. That we did not foresee.	. . . .	. . . . . .
6. The police gave them valuable information.	. . . .	. . . . . .
7. No one would believe me.	. . . .	. . . . . .
8. Mr. Silver told us the answers to the test.	. . . .	. . . . . .
9. Our new car is a station wagon.	. . . .	. . . . . .
10. Regina reached second base safely.	. . . .	. . . . . .

D Each of the following sentences contains a phrase or a subordinate clause. Underline each phrase and clause. In the first space at the right, state whether the underlined group of words is a phrase or a clause. In the second space tell whether it is used as an adjective or an adverb or a noun. (Add 5 points for each correct answer.)

	Phrase or clause	Kind
1. The audience roared when the ventriloquist outfrowned his dummy.	. . . .	. . . .
2. Near the wigwam stood a totem pole.	. . . .	. . . .
3. The palm is the symbol of victory.	. . . .	. . . .
4. What you said makes no sense.	. . . .	. . . .
5. Joni Mitchell is a singer who moved to California.	. . . .	. . . .
6. This is a time for action.	. . . .	. . . .
7. Who is going with you?	. . . .	. . . .
8. He remembered the egg in his pocket.	. . . .	. . . .
9. Mom asked where you were.	. . . .	. . . .
10. At the end of her speech, Ms. Sandlov demanded action.	. . . .	. . . .

100

Spelling: Using -ent and -ence

Among the trickiest words to spell are those that end in *-ent* and *-ence* or *-ant* and *-ance*. Because each of these suffixes is an unstressed syllable, the vowel becomes the indistinct schwa sound /ə/. How then can you tell whether a word ends in *-ent* or *-ant; -ence* or *-ance*?

Unfortunately, there are few generalizations that are really helpful. Mostly, words with these endings have to be memorized. Since they are so easily confused, they will be taught separately; *-ent* and *-ence* in this lesson, *-ant* and *-ance* in Lesson 60.

Here are the only useful guides available for words ending in *-ent* and *-ence:* (Memorize the words given as examples.)

● The suffix *-ent* (which is the more common form) is added to a verb to make it an adjective, as in list *1* below. Sometimes there is no separate verb in English, as in list *2*. Only the adjective form (derived from a Latin verb) exists.

1		*2*
confide	confident	prominent
depend	dependent	violent
insist	insistent	innocent
differ	different	obedient
revere	reverent	eminent
emerge	emergent	permanent

● Many adjectives ending in *-ent* have related nouns which end in *-ence*. If you can spell one, you can spell the other.

Here are the noun forms of the *-ent* adjectives given under the first guide above:

confident	confidence	prominent	prominence
dependent	dependence	violent	violence
insistent	insistence	innocent	innocence
different	difference	obedient	obedience
reverent	reverence	eminent	eminence
emergent	emergence	permanent	permanence

EXERCISE A Add the suffix *-ent* to each of the following verbs to change the verb to an adjective. Write the adjective in the blank. Remember the rule about dropping final *e* before adding a suffix beginning with a vowel. (Add 10 points for each correct answer.)

EXAMPLE   exist + ent = . *existent*

1. consist + ent = ...   4. inhere + ent = ...

2. indulge + ent = ...   5. diverge + ent = ...

3. reside + ent = ...   6. precede + ent = ...

7. cohere + ent = ...   9. persist + ent = ...

8. converge + ent = ...   10. urge + ent = ...

EXERCISE B   For each adjective below, write the corresponding noun form ending in *-ence*. (Add 5 points for each correctly spelled word.)

A. convenient   *convenience*

1. lenient	....	11. indulgent	....
2. absent	....	12. recurrent	....
3. irreverent	....	13. violent	....
4. competent	....	14. excellent	....
5. evident	....	15. present	....
6. magnificent	....	16. impudent	....
7. silent	....	17. penitent	....
8. independent	....	18. patient	....
9. diligent	....	19. adolescent	....
10. prominent	....	20. intelligent	....

EXERCISE C   Be ready to write from dictation all of the words taught in this lesson. (Add 2 points for each correctly spelled word.)

REVIEW EXERCISE   Complete each word by writing in the blank *-le, -al,* or *-el,* whichever is correct. (Add 10 points for each correct answer.)

1. dent....   6. ank....

2. origin....   7. annu....

3. quarr....   8. kenn....

4. stab....   9. barr....

5. hospit....   10. puzz....

Building Vocabulary: Analysing Words

When chemists analyse chemical compounds, they break them down into their parts to see what they are made of. You do much the same thing when you analyse words. By breaking a new word down into its parts, you can often see that its root, or main part, is a word whose meaning you already know. If you know the meaning of a few common prefixes and suffixes, you can usually form a good idea of the meaning of the new word.

EXAMPLE   An ungovernable temper is a serious fault.

The word printed in red consists of three main parts: the prefix *un-*, the root *govern,* and the suffix *-able. Govern,* of course, means "to rule" or "control." Combined with the prefix *un-* (*not*) and the suffix *-able* (*able, capable*), it means "not capable of being controlled," hence "wild, unruly, violent."

Usually, a suffix changes the part of speech of the word to which it is added (*-able* turns the verb *govern* into an adjective). A prefix, on the other hand, usually does not change the part of speech (*governable* and *ungovernable* are both adjectives). Study the meanings of these common suffixes and prefixes and try to think of words in which they are used.

PREFIXES   un- (in-, il-, im-, ir-) *meaning* not—un necessary
re- *meaning* back, again, backward—re make

SUFFIXES   -able (-ible) *meaning* able, capable—usable
-al (-ial) *meaning* concerning, pertaining to, according to—sensational

EXERCISE A   Without using a dictionary, divide the following words into prefix, root, and suffix, as in the example. Then write a short definition that shows how the prefix or suffix affects the root meaning of the word. Afterward, check your answers in a dictionary. You will not be scored on this exercise. Note that some words have both prefix and suffix.

A. im|mater|ial /ím ə tír ē əl/ *adj.* ... *not pertaining to matter* ...

1. controversial /kón trə vúr shəl/ *adj.* ....

....

2. incompetent /in kóm pə tənt/ *adj.* ....

3. managerial /mán ə jír ē əl/ *adj.* ....

4. inadequate /in ád ə kwit/ *adj.* ....

5. cultural /kúl chər əl/ *adj.* ....

6. unintelligible /ún in tél ə jə bəl/ *adj.* ....

....

7. reconcile /rék ən sīl/ *v.* ....

8. inflexible /in flék sə bəl/ *adj.* ....

9. unpalatable /un pál it ə bəl/ *adj.* ....

....

10. refrain /ri frán/ *v.* ....

EXERCISE B In the space to the left of each sentence, write the letter of the definition below that best explains the italicized word. (Add 10 points for each correct answer.)

.... 1. The constant discussion in the newspapers has made the new school policy an extremely *controversial* matter.

.... 2. *Incompetent* drivers are as dangerous to others as to themselves.

.... 3. Maggie Lena Walker's *managerial* skills made her a successful insurance and banking executive.

.... 4. You can't do your best work with *inadequate* food and sleep.

.... 5. Most large cities offer far greater *cultural* opportunities than do small towns.

.... 6. Even today, Einstein's theories are *unintelligible* to all but a few highly trained mathematicians.

.... 7. We hoped to *reconcile* the former enemies after the war.

.... 8. One MP's *inflexible* opposition prevented the bill from passing.

.... 9. A bad cold may make ordinary food seem quite *unpalatable*.

.... 10. Please *refrain* from whispering while I am talking.

a. Subject to argument and strong disagreement.
b. Having to do with things that show mental and artistic refinement.
c. Not enough; insufficient.
d. Lacking the strength, training, or other qualifications for an activity.
e. Firm, unyielding, rigid.
f. Like a manager; reflecting the skills, abilities, and outlook of a trained business executive.
g. To bring back into harmony persons or ideas that have been opposed.
h. To hold back from doing something.
i. Impossible to understand.
j. Not pleasing to the taste.

CHAPTER SIX

Capital Letters

What is the distinction in meaning between *girl* and *Pam*, between *school* and *Stewart School*, between *river* and *Columbia River?* If you understand the difference between the words in each of these pairs, you understand the basic rule governing the use of capital letters. The words without capitals refer to *any* girl, *any* school, *any* river. They are *common* nouns. Those words with capitals name a *particular* girl, school, and river. They are proper nouns. The basic rule is that you use a capital letter when you write a proper noun, one which singles out a particular person, place, or thing. An adjective formed from a proper noun is a proper adjective. Proper adjectives are also capitalized: English (from England); Canadian (from Canada); African (from Africa). This chapter will call your attention to the various kinds of proper nouns and adjectives and give you practice in recognizing and capitalizing them.

LESSON 54

Capitals for Geographical Names

Capitalize geographical names.

CITIES AND TOWNS   Quebec City, Charlottetown
COUNTIES AND TOWNSHIPS   Lacombe County, Township of Whitchurch-Stouffville
PROVINCES   Manitoba, Newfoundland, Alberta
COUNTRIES   Brazil, Canada
CONTINENTS   Africa, Asia
ISLANDS   Vancouver Island, Baffin Island
BODIES OF WATER   Atlantic Ocean, Lake Louise, Red River
MOUNTAINS   Rocky Mountains, Laurentian Mountains
STREETS   Ross Street, Avenue Road
PARKS   Prince Albert National Park
SECTIONS OF THE COUNTRY   the North, the Far West

1. Capitalize words like city, street, lake, river, park, mountain, and ocean when they are part of a proper name.

EXAMPLES   Lake Simcoe, Mount Logan, Bay of Fundy

105

2. Capitalize east, west, north, and south when they name a section of the country. Do not capitalize east, west, north, and south when they name directions.

EXAMPLES I have lived in the *West* longer than in the *East*. (sections of the country)
Go *south* to the hospital and turn *east*. (directions)
The *east* wind brought rain. (direction)

3. Do not capitalize a common noun modified by a proper adjective unless it is part of a name.

EXAMPLES a Spanish *city*   Quebec *City*
a Manitoba *lake*   Clear *Lake*

EXERCISE Find the twenty-five incorrect items and add capital letters where they are needed. (Add 4 points for each corrected item.)

A. Main street

1. Peace river
2. a Calgary firm
3. Macdonald-Cartier freeway
4. Strathcona county residents
5. the Rocky Mountains
6. the atlantic ocean
7. Algonquin park
8. great bear lake
9. an Ojibwa leader
10. the canadian ambassador
11. the south side of nineteenth street
12. the capital of new brunswick
13. the spanish people
14. an acadian village
15. an alberta lake resort
16. red deer, alberta
17. fundy national park

B. a swiss town

18. seventh avenue
19. a city in the middle west
20. the nations of Europe and Asia
21. a Chinese village
22. Main street runs north and south
23. an african country
24. the sahara desert
25. nations of the far east
26. the pacific northwest
27. Mont Tremblant
28. an ocean beach
29. Huron county
30. Cavendish beach
31. a university in the East
32. Queen Anne road
33. two km east
34. a french restaurant

Capitals for Special Groups and Events

Capitalize words like club, corporation, hotel, building, theatre, high school, and college when they are part of a proper noun.

PART OF A PROPER NOUN	COMMON NOUN
Carmen's *club*	a dinner *club*
Orlando Building *corporation*	a large *corporation*
The Empress *hotel*	an old *hotel*
The Hydro *building*	a tall *building*
National Arts *centre*	a *centre* in Ottawa
Alpha *secondary school*	a *secondary school* in Alpha
Simon Fraser *university*	a *university* in British Columbia

Capitalize names of special events and calendar items (days of the week, months, and holidays).

EXAMPLES   Battle of Waterloo   Thanksgiving Day
French Revolution   Monday, July 1

Capitalize names of races and religions.

EXAMPLES   a Baptist, a leader of the Jews, a Polynesian

Do not capitalize seasons, school years, or school subjects except languages and the names of specific courses.

EXAMPLES   summer, fall, spring, winter
junior, senior, graduate
English, French, algebra, history (*but:* History I)

EXERCISE A   Change each proper noun below to a corresponding common noun. Change each common noun to a corresponding proper noun. (Add 10 points for each correct item.)

A. Future Scientists Club   *a club for future scientists*

B. sometime next spring   *on Thursday, May 14*

1. Parent-Teacher Association   ....

2. a hospital in the city   ....

3. two holidays   ....

4. my school   ....

5. the War of 1812   ....

6. a war involving the world   . . . .

7. Algebra I   . . . .

8. two foreign languages   . . . .

9. on Main Street   . . . .

10. a native of this country   . . . .

EXERCISE B   Draw a line through any word that begins incorrectly. Write the word correctly in the blank to the right of the line. If there is no error in a line, write C (for *correct*) in the blank. (Add 5 points for each correct answer.)

A. When my ~~Sister~~ finished ~~School,~~ she went away   *sister, school,*

    to ~~Camp.~~   *camp*

B. The Rialto Theatre is on Main Street.   *C*

1   When I finished High School, my parents took   . . . .

2   me to the Calgary stampede. Stampedes, or   . . . .

3   Rodeos, are very popular forms of western   . . . .

4   entertainment. Colourful and exciting, stampedes   . . . .

5   recapture and preserve the flavour of life on the   . . . .

6   North American Cattle Range. Of course, the   . . . .

7   Calgary stampede is the most famous of all. The   . . . .

8   first one was held in 1912, organized and directed   . . . .

9   by Guy Weadick, a wyoming cowboy. A feature   . . . .

10 of this Stampede, and all subsequent ones, was the   . . . .

11 Street Parade on Opening Day. Hundreds of   . . . .

12 indians, RCMP, cowboys, Cowgirls and floats   . . . .

13 presented a grand spectacle. Today, the Calgary   . . . .

14 Stampede is a true Fiesta. Hundreds of Thousands   . . . .

15 attend and most wear cowboy costumes and   . . . .

16 Ten-gallon hats. Everyone loves to watch the Calf-   . . . .

17 roping, Bareback riding and the Chuckwagon Race.   . . . .

18 There are Street Shows each morning and Square   . . . .

19 Dancing in the streets at night. At the end of the   . . . .

20 Stampede, there is a grand Cowboy-Ball Finale.   . . . .

Capitals for Titles

Capitalize titles of persons when used before the person's name.

EXAMPLES   Captain Brown, Superintendent Ieradi, Judge Hanlon.

Do not capitalize titles used alone or after the person's name unless they are titles of current high government officials.

EXAMPLES   The Prime Minister lives on Sussex Drive.
Mr. Herbert Cameron, *vice-president* of the bank, is in his office.
Reporters interviewed the Minister of Natural Resources.

Capitalize mother, father, sister, etc., when they are used as names.
Do not capitalize mother, father. sister, etc., when they are preceded by a possessive: his, her, my, John's, etc.
Capitalize words of family relationship preceding a name.

USED AS NAMES   I will ask Mother for her permission.
Hello, Father.

NOT USED AS NAMES   The *mother* of the children was away from home.
This is my *mother.*   (preceded by a possessive)

TITLES PRECEDING NAMES   We visited Grandmother Owen and my Aunt Jane.

Modern usage does, however, permit the writing of *mother, father, sister,* etc., without a capital even when they are used as names. Hence either way is acceptable, but most writers follow the rule given here.

Capitalize the first word and all important words in titles of books, magazines, poems, stories, movies, and works of art.

EXAMPLES   The Last Spike (book)
the Toronto Star (newspaper)
Saturday Night (magazine)
Rain In The North Country (painting)

Note: Within a sentence the word *the* before the title of a magazine or newspaper is not capitalized. At the beginning of book and art titles it is always capitalized.

Capitalize nouns and pronouns referring to God.

EXAMPLE   The congregation prayed to God, asking for His blessing.

Note: Do not capitalize words referring to the gods of primitive religions and ancient mythologies.

EXAMPLE   The ancient Greek gods interfered in the affairs of mortals.

109

EXERCISE A   Correct the capitalization in the following paragraph by inserting capitals where they should be and by drawing a slanting line through capitals that should be small letters. (Add 5 points for each correct answer.)

1   As an assignment for latin class, we read the tale of Orpheus and

2   Eurydice in Robert Graves's book, *the Greek myths.* I enjoyed the story of

3   the musician from thrace who charmed Hades, the God of the under-

4   world, with his music. The god was persuaded to allow Orpheus' Wife,

5   Eurydice, to return to life. But hades set one condition. If Orpheus

6   looked back to see if his Wife was behind him before they both reached

7   the upper world, Eurydice would have to return to the land of the dead.

8   On the brink of the upper world, the Master Musician looked back, and

9   Eurydice was lost to him forever. Our Teacher played parts of Gluck's

10   opera, *orpheus and eurydice.* She arranged for us to obtain discount

11   tickets to a film by the french director, Jean Cocteau. His film, *orpheé,*

12   was based on the ancient legend. It seems the tale has influenced many

13   artists. Last night, uncle Ernest showed me a print of a Mosaic by an

14   unknown roman artist entitled *Orpheus charming the beasts.*

EXERCISE B   Write a brief sentence using each word below correctly (and *not* at the beginning of the sentence). (Add 10 points for each correct sentence.)

A. *Ambassador:* Canada's representative was Ambassador Barton.

B. *ambassador:* He was an ambassador ten years ago.

1. *God:* ....

2. *god:* ....

3. *Minister:* ....

4. *minister:* ....

5. *Father:* ....

6. *father:* ....

7. *Captain:* ....

8. *captain:* ....

9. *Aunt:* ....

10. *aunt:* ....

Practice with Capital Letters

EXERCISE A Correct the capitalization in the following sentences by inserting capitals where they should be and by drawing a slanting line through capitals that should be small letters. (Add 2 points for each correct answer.)

1. Members of the brownies and girl guides went to see *The Nutcracker*. Every year at christmas, the National Ballet performs this classic at o'keefe centre.

2. Like many Western communities, calgary began as a NWMP post. The stockaded log fort was called fort Calgary after a gaelic word said to mean 'clear, running water'. The head of the Bow river valley was chosen as the site for the cpr pass through the rockies, thereby placing fort Calgary on the main line.

3. Gordon Lightfoot's "Canadian railroad trilogy" is a traditional Ballad and one of Lightfoot's Best Known songs.

4. Sir John a. Macdonald was the First Prime minister of Canada.

5. Cape Breton island, part of Nova Scotia, is separated from the Mainland by the strait of Canso.

6. Lester B. Pearson, a former prime minister of Canada, was awarded the Nobel Peace prize in 1957 for his efforts in creating the UN emergency force in the middle east.

7. Mrs. Stratton, Head of the English department, discovered that book reports on such classics as *Great expectations* by Dickens and *Wuthering Heights* by Brontë were actually based on the *classic comics* versions sold in the local smoke shop.

8. Chatsworth, ontario in Grey county is the Birthplace of Nellie McClung, who fought for Women's Rights.

9. A major Collection of Emily Carr's work was bequeathed to the Vancouver art gallery by the Artist.

10. The cbc produced a Television Special on Emily Carr and her work.

EXERCISE B Insert the necessary capital letters in the following paragraphs. (Add 2 points for each correct answer.)

1   After we had finished reading selections from dante's *the divine*

2   *comedy* in english class last wednesday, ms. portinari asked us to write a
3   composition. She said that most religions, whether current or past, have
4   some concept of an afterlife. Our assignment was to compare dante's
5   idea of an afterlife with one found in another religion or in mythology.
6   Although I did my ukrainian and history assignments quickly, I spent
7   most of the evening working on this task for english. It was the most
8   thought-provoking assignment I had had since entering sir john a.
9   macdonald high school.

10   I decided to investigate the ideas found in buddhism. My aunt, who
11   teaches a course in philosophy and religion at the university of alberta
12   in calgary, told me that although buddhism is largely an oriental relig-
13   ion, its ideas and dogmas are quite familiar to people living in the occi-
14   dental world. This religion was an outgrowth of hinduism. Gautama
15   siddhartha became the buddha when he received enlightenment after
16   meditating in a forest near the town of varanasi. Followers of buddhism
17   believe that people experience a series of reincarnations. According to
18   aunt Sylvia, buddhists feel that people control their destinies. The good
19   or evil they do in this life controls the type of life they will have in their
20   next reincarnation. Since buddhists consider life to be full of suffering,
21   their ultimate goal is to end the series of reincarnations. This state is
22   called *nirvana*.

23   Actually, the ideas of dante and the ideas of buddhists are very far
24   apart. While the italian master presented a world in which good and evil
25   were rewarded or punished after death, the buddhists present a world in
26   which people are remunerated for their actions in their next life. In
27   dante's christian philosophy, the good are rewarded with paradise. For
28   buddhists, the good are rewarded by ceasing to exist.

29   Last night father brought home a copy of a novel by a german writer,
30   hermann hesse. His novel, *siddhartha,* is based on the life of the buddha.
31   Both mother and father saw a movie version of *siddhartha* last july at the
32   art centre's theatre.

Chapter Review

EXERCISE A   Write the letter of the correct form (*a* or *b*) in the blank. (Add 4 points for each correct answer.)

a	A. a. Lake Ontario	b. lake Ontario
....	1. a. Banks Island	b. Banks island
....	2. a. a Provincial Park	b. a provincial park
....	3. a. the aim of the West	b. the aim of the west
....	4. a. a km North of here	b. a km north of here
....	5. a. the St. Lawrence River	b. the St. Lawrence river
....	6. a. a City in Nova Scotia	b. a city in Nova Scotia
....	7. a. Quebec City	b. Quebec city
....	8. a. next Sunday	b. next sunday
....	9. a. next Spring	b. next spring
....	10. a. a few Girl Guides	b. a few girl guides
....	11. a. our English teacher	b. our english teacher
....	12. a. courses in Mathematics	b. courses in mathematics
....	13. a. taking Geometry I	b. taking geometry I
....	14. a. a Polynesian dance	b. a Polynesian Dance
....	15. a. Parry Sound High School	b. Parry Sound high school
....	16. a. Eddy Match Company Limited	b. Eddy Match company limited
....	17. a. for my Father	b. for my father
....	18. a. a mythic God	b. a mythic god
....	19. a. faith in God	b. faith in god
....	20. a. *The Diary of Anne Frank*	b. *the Diary of Anne Frank*
....	21. a. Twenty-First Street	b. Twenty-first Street
....	22. a. the Norman Conquest	b. the Norman conquest
....	23. a. the President of the club	b. the president of the club
....	24. a. the Red Cross President	b. the Red Cross president
....	25. a. several Catholics	b. several catholics

EXERCISE B   If a sentence below contains no errors in capitalization, write *C* (for *correct*) in the blank. If a sentence contains a word or words with an incorrect capital or small letter, draw a line through the error and write the word or words correctly in the blank. (Add 5 points for each correctly marked item.)

A. I am learning a great deal about ~~Soil Conservation~~.   *soil conservation*

1. Soil is one of the most important Natural Resources of Canada.   . . . .

2. Agriculturally, Canada may be divided in three Geographic Regions: eastern Canada, the Prairie provinces and the mountainous province of British Columbia.   . . . .

3. In eastern Canada, the forest soils are never very rich and they must be treated with farm manure and Commercial Fertilizers if satisfactory crops are to be grown.   . . . .

4. In Nova Scotia and New Brunswick there are some 87 000 acres protected from the sea by dikes.   . . . .

5. The Early Settlers of the bay of Fundy area came from the Loire valley in France, where much of the farming was conducted on land reclaimed from the Sea.   . . . .

6. These French Settlers built the first Dike near annapolis royal in 1617.   . . . .

7. Some Government soil-conservation projects are the prairie farm rehabilitation Act, the eastern Rocky Mountain conservation board, the river valley Development Project and the Reclamation of the maritime marshland Project.   . . . .

8. All of these facts are things we learn in School.   . . . .

9. We also learned about Reforestation, because this is an important aspect of soil conservation.   . . . .

10. Forest management is also called Silviculture.   . . . .

11. In 1907, sir Wilfred Laurier arranged the first General Conference on Canadian Forestry.   . . . .

12. Scientific inquiries did not begin until after the second world war, when several royal commissions were established.   . . . .

Cumulative Review

A The questions below each italicized sentence refer to words and word groups in the sentence. Answer the questions in the spaces provided. (Add 4 points for each correct answer.)

The Nile River always floods the delta lands of Egypt.

1. The subject is: . . . .

2. The verb is: . . . .

3. The complement is: . . . .

4. What kind of complement is it? . . . .

5. What part of speech is *lands?* . . . .

6. What part of speech is *delta?* . . . .

7. What part of speech is *always?* . . . .

8. Write the prepositional phrase. . . . .

9. What word does the phrase modify? . . . .

10. Is it an adjective or an adverb phrase? . . . .

The rise and the fall of the Nile River are important because the farmer must irrigate his arid land.

11. The compound subject of the main clause is: . . . .

12. The verb of the main clause is: . . . .

13. The complement of the main clause is: . . . .

14. What kind of complement is it? . . . .

15. What part of speech is *arid?* . . . .

16. What part of speech is *rise?* . . . .

17. Write the first and last words of the subordinate clause. . . . .

18. Is it an adjective or an adverb clause? . . . .

19. Write the prepositional phrase. . . . .

20. Is it an adjective or an adverb phrase? . . . .

In the spring, the rising river will cover the exposed riverbed, will flood the banks, and will fill the canals.

21. The compound verbs are ...., ..., and ....

22. What kind of complement is *banks?* ....

23. What kind of complement is *riverbed?* ....

24. What kind of complement is *canals?* ....

25. Is *In the spring* an adjective or an adverb phrase? ....

B Place an *S* before the items which are complete sentences. Place an *F* before those which are or contain fragments. (Add 20 points for each correct answer.)

.... 1. Have you done the problems? The ones in today's assignment?

.... 2. The train roared through the night. Thundering over bridges, shouting through tunnels, hooting at every village and crossroad.

.... 3. By staying in tourist houses and cabins instead of hotels, we saved money. As a result we had enough money for a trip to Mexico.

.... 4. The old nag that had pulled Mr. Grady's milk wagon for years.

.... 5. All day the entire neighbourhood was covered with smoke. As all the homeowners burned the leaves raked from their lawns.

C Change the punctuation and capital letters in the following paragraph to remove all fragments and run-on sentences. (Add 10 points for each corrected fragment or run-on.)

1 Have you ever heard a jug band? These bands are composed of
2 instruments. You can make yourself. From items commonly found
3 around the house. The next time you buy cider. Save the jug it produces
4 a bass throb when the player blows across the top of it. Providing the
5 horn section for the band. A comb covered with tissue also produces
6 interesting music. Central to the jug band is an old-fashioned wash-
7 board. With a few tin plates and cups attached to the side of it. Wash-
8 boards are played with metal thimbles used as picks. Metal washtubs can
9 be used as drums this versatile item can also be played as a string
10 instrument. Simply turn the washtub upside down. And attach a pole to
11 its side. Make a hole in the centre of the tub. For a string to go through.
12 The top of the string attaches to the top of the pole. So that the pole,
13 string, and tub assume a triangular formation. Then get your friends
14 together and play.

Spelling: Using *-ant* and *-ance*

In this lesson, you will study words that end in *-ant* and *-ance,* the other forms of the endings *-ent* and *-ence* that you learned in Lesson 52.

Here are some guides for the use of *-ant* and *-ance:* (Memorize the example words.)

● The suffix *-ant* is usually added to a verb to form an adjective, as in list *1.* The words in list *2* have no separate English verbs. (Note the dropping of final *e* and the changing of *y* to *i* in some of the words.)

1		*2*
resist	resistant	arrogant
assist	assistant	elegant
defy	defiant	vigilant
ignore	ignorant	abundant
rely	reliant	distant
attend	attendant	exuberant

● Many adjectives ending in *-ant* have related nouns which end in *-ance.* Knowing how to spell either form means you can spell the other.

Here are the noun forms of the adjectives above:

resistant	resistance	arrogant	arrogance
assistant	assistance	elegant	elegance
defiant	defiance	vigilant	vigilance
ignorant	ignorance	abundant	abundance
reliant	reliance	distant	distance
attendant	attendance	exuberant	exuberance

● The suffixes *-ant* and *-ance* are added to verbs ending in *-ate.* This is one group of words that is easy to remember. The *a* in *-ate* is your clue to use *-ant* and *-ance*—all three endings have an *a* in the last syllable.

radiate	radiant	radiance
tolerate	tolerant	tolerance
dominate	dominant	dominance

EXERCISE A   Add the suffix *-ant* to each of the following verbs to change the verb to an adjective. Write the adjective in the blank. Remember the rules about final silent *e* and *y.* (Add 20 points for each correct answer.)

1. observe + ant = ...   4. please + ant = ...

2. pend + ant = ...   5. comply + ant = ...

3. exult + ant = ...

117

EXERCISE B   For each verb ending in *-ate* below, write the related *-ant* form. (Add 10 points for each correct answer.)

EXAMPLE   irritate *irritant*.

1. stimulate ....   6. luxuriate ....

2. resonate ....   7. participate ....

3. lubricate ....   8. vacate ....

4. stagnate ....   9. immigrate ....

5. vibrate ....   10. celebrate ....

EXERCISE C   For each word below, write the related form ending in *-ance*. (Add 10 points for each correct answer.)

1. fragrant ....   6. instant ....

2. significant ....   7. important ....

3. reluctant ....   8. entrant ....

4. repugnant ....   9. repentant ....

5. brilliant ....   10. recalcitrant ....

EXERCISE D   Be ready to write from dictation all of the words taught in this lesson. (Add 10 points for each correctly spelled word.)

REVIEW EXERCISE   For each word below, write the corresponding adjective form in the blank. (Add 10 points for each correctly spelled word.)

EXAMPLE   indulge *indulgent*

1. consist ....   6. depend ....

2. converge ....   7. inhere ....

3. confide ....   8. urge ....

4. reside ....   9. insist ....

5. cohere ....   10. precede ....

Building Vocabulary: Words to Learn

atrocious /ə trố shəs/ *adj.* Savage, extremely cruel, wicked: *The prisoner was found guilty of an atrocious crime and sentenced to life imprisonment.*

contagion /kən tấ jən/ *n.* The spreading of a disease from person to person through physical contact; hence, any disease spread in this way: *The government controls entrance into the country in order to combat contagion.*—contagious, *adj.*

denounce /di noúns/ *v.* To state strongly that someone is deserving of blame; also, to give information against someone: *The newspapers have denounced the mayor for not carrying out his election promises.* —denunciation /di nún sē ấ shən/ *n.*

discreet /dis krḗt/ *adj.* Careful; showing forethought and good judgment: *Lawyers must be very discreet in discussing their clients with others.*

impact /ím pakt/ *n.* The forceful striking together of two objects: *The impact of the bullet knocked the tin can 50 m.*

insoluble /in sól yə bəl/ *adj.* Impossible to solve or explain: *How the robber got into the bank vault remains an insoluble mystery.*

pessimism /pés ə míz əm/ *n.* A tendency to look on the dark side of things; lack of hope that things will turn out well: *The team's pessimism about their chances today is because of the fact that they have lost the last three games.* pessimist ,*n.*—pessimistic ,*adj.*

recuperate /ri kű pə rāt/ *v.* To get well again after an illness, accident, etc.: *It will be a week before Jerry recuperates fully from his operation.*

subsist /səb síst/ *v.* To have enough food to keep alive but no more; to live: *People can subsist on 4000 KJ per day, but their health may suffer.*

vivacious /vi vấ shəs/ *adj.* Lively and spirited: *Mark's vivacious personality makes him a pleasant and amusing companion.*

EXERCISE   Fill each blank with the word from this lesson that makes the best sense in the context. (Add 10 points for each correct answer.)

1. When the ship struck the iceberg, the . . . . knocked most of the passengers off their feet.

2. Even after leaving the hospital, Mike still did not . . . . fully from his pneumonia for at least two more weeks.

3. It was hardly . . . . of Willis to boast to the police officer that he had never been caught speeding before.

4. We do not think that the problem is . . . ., but it will need all our efforts to overcome it.

5. To prevent . . . ., the doctor washed her hands thoroughly after examining the patient.

6. They . . . . him to the police as a criminal.

7. The man's . . . . crimes horrified the entire community.

8. Maria is an extremely . . . . person who is the centre of attention at every party.

9. While travelling, the Plains Indians were able to .... on a diet of dried meat and berries.

10. Sandra was only expressing her usual .... when she said that she had probably flunked the examination.

REVIEW EXERCISE In the space to the left of each sentence, write the letter of the word from the list below that could best fill each blank. (Add 10 points for each correct answer.)

a. agile
b. aspiration
c. contemptible
d. controversial
e. degenerate
f. delicate
g. ensue
h. faction
j. heedless
k. reconcile
l. supersede
m. unintelligible
n. valid

.... 1. Garry's first enthusiasm for the plan will ____ into indifference when he realizes how much work it will involve.

.... 2. It was ____ to take the smaller child's books and throw them in the mud.

.... 3. A person in ____ health should not take up mountain climbing as a hobby.

.... 4. The ____ little dog leaped through the paper-covered hoop and then trotted out of the ring on its hind legs.

.... 5. Youth should be a time of deep dreams and high ____.

.... 6. The revised schedule of lunch hours will ____ the one that is now in effect.

.... 7. A subject as ____ as politics is not usually a good one for conversation with strangers.

.... 8. Liz and Ella were not on speaking terms for weeks, but we have at last been able to ____ them.

.... 9. The Latin oration at my brother's graduation was —— to nearly everyone in the audience.

.... 10. ____ of our warnings, Gabby went right on tugging at the drawer until he broke it.

120

CHAPTER SEVEN

Punctuation

This chapter will teach you the correct use of three marks of punctuation —the comma, quotation marks, and the apostrophe. You have already learned the use of end marks (period, question mark, and exclamation mark) in your study of sentence completeness in Chapter Five.

LESSON 62

The Comma: In Series

Use commas to separate items written in a series.

EXAMPLES You will be required to read short stories , plays , poems , and essays. (series of nouns)

That is a long , childish , uninteresting book. (series of adjectives)

We stumbled into the hall , bumped into the chair , turned on the light , and laughed in relief. (series of predicates)

I did not know where you were , how you were , or when you would return. (series of clauses)

When the last two items in a series are joined by *and,* you may omit the comma before the *and* if the comma is not necessary to make the meaning clear.

COMMA NOT NECESSARY   The cloverleaf connects *Main Street, River Road* and *Highway 10.* (A comma before *and,* while perfectly correct, would not affect the meaning of the sentence.)

COMMA AFFECTS MEANING   For lunch we served soup, tomato juice, ham and cheese sandwiches. (Without a comma before *and,* the sentence suggests that we served only three items: soup, juice, and sandwiches.)

For lunch we served soup, tomato juice, ham , and cheese sandwiches. (With a comma before *and,* the sentence says that we served four items.)

Follow your teacher's directions concerning the use of the comma before *and.* Some teachers may prefer that you use it always because it is almost always correct, and the habit of using it may prevent your writing unclear sentences.

Do not use a comma (1) between an adjective and the noun it modifies or (2) before an adjective which is thought of as part of the noun.

121

A good rule to follow when punctuating a series is to use a comma between words when you can logically put the word *and* (or *or*) in place of the comma.

INCORRECT   This part of Quebec City is full of narrow, winding, crowded, streets. (Illogical: "narrow and winding and crowded *and* streets." The noun *streets* is not a part of the series.)

CORRECT   This part of Quebec City is full of narrow, winding, crowded streets. (Logical: "narrow *and* winding *and* crowded streets.")

INCORRECT   Sam is an alert, left guard. (Illogical: "alert *and* left guard." The adjective *left* is thought of as part of the noun *guard*.)

CORRECT   Sam is an alert left guard.

If all items in a series are joined by <u>and</u> or <u>or</u>, do not use commas.

EXAMPLES   You will read short stories and plays and poems and essays.

Should assemblies be planned by students or teachers or a committee of students and teachers?

EXERCISE   Insert commas where they are needed in the following sentences. (Add 10 points for each correctly marked sentence.)

1. Janet Susan and I use various remedies for insomnia.

2. When she can't get to sleep, Janet takes a relaxing bath drinks hot chocolate or reads a telephone book.

3. To fall asleep quickly, Susan requires three things: fresh air and soft music and complete darkness.

4. Not concerned about baths and food dull reading and soft music lighting and ventilation, I use my imagination to go to sleep.

5. I visualize something that is quiet pleasant and peaceful.

6. I often imagine that I am an astronaut touring the vast mysterious universe an explorer all alone in the silence of a huge untouched forest or an aborigine quietly enjoying the beauties of nature.

7. Sitting near my cave door and watching a beautiful sunset, I am not disturbed by such noises as a neighbour's blaring television set or a loud ambulance siren or noisy highway traffic.

8. Sometimes I try to discover for myself ways of taming animals raising crops or inventing a language.

9. I grow weary and fall asleep as I try to invent my own alphabet sign language and smoke signals.

10. The sound symbols I devise are far cruder than those found in the early Chinese Egyptian or Semitic languages.

The Comma: Appositives

Use commas to set off expressions which interrupt the sentence.

In this lesson and in the next two lessons, you will learn how to punctuate various kinds of expressions which interrupt the sentence. The kind of interrupter you will study in this lesson is the appositive. An appositive is a noun or pronoun, often with modifiers, used to explain or identify another noun or pronoun. It usually follows the word it explains or identifies.

Appositives with their modifiers are set off by commas.

EXAMPLES Toller Cranston , a superb skater , is also a painter.
Next on the program was Hagood Hardy , the pianist.

A short appositive, especially if it is a single word, may be so closely related to the noun preceding it that it need not be set off by commas.

EXAMPLES My friend Mrs. Silver   The play *Macbeth*
Your sister Fran   The author **Mowat**

EXERCISE A   Insert commas where they are needed in the following sentences. (Add 10 points for each correctly marked sentence.)

1. According to Jung a famous psychologist the "whole" person consists of two parts the conscious and the unconscious.

2. In one book *Modern Man in Search of a Soul* Jung discusses dreams.

3. He disagrees with his predecessors people who said that all dreams reflect hopes or fears the basic emotions.

4. According to Jung, other things memories or fantasies also appear in dreams.

5. Most psychoanalysts people who are trained to study unconscious mental processes ask their patients to recall their dreams.

6. REM sleep is characterized by rapid eye movement a physical aspect that can be easily observed.

7. People awakened during REM sleep usually participants in laboratory experiments have been able to recall their dreams in great detail.

8. Aserinsky and Kleitman two scientists investigating the phenomenon of sleep claim that dreams during REM sleep can be vividly recalled.

9. Some scientists feel that dreams are a defence mechanism a protective device the mind uses to keep the person from waking up.

10. This would explain why a loud noise a car backfiring or a dog barking usually becomes part of a dream.

EXERCISE B   By using correctly punctuated appositives, revise the following sentences to eliminate wordiness. (Add 10 points for each correct sentence.)

1. The entire truckload spilled onto the middle of the highway. The truck-load consisted of four tonnes of gravel. . . . .
. . . .

2. Ike blew the fuses again. He is one of our scientific geniuses. . . . .
. . . .

3. Mr. Nevins discovered the cause of the million-dollar blaze. He is the chief of the fire department. . . . .
. . . .

4. I am working on Unit Five. The title of the unit is "The Westward Movement." . . . .
. . . .

5. I saw Judy on the train. Judy is my cousin. . . . .
. . . .

6. The class read "Atlantic Door". Earle Birney wrote this poem. . . . .
. . . .

7. The house was built in 1860. It is an ornate mansion. . . . .
. . . .

8. Mr. Ahmed asked us to ride in the plane. It was a tiny Piper Cub.
. . . .

9. Do you remember Sue? She is the girl I told you about. . . . .
. . . .

10. Aunt Kate arrived on Tuesday and asked Mom to accept a job in Saskatoon. It was the day after Thanksgiving. . . . .
. . . .
. . . .

The Comma: Direct Address; Introductory Words

Words used in direct address are set off by commas.

EXAMPLES   Bob , do you know my sister?
Please come here a minute , Marcia.
Now , my son , tell me the truth.

Words such as well, yes, no, and why are followed by a comma when they are used to introduce a sentence or remark.

EXAMPLES   No , you may not go out tonight.
Why , what a surprise!

EXERCISE   Insert commas where they are needed in the following sentences. Not every sentence requires commas. Be able to explain your punctuation. (Add 5 points for each correctly marked sentence.)

1. Yes air pressure can be tremendously important.
2. Suppose Clara that you fell out of a high-flying airplane.
3. Well air is very thin 24 km up.
4. Why the air pressure inside your body would cause death.
5. Seriously Clara you can test this principle in your kitchen.
6. Does a pressure cooker have a safety valve Clara?
7. I did a research paper on air pressure last year Teresa.
8. Why changes in pressure can be quite dangerous.
9. Oh then you know about the problems faced by divers.
10. Yes flyers experience relatively slow changes in pressure compared to divers.
11. One of the first places a diver feels pressure changes Teresa is the eardrum.
12. Why rapid changes in pressure can cause the drum to burst.
13. I've heard Clara that divers hold their noses and blow when they start to feel pain in their ears.
14. Yes swallowing also helps to equalize pressure.
15. Do you know Clara why your ears pop when you go up a mountain?
16. Why I think it's a result of the pressure on the inner ear equalizing the pressure on the outer ear.

17. Why is it better for a diver to have perfect teeth than teeth with fillings Teresa?

18. Well I don't think I know the answer to that question.

19. Really Teresa it's a serious problem.

20. Air pressure exerts a different force on the filling than on the tooth, and Teresa under severe conditions it can cause a tooth to collapse.

REVIEW EXERCISE Insert commas where needed in the following sentences. In the blank at the left of each number write the letters, *in order,* of the appropriate reason for each comma used. (Add 10 points for each correctly marked sentence.)

a. in series   c. with words in direct address
b. with appositives   d. after introductory words

.... 1. Oh I know the definition of *esprit de corps* a French phrase meaning "team spirit."

.... 2. In your class Mr. Melton I have learned that a good explanatory paragraph has more than one sentence develops a central idea and presents specific details.

.... 3. The new shortstop a fellow named Ted Anderson boasted that he could catch pitch and play first base better than we could.

.... 4. No this machine a recent model does not use so much electricity oil and water as the older models.

.... 5. School-building alterations a large item in the budget are necessary because of the present inadequate cafeteria facilities the crowded classrooms and the undersized auditorium.

.... 6. Lorne Greene a famous actor starred in the series *Bonanza*.

.... 7. Yes this graceful towering pine tree a village landmark faces destruction.

.... 8. On Saturday Angelo Santi our best trumpet player rehearsed with the school band in the morning marched with the band at the game in the afternoon and played in a dance orchestra at night.

.... 9. For lunch we had trout green beans fried potatoes and hot rolls.

.... 10. Yes in late January a series of arctic blasts hit Europe and Canada and set new records for all-time low temperatures.

The Comma: Parenthetical Expressions;
Dates and Addresses

Parenthetical expressions are set off by commas.

A parenthetical expression is one which is put into the sentence as an added thought of the writer's. It interrupts the main thought of the sentence. Expressions commonly used parenthetically are *I believe (think, hope, etc.), on the contrary, on the other hand, of course, in my opinion, for example, however, to tell the truth, nevertheless, in fact, generally speaking.* Because it is not essential to the sentence, a parenthetical expression is always set off by commas.

EXAMPLES   The majority, on the other hand, voted for Ruth.
This book is, I believe, the best book I have ever read.

EXERCISE A Insert commas where needed in the following sentences. (Add 10 points for each correctly marked sentence.)

1. In my opinion most people in the Western world have an intrinsic dislike of snakes.

2. Westerners in fact use the term *a snake in the grass* to describe a treacherous person.

3. Snakes of course are often portrayed as embodiments of evil in Western literature.

4. However in many Eastern cultures the snake is revered.

5. The Hindus for example venerate the snake.

6. Generally speaking they see snakes as protecting rather than harming humans.

7. Snakes also figure predominantly I believe in the myths of the Cretans.

8. Several Minoan goddesses were in fact actually snake goddesses.

9. On the other hand North American Indians also placed high value on the snake.

10. In times of famine for example snake dances were performed.

In a date or address consisting of two or more parts, put a comma after every part—except, of course, when the final part comes at the end of a sentence.

Note: Each of the following is considered *one* part of a date or address:

March 15 (the month followed by the day)

127

55 Barber Greene Road (the street number and street name)
Don Mills, Ontario (the city, followed by the province)
M3C 2A1 (the postal code)

EXAMPLE   A letter addressed on May 10 , 1976 , to Mr. Leonard Hudspeth , 155 Tallon Road , Montreal , Quebec H3G 2A5 , was lost. (Notice that the comma after the man's name is needed because the address interrupts the sentence.)

EXERCISE B   Insert commas where needed in the following sentences. (Add 20 points for each correctly marked sentence.)

1. On July 1 1967 Canadians celebrated their Centennial.

2. Peter wrote to the General Electric Company Limited Toronto Ontario to obtain information about the engines of atomic submarines.

3. Mr. Van Dunk may be reached at 1120 Four Brooks Road Edmonton Alberta T5X 2S7 or at 420 Main Street Coquitlam British Columbia V3J 4A2.

4. The letter addressed to 1425 Ocean Drive Prince Edward Island was forwarded to Halifax Nova Scotia after a delay of several days.

5. The letter from Medicine Hat Alberta was dated December 5 1980.

REVIEW EXERCISE   Write brief, correctly punctuated sentences containing answers to the questions. (Add 20 points for each correct sentence.)

1. When and where were you born? ....
....

2. What are three of your favourite foods? ....
....

3. What is the date of Confederation? ....
....

4. What is your address? ....
....

5. On what date did men first land on the moon? ....
....

The Comma: Compound Sentences

Use a comma before and, but, or, or nor when it joins independent clauses.

EXAMPLES   At the airport check your suitcases, and Frank will help you carry the packages.

No one knew the route, but Bob thought he could figure it out.

A compound sentence is a sentence composed of two or more independent clauses joined together, but not containing any subordinate clauses.

Do not confuse a sentence in which two *verbs* are joined by a conjunction with a compound sentence, in which two *independent clauses* are joined by a conjunction.

EXAMPLE   Darlene limped off the field and collapsed on the players' bench.

The second part, "collapsed on the players' bench," is not an independent clause; it has no subject. The subject of *collapsed* is *Darlene; Darlene* is also the subject of the first verb *limped.* Two or more verbs having the same subject are called a *compound verb.* Do not use a comma between parts of a compound verb.

EXAMPLE   The clerk wrote down my order and handed me a receipt.

In the following examples, the first sentence has a compound verb and does not need a comma. The second sentence is composed of two independent clauses and does need a comma. It is a compound sentence.

COMPOUND VERB   We met Alex and asked him to go with us. (no comma)

COMPOUND SENTENCE   We met Alex, and Ed asked him to go with us. (comma)

EXERCISE A   Insert commas where needed in the following sentences. Do not be misled by compound verbs. Not all sentences require commas. (Add 10 points for each correctly marked sentence.)

1. Christopher always does the cooking and his roommate cleans up.

2. The hero kissed the heroine and her jealous dog bit him.

3. The logs will be hauled by truck or they will be floated down the river.

4. Tomás does not fear lightning nor do tornadoes frighten him.

5. Most of us thought the movie was dull but Abby liked it.

6. The crowd swarmed onto the field and carried off the goal posts.

7. You must obey the rules of the school or suffer the consequences.

8. Put covers on all your textbooks and your teachers will be pleased.

9. Our small vessel weathered every storm and brought us safely into port.

10. Father believes everyone but Mother is more cautious.

REVIEW EXERCISE Insert commas where needed in the following story. Give the reason for your punctuation by writing at the end of each corrected line the letter of the comma use it illustrates. (Add 5 points for each correctly marked line.)

a. in series
b. with appositives
c. in direct address
d. with parenthetical expressions
e. after introductory words
f. with dates and addresses
g. with main clauses
h. no comma necessary

On June 16 1979 my family left Fredericton and moved to   1. . . . .

R.R. #2 Springfield Nova Scotia. I was very lonesome in my   2. . . . .

surroundings for a while but soon I became acquainted with   3. . . . .

Bud my next-door neighbour. We have already found a   4. . . . .

number of interesting amusing things to do together.   5. . . . .

Last Saturday night for instance Bud exclaimed, "I'd   6. . . . .

like some large ripe juicy peaches right now!" He added that   7. . . . .

Mr. Heston a nearby farmer had an orchard full of "wonderful"   8. . . . .

peach trees. "Are you game Phil?" he asked me shyly.   9. . . . .

We quickly left town crossed a cornfield and invaded   10. . . . .

the orchard. Oh what a grand time we had shaking the trees   11. . . . .

for peaches! Before long however I saw a flashlight glint   12. . . . .

in Mr. Heston's hand. "Run Bud! Run!" I yelled. We carried   13. . . . .

our booty two baskets on our fast retreat. Mr. Herston did   14. . . . .

not run or follow us. All that he did in fact was stand there   15. . . . .

and laugh at us.   16. . . . .

At last we reached my quiet safe backyard. We rolled   17. . . . .

the peaches on the ground shone a flashlight on them and   18. . . . .

saw that they were full of wormholes. We realized of course   19. . . . .

that we deserved what had happened to us.   20. . . . .

The Comma: Introductory Phrases and Clauses

An introductory expression is one which comes first in the sentence. It *introduces* the sentence.

Use a comma after an introductory adverb clause.

EXAMPLES   If the weather is bad, commencement exercises will be held indoors.
Because the school is overcrowded, double sessions will be necessary.

Introductory adverb clauses usually begin with one of the following words:

after	as though	since	whenever
although	because	unless	where
as	before	until	wherever
as if	if	when	while

Use a comma after an introductory phrase containing a participle.

EXAMPLES   Expecting the worst, we armed ourselves.   (introductory phrase containing a present participle)
Badly broken by its fall, the lamp could not be repaired.   (introductory phrase containing a past participle)

Use a comma after two or more introductory prepositional phrases.

EXAMPLES   Because of the curve in the glass window, you cannot see your reflection.
Like a lost puppy among strangers on a crowded street, the child tried desperately to find a friend.

EXERCISE   Insert commas where needed in the following sentences. Not all sentences require a comma. Before each corrected sentence write the letter of the comma use it illustrates. (Add 10 points for each correctly marked sentence.)

    a. after an introductory adverb clause
    b. after an introductory participial phrase
    c. after two or more introductory prepositional phrases

.... 1. Since water is deeper than it looks good spear fishers shoot below rather than at their apparent target.

.... 2. If a fish underwater sees you on a pier you probably look as though you are higher than you really are.

131

.... 3. By an explanation of refraction I can give sensible reasons for these strange appearances.

.... 4. Although she is our best tennis player Sally is out for the year.

.... 5. While I was working at the gas station I learned a lot about cars.

.... 6. Complete your homework assignments before you go home.

.... 7. Chasing the puck down the ice Guy hit the boards and sprained his elbow.

.... 8. Angered by her brother's remarks Jan stamped out of the room.

.... 9. A display of school spirit often helps the team to play better.

.... 10. If people object to my suggestion let them state their reasons.

REVIEW EXERCISE Insert commas where needed in the following paragraphs. (Add 4 points for each correct answer.)

WHAT IS IT?

1   "As this animal a nocturnal creature stepped from the entrance of its
2   home it looked warily around. Its long large ears listened for any sound
3   which might mean danger. Sensing no immediate threat it thrashed its
4   heavy fleshy tail twitched its piglike snout, and made its way through the
5   underbrush. Shadowed by the thick foliage the moonlight illuminated
6   the well-beaten paths and it avoided these paths because of its timidity.
7   Its short powerful limbs carried it along to a newly found feeding
8   ground. The thought of the waiting meal hundreds of fat termites caused
9   its long sinewy tongue to tingle with anticipation. While it was eating
10 however the creature heard an ominous noise a danger signal. Using its
11 strong claws it quickly and efficiently buried itself waited until the peril
12 had passed, and then returned to its underground burrow in the dark
13 jungle."

14 "Edith could you be describing a termite eater?" Doris asked.

15 "That I believe is obvious but what's its name?" she said.

16 No one of course guessed its real name aardvark.

Quotation Marks

Use quotation marks to enclose a direct quotation—a person's exact words. Do not use quotation marks to enclose an indirect quotation—not a person's exact words.

EXAMPLES   Dorothy said, "I'd like to go with you." (Direct quotation. The words enclosed by quotation marks are Dorothy's exact words.)

Dorothy said that she'd like to go with us. (Indirect quotation. The sentence tells what Dorothy said but not in her exact words.)

A direct quotation begins with a capital letter.

EXAMPLE   She said, "Turn to the back of the book."

When one quoted sentence is divided into two parts by such interrupting expressions as *he said* and *I replied,* the second part begins with a small letter.

EXAMPLE   "This book," she said, "was written by two reporters for the *Ottawa Journal.*"

Of course, if an expression like *he said* or *I replied* comes at the end of a sentence, the following sentence must begin with a capital letter.

EXAMPLE   "We're late," whispered Phyllis . "The show has already begun."

A direct quotation is set off from the rest of the sentence by commas.

EXAMPLE   "That ," he said , "is a very poor excuse."

Commas and periods are always placed *inside* closing quotation marks. Question marks and exclamation points are placed inside when the *quotation* is a question or an exclamation. Otherwise they are placed outside.

EXAMPLES   "The first prize ," the announcer said, "goes to Setsu Uchiyama ."
"Where have you been ?" she asked.
"Look out !" we cried.
Did you hear him say, "Get out "?

In a quotation of several sentences, do not put quotation marks around each sentence, but only at the beginning and end of the entire quotation.

INCORRECT   Terry said, "If you do not join the G.A.A., you will not be supporting school activities." "You will have to pay twice as much for tickets to games and plays." "The whole activity program will be hindered."

CORRECT   Terry said "If you do not join the G.A.A., you will not be supporting school activities. You will have to pay twice as much for tickets to games and plays. The whole activity program will be hindered. "

133

When you write dialogue (a conversation), begin a new paragraph every time the speaker changes.

"What time is it, Mother?" called Frances.

"Just a minute, dear. It's almost six o'clock by my watch," her mother answered.

"Do you think we can catch the 6:10 bus?" Frances asked.

"You're the only reason we can't," replied Mrs. Stevens. "Hurry, will you?"

EXERCISE A   Correctly punctuate the following dialogue. (Add 4 points for each correct answer.)

1   Many former expressions Dr. Lacy explained are now outdated

2   because of metric conversion. Expressions involving the words 'weight'

3   and 'weigh' he added are especially difficult.

4   Do you mean asked Bea that I can't say I weigh 100 pounds?

5   Dr. Lacy shook his head. No he stated. From now on your mass

6   is 45.5 kg.

7   Hey exclaimed Sue, a popular girl in the back row. What happens

8   to this paperweight on my desk?

9   That question laughed Dr. Lacy is a weighty matter. He added

10   obviously some expressions will not change.

EXERCISE B   Change each indirect quotation below to a direct quotation, and change the punctuation accordingly. (Add 20 points for each correct sentence.)

A. I asked Tom to paint the trellis.

"Tom, will you paint the trellis?" I asked.

1. Christina announced that she knew that Billy would apologize. .

....

2. Dad wondered where we were going and when we would return.

....

3. The coach advised us to keep our heads up.

....

4. Debby shouted that she did not want to watch television.

....

5. Sue asked me why I had not kept my promise to her.

....

The Apostrophe to Show Ownership

The apostrophe is used for two important purposes: (1) to show ownership or possession, and (2) to show where letters have been left out in contractions.

To form the possessive of a singular noun add an apostrophe s ('s).

EXAMPLES   one boy's coat, the boss's job, Jim's dog (one boy, one boss, one Jim)

To form the possessive of a plural noun ending in s, add only an apostrophe (s').

EXAMPLES   birds' nesting ground (nesting ground of many *birds*)
birds' voices (voices of many *boys*)

Most plural nouns end in *s*. A few, however, do not end in *s*: *children, men, women, people,* etc. These few words are made possessive in the same way that singular nouns are made possessive.

To form the possessive of a plural noun not ending in s, add an apostrophe s ('s).

EXAMPLES   a men's club, children's games, people's government

When you are deciding how to make a word possessive, you must ask yourself whether the word is singular or plural; that is, whether it refers to one person or thing or to several persons or things. A good way to decide is to substitute in your mind a prepositional phrase.

EXAMPLES   a boy's coats (coats *of a boy—boy* is singular)
several boys' coats (coats *of several boys—boys* is plural)

EXERCISE A   Each group of words below shows possession. In Column *A*, rewrite the words to include a prepositional phrase beginning with *of*. In Column *B*, write S or P to indicate whether the object of the preposition *of* is singular or plural. In Column *C*, write the object of the preposition (the possessive word) with the apostrophe in place to indicate that the possessive word is singular or plural. (Add 5 points for each correct line.)

	A	B	C
A. Bills friends	*friends of Bill.*	(S)	*Bill's* friends
B. the dogs tails	*tails of the dogs*	(P)	*dogs'* tails
1. a friends family	....	( )	.... family
2. friends families	....	( )	.... families

135

3. the girls locker room .... ( ) .... locker room

4. Guss hat .... ( ) .... hat

5. the boys gym .... ( ) .... gym

6. the babys playpen .... ( ) .... playpen

7. Margaret Atwoods poems .... ( ) .... poems

8. the Premiers speech .... ( ) .... speech

9. the cars front bumpers .... ( ) .... bumpers

10. the cars front bumper .... ( ) .... bumper

11. an employees welfare .... ( ) .... welfare

12. all employees welfare .... ( ) .... welfare

13. many trees branches .... ( ) .... branches

14. a trees branches .... ( ) .... branches

15. an officers uniforms .... ( ) .... uniforms

16. some officers uniforms .... ( ) .... uniforms

17. Vics brother .... ( ) .... brother

18. Willies sister .... ( ) .... sister

19. several voters opinions .... ( ) .... opinions

20. Mexicos history .... ( ) .... history

Do not use an apostrophe in plurals unless they are possessive.

EXAMPLES Her **pupils** respect her. (*pupils* is simply plural, no apostrophe)
Her **pupils'** respect pleases her. (*pupils* is possessive)

EXERCISE B Insert apostrophes where needed in the following paragraph. (Add 20 points for each correct answer.)

1   Picassos painting, *Guernica,* had been on exhibit at New York Citys

2   Museum of Modern Art since 1939. *Guernica* is a 8-m-wide mural

3   of protest against the bombing of a Basque town during the Spanish

4   Civil War. The artists portrayal of the villages devastation is quite

5   unforgettable. Agony is expressed by the many figures distorted shapes.

6   When the museums recent exhibition, called "Pablo Picasso: A Retro-

7   spective" was over, *Guernica* went to Spain, according to the artists

8   wishes.

The Apostrophe in Pronouns and Contractions

The possessive pronouns his, hers, its, ours, yours, theirs, and whose do not require an apostrophe.

EXAMPLES This campaign button is hers.
I like its colour.
Theirs are better than ours.

To form the possessive of pronouns like one, everyone, and anybody, add an apostrophe s ('s).

EXAMPLES Everyone's answers were incorrect.
Has anybody's invitation been sent?

When you combine two words into one word by omitting one or more letters, you are forming a contraction.

Use an apostrophe to indicate where letters have been left out in a contraction.

EXAMPLES should not = shouldn't   they have = they've
I will   = I'll   it is   = it's

Note: Its (without an apostrophe) is the possessive form of *it. It's* (with an apostrophe) is a contraction of *it is.* Never put an apostrophe in *its* unless you mean *it is.*

EXAMPLES The French Club enlarged its treasury by giving a bake sale.
It's a good way to make money.

EXERCISE In the blank spaces, write contractions of the words at the left. (Add 5 points for each correct answer.)

1. we have   ....
2. is not   ....
3. you are   ....
4. does not   ....
5. she will   ....
6. were not   ....
7. cannot   ....
8. he is   ....
9. Dominic is ....
10. they had   ....
11. do not   ....
12. let us   ....
13. who is   ....
14. it is   ....
15. must not   ....
16. he would   ....

137

17. we will ....   19. will not ....

18. they are ....   20. I shall ....

REVIEW EXERCISE Circle any word below that should have an apostrophe and write the word correctly in the blank to the left of the line. If there is no error in a line, write *C* (for *correct*) in the blank. (Add 4 points for each correctly marked line.)

BANKING DISMAY

1. ....   One of Stephen Leacocks funniest short stories is

2. ....   called "My Financial Career". Its about his attempt

3. ....   to deposit money for the first time in a bank. In

4. ....   Leacocks tale, he calls himself an 'irresponsible

5. ....   idiot' and says its because he gets rattled as soon as he

6. ....   enters a bank. On this occasion, he has only fifty-six

7. ....   dollars to deposit and he gets in difficulties because

8. ....   he acts as though the sums enormous. At first the

9. ....   bank manager believes hes one of Pinkertons men,

10. ....   come to investigate security. Then the manager

11. ....   guesses he must be Baron Rothschilds son. When the

12. ....   truths explained, the manager coldly sends Leacock

13. ....   to the accountants wicket. First, however, Leacock

14. ....   steps through the safes doorway, rather than the

15. ....   office door, further embarrassing himself. He sheep-

16. ....   ishly heads in the right direction, under the managers

17. ....   scornful eye. His moneys been rolled into a tight

18. ....   wad, and he thrusts it at the accountant. When the

19. ....   entire amounts deposited, Leacock tries to withdraw

20. ....   a few dollars. He cant think straight now at all and

21. ....   ends up getting back the whole sum hes just banked.

22. ....   Too far gone now, Leacocks determined to escape.

23. ....   He asks for his money in fifties and sixes and doesnt

24. ....   catch his own mistake. As he rushes through the

25. ....   banks doors, he hears a great roar of laughter behind

26. ....   him.

Chapter Review

EXERCISE A Insert punctuation marks where needed in the following sentences. (Add 2 points for each correct answer.)

1. Theres one in every class said Mr. Papas as Dick came in late without his notebook textbook, or pencil.

2. Arnold Freiberg captain of the grey team tells me that hes confident of victory in tonights meet.

3. No Im afraid youre wrong about that Dan I said Its hard to get a whole class to change its mind

4. When you approach a green light dont go too fast If youre going fast youll not be able to stop if the light changes

5. If youd show a little more patience said Mrs. Chambers people would like you better and your friends wouldnt drift away from you.

6. At yesterdays track meet in Coquitlam our opponents excelled in almost every event but the relays were very closely contested.

7. On May 1 1976 her address was 72 Park Terrace Montreal Quebec H7S 4B3.

8. At Amoss party we had Mrs. Kings potato chips, Mr. Bauers pretzel nuggets and Nancys punch.

EXERCISE B Insert punctuation marks where needed in the following passage. (Add 2 points for each correct answer.)

1   The popcorn man is a common sight in many large cities selling
2   popcorn nuts and candy apples. Downtown when the movie is over
3   the hockey game finished or the stores all closed the popcorn man is
4   still open for business He appears at his usual corner anchors his high
5   glass-enclosed pushcart at the curb lights its wavering gas burner and
6   proceeds with the ritual of popping corn. A small purring jet burner
7   beneath the pot of melting butter lights the vendors face with a warm
8   ruddy glow as he stands beside his cart an island of light in the dark-
9   ening street. The aroma so very mouthwatering is one that can't be
10   resisted on a cold winter's night.

11   "A bag of popcorn, please." Then comes the deft scoop into the
12   snowy pile the shake down of the bag before the second scoop, and the
13   professional, swirling dip of the butter can usually an old enamel
14   coffeepot over the overflowing bag. A dash of salt is the finishing
15   touch. Well my friends this warm aromatic bag of popcorn is surely a
16   taste of heaven.

17   There are other vendors who are also very popular around town
18   especially with children. They have gleaming mobile "stores" with
19   posters splashed across them, advertising the latest flavours: pineapple
20   banana coconut chocolate tropical fruit, and butter crunch. These
21   "stores" may be pushcarts motor scooters or small trucks. They are
22   refrigerators on wheels and these people sell ice cream. Theres nothing
23   quiet hidden, or mysterious about them. As they jingle loudly down
24   the blocks the streets come to life. Children burst from backyards cel-
25   lars vacant lots, and front doors. Parents dig into pocketbooks purses,
26   and trouser pockets for requested coins. When each truck stops the
27   person in the crisp white uniform swings open the thick door. Plunging
28   into the smoking interior, the vendor brings out the requested delica-
29   cies. Everyones familiar with the shrill screams of Johnny Merkle the
30   three-year-old as he races after the truck. Hes afraid hes going to be too
31   late but Johnnys not one to be left behind. Got any lemon-orange to-
32   day?" he asks breathlessly as he holds out a fist full of moist pennies.

33   For five minutes the childrens games are stopped and parents activities
34   are interrupted. The ice cream provides a welcome relief on a hot
35   summer day but in my opinion it cant equal the popcorn vendors wares.

Cumulative Review

A   Below each italicized sentence in this exercise there are questions about parts of the sentence. Write the answer to each question in the space at the right. (Add 5 points for each correct answer.)

The title of Carl's talk was "Early Autos."

1. What is the subject of this sentence?   . . . .

2. What is the verb in this sentence?   . . . .

3. What part of the sentence is *"Early Autos"*?   . . . .

4. What part of speech is *talk?*   . . . .

5. Is *of Carl's talk* a phrase or a clause?   . . . .

6. What word does *of Carl's talk* modify?   . . . .

7. Is *of Carl's talk* used as an adjective or an adverb?   . . . .

Did Carl give you any facts about Henry Ford yesterday?

8. What is the subject of the sentence?   . . . .

9. What is the verb in the sentence?   . . . .

10. What part of the sentence is *you?*   . . . .

11. What part of speech is *you?*   . . . .

12. What part of speech is *any?*   . . . .

13. What part of the sentence is *facts?*   . . . .

14. What part of speech is *yesterday?*   . . . .

15. What word does *about Henry Ford* modify?   . . . .

Because Ford used accelerated mass production, he could by 1914 assemble a car in ninety-three minutes.

16. What is the subject of the independent clause?   . . . .

17. What is the verb in the independent clause?   . . . .

18. What part of the sentence is *car?*   . . . .

19. What word introduces the subordinate clause?   . . . .

20. Is the subordinate clause used as an adjective or an adverb?   . . . , ...

B   In the following paragraphs, punctuation marks and capital letters have been either omitted or used incorrectly. Correct the paragraphs by inserting punctuation and capitals in the proper places and removing those which are incorrect. (Add 2 points for each correct answer.)

1   When Mr. Coleman the principal of Laurier high school, asked Earl
2   the reason for his eight tardinesses this month Earl explained about his
3   alarm clock. Determined not to be late to school this year he had
4   bought the clock from Mr. Stephenson. Proprietor of Stephensons
5   Canadian secondhand emporium on First street. The alarm had work-
6   ed very well. Until the day Earl knocked the clock off the window sill.
7   From that day on, however he had had trouble. Because he could no
8   longer set the alarm properly. The clock survived its fall into the
9   bushes outside Earls window but the alarm indicator had been shifted.
10 As the clocks owner explained. He couldn't tell how the alarm was set.

11   Earl had he believed figured out a solution. He waited until the alarm
12 went off, then he checked with his wristwatch. When the indicator on
13 the clock pointed to 7:00 the alarm went off at 2:15. Making use of this
14 information Earl set the clock for 12:15. Expecting it to ring at 7:30 the
15 time he had to get up. This careful figuring did not help the clock rang at
16 8:30, leaving him no time for eating breakfast and getting to school. The
17 next day he set the alarm for 11:15. Which was one hour earlier. He was
18 awakened at 9:00.

19   Finally Earl decided to push the clock out the window again, In the
20 hope that the second crash would knock the alarm back into working
21 order. The second tumble changed everything. By completely breaking
22 the clock.

23   "Now, said principal Coleman you had better give in and buy another
24 clock." He sent Earl to the Fixit clock hospital, where Earl bought
25 another secondhand model.

26   I think Ill not keep this one on the window sill, Mr. Coleman"
27 declared Earl. As he displayed his purchase. Itll be safer on the table."

Usage: Avoiding "Is when," "Being as," and "Had ought"

Do not use is when or is where in writing a definition.

NONSTANDARD   A catboat is *where a boat has* one mast and no jib.
STANDARD   A catboat is a boat with one mast and no jib.

NONSTANDARD   An anthology is *when a book contains* many selections.
STANDARD   An anthology is a book containing many selections.

Do not use being as or being that for since or because.

NONSTANDARD   *Being as* I am a new student, I have few friends here.
STANDARD   Since (or *because*) I am a new student, I have few friends here.

Do not use had with ought.

NONSTANDARD   We *had ought* to start.
STANDARD   We ought to start.

NONSTANDARD   You *hadn't ought* to do it.
STANDARD   You ought not to do it.

EXERCISE If a sentence below contains one or more usage errors, write (0) in the blank, cross out the error, and write your correction above it. (If a word or letter is unnecessary, merely cross it out.) If a sentence is correct, write (+) in the blank. (Add 5 points for each correctly marked sentence.)

....   1. Someone had ought to tell her the truth.

....   2. You had ought to learn to play backgammon.

....   3. That fire must be somewhere near here!

....   4. A satellite is when a small planet goes around a larger one.

....   5. Since a hurricane was approaching, we left the island.

....   6. Being as Joan is only twelve, she doesn't understand irony.

....   7. A dune is where a sandhill has been formed by the wind.

....   8. An air-cooled engine is where a radiator is not needed.

....   9. If you have nothing to do, you can take this note to Mrs. James.

.... 10. You hadn't ought to complain.

.... 11. We did the work badly, being as we were in a hurry.

.... 12. She had ought to do as well as Ana.

.... 13. Being that the weather looked bad, we postponed our trip.

.... 14. When you come back from town, please bring my mail.

.... 15. Why didn't you take the supplies with you when you came?

.... 16. If you come in the morning, bring your lunch.

.... 17. An I-beam is where a beam is shaped like a capital *I*.

.... 18. Being as she is older, she should set a good example.

.... 19. They had ought to remember what you said.

.... 20. I didn't want to hurt his feelings, being as he's so new.

REVIEW EXERCISE   Select the correct one of the two words in parentheses and copy it in the space at the right. Cross out the incorrect word. (Add 5 points for each correct answer.)

1. We were playing fairly (good, well) in the first half.   . . . .

2. May I (bring, take) this home?   . . . .

3. Someone (ought, had ought) to bring refreshments.   . . . .

4. May I (bring, take) this paper down to Miss du Boise?   . . . .

5. Charlie pitches (good, well) in a tight spot.   . . . .

6. (Being, Because) I am tall, I tend to slouch.   . . . .

7. She did not perform so (well, good) in the rehearsal.   . . . .

8. In the store I asked her to (take, bring) the meat home.   . . . .

9. How (well, good) they sing the songs.   . . . .

10. We (hadn't ought, ought not) to copy.   . . . .

11. Go to the office and (take, bring) your books with you. . . . .

12. She (ought not, hadn't ought) to be so critical.   . . . .

13. I'll run over to Pauline's and (bring, take) her this book. . . . .

14. Someone (ought, had ought) to find out the truth.   . . . .

15. Mary did (good, well) in math.   . . . .

16. I often (bring, take) an extra blanket when I go camping.   . . . .

17. You (ought, had ought) to pay your debts promptly.   . . . .

18. Would you mind (bringing, taking) me the newspaper? . . . .

19. Because of his cold, Don did not play very (good, well). . . . .

20. She will (bring, take) us a surprise when she comes.   . . . .

144

Spelling: The Four Forms of *in-*

The common prefix *in-* (meaning "not") can be spelled in three other ways besides *in-*. A knowledge of these ways will help you to avoid misspelling many common words. The other three forms of *in-* are *im-*, *il-*, and *ir-*. Look at the following lists of words, which illustrate all four forms of *in-*, and see if you can decipher any patterns or rules concerning when to use which form of this prefix.

(Hint: Look at the letter immediately following the prefix in each word.)

1	2	3
inappropriate	imbalance	illegal
inefficient	impolite	illiterate
inimitable	impossible	illogical
inoffensive	impartial	
incorrect	imperfect	4
indecent	immortal	irregular
inhuman	immoderate	irreligious
insane	immodest	irresponsible

Here are some rules concerning the forms of the prefix *in-*:

Change *in-* to *im-* before words beginning with *b*, *p*, or *m*.

Change *in-* to *il-* before words beginning with *l*.

Change *in-* to *ir-* before words beginning with *r*.

Keep the *in-* form before words beginning with any letter other than those covered in the first three rules above.

The process in which a sound in a word tends to become like the sound that follows it is known as **assimilation**. It is hard to say the /n/ sound in *in-* when the very next sound is /b/, /p/, or /m/. The lips begin to form the /p/ in *possible,* for example, before they finish saying the /n/ of *in-*. Try putting *in-* and *possible* or *in-* and *mortal* together and saying the resulting words. Do the same with *in-* plus *responsible* and *in-* plus *literate.* Your tongue almost automatically changes the *n* to fit the letter that comes right after the *n.*

Knowing that *in-*, *im-*, *ir-*, and *il-* mean "not," and keeping in mind the rules concerning assimilation, you can add these prefixes to such words as *movable, regular,* and *rational* and come up with the correctly spelled (two consonants) "new" words: *immovable, irregular,* and *irrational.* On the other hand, you will never be tempted to put two *n*'s at the beginning of *inefficient,* for example, because you know that this word is made up of the prefix *in-* plus *efficient,* and means "not efficient."

EXERCISE A Use your knowledge of assimilation to join the prefix *in-* to each word below to make a new word meaning "not" plus the meaning of the word given. Write *in-*, *im-*, *il-*, or *ir-*, whichever is the correct form, in front of each word below. (Add 5 points for each correct answer.)

1. ....mortal

2. ....comparable

3. ....legible

4. ....personal

5. ....material

6. ....reconcilable

7. ....numerable

8. ....exact

9. ....passable

10. ....sanity

11. ....liberal

12. ....patient

13. ....active

14. ....mature

15. ....reducible

16. ....practical

17. ....formal

18. ....legitimate

19. ....resolute

20. ....mobile

EXERCISE B Write five words (other than those taught in this lesson) that contain the *im-* form of *in-* (meaning "not"); five that contain the *il-* form; five that contain the *ir-* form; five that contain the original *in-* form. (Add 5 points for each correct answer.)

im-	*il-*	*ir-*	*in-*
1.	1.	1.	1. ....
2.	2.	2.	2. ....
3.	3.	3.	3. ....
4.	4.	4.	4. ....
5.	5.	5.	5. ....

EXERCISE C Be ready to write from dictation the words taught in this lesson. (Add 2 points for each correctly spelled word.)

REVIEW EXERCISE In the blank, write the related *-ant* form of each word below. (Add 10 points for each correctly spelled word.)

1. reluctance   ....

2. defy   ....

3. distance   ....

4. stagnate   ....

5. fragrance   ....

6. comply   ....

7. vacate   ....

8. ignore   ....

9. rely   ....

10. instance   ....

Building Vocabulary: How Words Are Defined

To define a word is simply to explain what it means. You can sometimes accomplish this by giving one or more close synonyms. More often, you must follow a formal, two-step process in defining a word—the same method by which most dictionary definitions are written.

To define a word, first relate it to other words that are close in meaning. Then show how it differs in meaning from these words.

The second step is important. To use words accurately, you must know not just their general meaning but how they differ from near synonyms. For example, how would you define *migraine* to fit this context?

EXAMPLE   The student was suffering with a terrible **migraine** and experienced shooting pains on the left side of his head.

Clearly, *migraine* must be a type of "headache." How does its meaning differ? A definition naturally falls into two parts:

DEFINITION   A migraine is (1) a headache (2) of a very severe nature, with distinctive characteristics.

Now see if you can work out a definition for the verb *to mar* in the same way—by thinking of a synonym and showing how the meanings differ.

EXAMPLES   That hot dish has **marred** the dining table.
Ken's pleasing personality is **marred** by his constant fault-finding.

To mar must have the general meaning of "to damage." But the damage, while real and troublesome, does not go too deep. The marred table is still usable. Ken's personality is pleasing except for his fault-finding. Here is a possible two-part definition of *to mar*.

DEFINITION   To mar is (1) to damage (2) superficially.

Notice that a good definition can usually be substituted in the original context for the word defined. When you explain a word, test your definition in this way.

EXAMPLES   The student was suffering from **headaches of a very severe nature** .
The hot dish **damaged** the dining table **superficially** .

EXERCISE   Study the context in which each italicized word is used. Then read the definitions of these words below and analyse them in this way: circle the broad, general synonyms that classify the meaning of each word; underline the rest of the definition that tells how the meaning of the word differs from that of its synonyms. (Add 10 points for each correctly marked definition.)

1. "I have long *advocated* a tax reform," said the Minister of Finance, "and I am happy to see that my views have at last become law."

2. The children often *bicker* among themselves, but no one takes it very seriously.

3. "If you don't get out of here this very minute," *blustered* Mr. Willing, "I'm going to call the police!"

4. The eruption of Mt. Vesuvius, which destroyed Pompeii, was perhaps the greatest *cataclysm* of ancient times.

5. After I had been waiting for a quarter of an hour, the salesperson at last *condescended* to notice that I was there.

6. The news commentator took lessons in *elocution* to improve his delivery on radio and television.

7. Sitting by the fire, the elderly woman often *laments* the days of her youth and prosperity.

8. The family is notable for its *piety*. They never miss church on Sunday and always begin their meals by saying grace.

9. When soldiers seized the palace, they said that they were protecting the queen, but this was merely a *pretext*.

10. It is absurd even to suggest that a person of such *rectitude* as Judge Wylie would ever accept a bribe.

DEFINITIONS

1. **advocate** /ád və kāt/ *v.* To speak or declare oneself in favour of an idea or action.
2. **bicker** /bík ər/ *v.* To quarrel or argue in a petty, fussy way.
3. **bluster** /blús tər/ *v.* To talk in a noisy, bullying, foolish way.
4. **cataclysm** /kát ə klíz əm/ *n.* A flood; any large and violent upheaval or natural change.
5. **condescend** /kón di sénd/ *v.* To behave toward a supposed inferior in a lofty or superior manner.
6. **elocution** /él ə ky-ū́ shən/ *n.* The art of reading aloud or speaking clearly, effectively, and correctly.
7. **lament** /lə mént/ *v.* To grieve deeply and openly.
8. **piety** /pī́ ə tē/ *n.* Reverent respect shown toward God or toward one's parents or country.
9. **pretext** /prḗ tekst/ *n.* A false reason or explanation for an action, stated in order to conceal the real one.
10. **rectitude** /rék tə tūd/ *n.* Moral uprightness; virtuous behaviour, in accordance with clear standards of right and wrong.

CHAPTER EIGHT

Making Words Agree

Number is a grammar term for the distinction between words which mean "one" and words which mean "more than one." Words which refer to one (single) thing are said to be *singular* in number. Words which refer to more than one thing are said to be *plural* in number.

For a sentence to be grammatically correct, certain parts of it must agree in number. If one of these parts is singular, the other must be singular. If one is plural, the other must be plural. The parts of a sentence which must agree in this way are the subject and verb, and pronouns and their antecedents (the words the pronouns refer to). Most of the time in your speaking and writing you automatically keep these parts in agreement, but there are certain constructions which present special problems. This chapter will tell you what these constructions are and give you practice in using them correctly.

LESSON 76

Agreement of Subject and Verb

A verb agrees with its subject in number.

In the following examples notice how the verb changes in number when the subject changes in number. This change is necessary to keep the verb and its subject in agreement.

EXAMPLES   The style has changed.

Styles have changed.

A satellite in orbit travels 8 km a second.

Satellites in orbit travel 8 km a second.

Using a singular verb with a plural subject or a plural verb with a singular subject is a grammatical error in agreement.

NONSTANDARD   The *children was* unusually quiet that night.
STANDARD   The children were unusually quiet that night.

NONSTANDARD   There *has been* many *complaints* about the proposed tax law.
STANDARD   There have been many complaints about the proposed tax law.

An *s* added to the end of most nouns makes the noun plural. An *s* added to the end of a verb makes the verb singular.

SINGULAR   This pen   *look*s expensive.
           This pen   *ha*s a ball point.
           This pen   *write*s under water.

PLURAL   These pen*s*   *look* expensive.
           These pen*s*   *have* ball points.
           These pen*s*   *write* under water.

EXERCISE A   After each of the following verbs, write *S* if the verb is singular, *P* if the verb is plural. Think of the verbs as they would be if used with the subjects *it* or *they*. (Add 5 points for each correct answer.)

1. walks   ....
2. tries   ....
3. make   ....
4. wishes ....
5. has   ....
6. are   ....
7. have   ....

8. was   ....
9. shine   ....
10. lies   ....
11. takes ....
12. go   ....
13. give   ....
14. leave ....

15. carries   ....
16. fly   ....
17. goes   ....
18. lose   ....
19. ask   ....
20. exists   ....

EXERCISE B   Some of the subjects and verbs paired in the following list agree in number; some do not agree in number. Write plus (+) before those which agree. Write zero (0) before those which do not agree. For those which do not agree, cross out the verb and write after it the correct form. (Add 5 points for each correct item.)

.... 1. planes fly ....
.... 2. pupils thinks ....
.... 3. motor runs ....
.... 4. cities is ....
.... 5. child asks ....
.... 6. players have ....
.... 7. horse looks ....
.... 8. tree grows ....
.... 9. flowers are ....
.... 10. dresses seems ....

.... 11. houses has ....
.... 12. woman write ....
.... 13. mountains stands ....
.... 14. guard waits ....
.... 15. cats jump ....
.... 16. dentist advise ....
.... 17. people was ....
.... 18. Liz give ....
.... 19. desk sits ....
.... 20. girls risk ....

150

Subjects Followed by a Phrase

The number of a subject is not usually changed by a prepositional phrase following the subject.

Sentences like the following sometimes cause an error in agreement because the speaker carelessly makes the verb agree with a word in the phrase instead of with the subject of the verb.

EXAMPLES   One of the children was absent. (*One* was, not children were)

This book of short stories is interesting. (*book* is, not stories are)

Mr. Auburn, with his sons, has gone shopping. (*Mr. Auburn* has gone *with his sons,* not sons have gone)

Members of the council enjoy special privileges. (*Members* enjoy, not council enjoys)

The following common words are singular: *each, either, neither, one, everyone, everybody, no one, nobody, anyone, anybody, someone, somebody.*

EXAMPLES   Each of the players was examined by a doctor.

Neither of the twins has been tardy all year.

The following common words are plural: *several, few, both, many.*

EXAMPLES   Few of the apples are ripe enough to eat.

Both of the lawyers have been highly recommended.

Some, any, none, all, and *most* may be either singular or plural, depending on the meaning of the sentence. These are the only subjects whose number may be affected by a word in a following phrase.

EXAMPLES   Some of the food was good.   All of the money is gone.

Some of the meats were good.   All of the pennies are gone.

EXERCISE A   In each sentence below, cross out the prepositional phrase, find the subject, and select the appropriate verb from the choice in parentheses. Then write the subject and verb in the space provided. (Add 10 points for each correct sentence.)

One was .... A. One ~~of the paper cups~~ (was, were) leaking.

.... 1. Cosmic rays in this room (is, are) striking us right now.

.... 2. The cause of her troubles (was, were) apparent.

.... 3. Each of you (has, have) heard this legend.

.... 4. (Do, Does) either of the girls own a bicycle?

.... 5. Everyone in my class (knows, know) that!

151

.... 6. The fibres of the wood (is, are) then crushed.

.... 7. Neither of the girls (plays, play) the piano.

.... 8. A few of your friends (were, was) here.

.... 9. The length of these boats (are, is) 6.3 m.

.... 10. (Is, Are) one of these notebooks yours?

EXERCISE B Underline the subject and the verb in each of the following sentences. If the verb agrees in number with the subject place a plus (+) before the sentence. If the verb does not agree with the subject, place a zero (0) before the sentence and correct the verb. (Add 5 points for each correctly marked sentence.)

.... 1. Merchandise on the lower shelves was damaged by flood water.

.... 2. Neither of the reports are clearly written.

.... 3. Not one of the bills were counterfeit.

.... 4. Both sentences in the paragraph say the same thing.

.... 5. A few members of the band was not in uniform.

.... 6. Neither of the rugs lie flat.

.... 7. Every one of these planes carries fifty passengers.

.... 8. Only one of us have a catcher's mitt.

.... 9. All of our supplies were bought at the supermarket.

.... 10. Nancy, along with other students, take gym three times a week.

.... 11. Some members of the team have played professionally.

.... 12. Each of us were acting selfishly.

.... 13. Some kinds of shellfish tastes delicious.

.... 14. Each of the organizations have a faculty sponsor.

.... 15. Frank, along with the other students, enjoys this kind of work.

.... 16. Has some of the students already returned?

.... 17. Traffic on the parkways seems heavy today.

.... 18. Empty seats on the bus is rare.

.... 19. The works of this writer have always been popular.

.... 20. One of those days was rainy.

The Compound Subject

A compound subject consists of two or more connected words. The words are usually connected by *and* or *or*.

EXAMPLES   A tree and a telephone pole were lying across the road.
Ed or his brother has to stay at home.

Most compound subjects joined by and are plural and take a plural verb.

EXAMPLES   Sally and Marie are in my class. (two people are)
The engine and one car were derailed. (two things were)

If a compound subject names only one person or thing, then the verb must be singular.

EXAMPLES   The medical director and chief surgeon is Doctor Church. (one person is)
Bacon and eggs is my favourite Saturday lunch. (the one dish is)

Singular subjects joined by or or nor are singular and take a singular verb.

EXAMPLES   Either the captain or the mate is aboard. (one, not both)
Paul or Carl has your notebook. (one, not both)

Do not confuse the *either . . . or, neither . . . nor* construction with the *both . . . and* construction, which requires a plural verb.

EXAMPLES   Both Mother and Dad are willing to help us.
Neither Mother nor Dad is willing to help us.

Plural subjects joined by or or nor are, of course, plural.

EXAMPLES   Neither the students nor the teachers are enthusiastic.
The juniors or the seniors have won the trophy.

EXERCISE   The following sentences contain compound subjects. In some of the sentences the verb and subject agree. In others, they do not agree. Place a plus (+) before the correct sentences and a zero (0) before the incorrect sentences. Then cross out each incorrect verb and write the correct form above it. (Add 10 points for each correctly marked sentence.)

.... 1. Either Felicia or Ellen is planning a hobo party.

.... 2. Both Dot and Avery have suggested a wiener roast.

153

.... 3. David or Maureen always lead our class discussions.

.... 4. Either Jan or Alison are going to meet us.

.... 5. Have either Andrea or Linda spoken to you?

.... 6. The winner and new champion is Lynn Contrucci!

.... 7. The team and the coach has already left.

.... 8. Franks and beans is a popular Saturday night meal.

.... 9. Bob and Sharon probably has the directions.

.... 10. Neither her books nor her papers was recovered.

REVIEW EXERCISE   Underline the subject in each sentence below. Then circle the correct one of the two verbs in parentheses. (Add 5 points for each correct answer.)

1. One of the most popular literary forms (is, are) the mystery.

2. The first mysteries in English (was, were) written by Wilkie Collins.

3. *The Moonstone,* the most successful of Collins' novels, (was, were) written in 1868.

4. Its plot complications and involvements (is, are) fascinating to readers.

5. Edgar Allan Poe, author of short stories, poems, and essays, (is, are) credited with developing the character of the modern detective.

6. The solution to the crimes (is, are) found by M. Dupin through ratiocination, or the process of logical thinking.

7. Neither the stories of Collins nor those of Poe (is, are) as widely read as those of Arthur Conan Doyle.

8. The facts of the case (presents, present) an elementary solution to his inimitable detective, Sherlock Holmes.

9. (Has, Have) either England or North America produced a current mystery writer as much in the reading public's favour as Conan Doyle?

10. (Is, Are) there anyone who has not read or seen a movie version of at least one mystery by Agatha Christie or Dorothy Sayers?

Subjects That Follow Verbs; Collective Nouns

When the subject follows the verb, as in sentences beginning with <u>here</u>, <u>there</u>, and <u>where</u>, be careful to find the subject and make the verb agree with it.

NONSTANDARD   There *is* several *routes* available.
STANDARD   There are several <u>routes</u> available.

NONSTANDARD   Here *is* your *papers.*
STANDARD   Here are your <u>papers</u>.

When the sentence is a question, the position of the verb may change.

EXAMPLES   The <u>apples</u> are in the bag.
Are the <u>apples</u> in the bag?

You must be especially careful not to use the contracted forms *here's,* *there's,* and *where's* with a plural subject.

NONSTANDARD   Where's your *friends?*
STANDARD   Where are your <u>friends</u>?

EXERCISE A   In the following sentences the subject comes after *here, there,* or *where.* Underline the subject and notice whether it is singular or plural. If the verb agrees with the subject, place a plus (+) before the sentence. If the subject and verb do not agree, place a zero (0) before the sentence. Then cross out the incorrect verb and write the correct form above it. (Add 10 points for each correctly marked sentence.)

.... 1. Where's Sheila and Julia?

.... 2. Here are the girls.

.... 3. There are numbers on all the parts to be cleaned.

.... 4. Here's some more parts that must be numbered.

.... 5. Where's that yellow chalk?

.... 6. Where are the gasoline and clean rags?

.... 7. There's the rags on that shelf.

.... 8. Where is the bolt that fits here?

.... 9. There's no numbers on these cleaned parts!

.... 10. Here's the reason.

155

Collective nouns may be either singular or plural.

A *collective noun* names a group of persons or objects. A collective noun may be used with a plural verb when the speaker is thinking of the individual parts of the group; it may be used with a singular verb when the speaker is thinking of the group as a unit.

EXAMPLES   The committee <u>was</u> appointed by the president. (Committee is thought of as a unit.)

The committee <u>have</u> been discussing the problem among themselves. (Committee members are thought of as individuals.)

The team <u>is</u> a strong one.

The team <u>do</u> not agree about their chances in the game today.

The following is a list of commonly used collective nouns:

army	committee	flock	squadron
audience	crowd	group	swarm
class	faculty	herd	team
club	fleet	jury	troop

EXERCISE B   The subjects in the following sentences are collective nouns. Think about the meaning of the sentence. Ask yourself whether the collective noun is thought of as a unit or as individuals. Then draw a line under the correct verb. (Add 10 points for each correct answer.)

1. A squadron of jets (were, was) flying overhead.

2. Our herd of Ayrshire cattle (is, are) the largest in the county.

3. The class (was, were) not in their seats when the bell rang.

4. The flock of wild geese flying above us (were, was) a beautiful sight.

5. Behind closed doors the jury (were, was) arguing among themselves.

6. The committee (was, were) angered by our refusal of its offer.

7. The faculty (are, is) not in agreement with one another.

8. The club (meet, meets) every Friday.

9. The entire team (has, have) been declared ineligible.

10. A group of pilots (was, were) discussing the weather among themselves.

Reviewing Agreement of Verb and Subject

EXERCISE A   In the spaces at the right of each sentence, write the subject and the correct one of the two verbs given in parentheses. (Add 2½ points for each correct answer.)

Subject   *Verb*

1. Both of the pies (look, looks) good.

2. Neither Al nor Sue (dance, dances).

3. One of the players (is, are) hurt.

4. This collection of poems (look, looks) interesting.

5. The crowd (was, were) angrily shouting at one another.

6. (There's, There are) only twelve students in the class.

7. Each of those jackets (costs, cost) too much.

8. Bread and butter (is, are) a fattening combination.

9. (Where's, Where are) the hammer or axe?

10. The rash on her hands (is, are) probably poison ivy.

11. Kathy, along with her sister, (has, have) chicken pox.

12. (Where's, Where are) Malcolm or Maria?

13. Every one of the actors (needs, need) another rehearsal.

14. After their defeat the team (was, were) wearing gloomy expressions.

15. (Is, Are) Stephen or Kay going to type my paper?

16. A ring of towering mountain peaks (enclose, encloses) the valley.

17. Jack or Isaac (is, are) awake. . . . .

18. A kilogram of tomatoes (costs, cost) eighty-nine cents right now. . . . .

19. (Here's, Here are) the bulbs. . . . .

20. Wires on the wing (discharges, discharge) static electricity. . . . .

EXERCISE B Underline the subject of the independent clause in each sentence. In some of the sentences, the verb and subject agree. In others, they do not agree. Place a plus (+) before the correct sentences and a zero (0) before the incorrect sentences. Then cross out the incorrect verb and write the correct form above it. (Add 5 points for each correctly marked sentence.)

. . . . 1. My science class has been experimenting with dry ice.

. . . . 2. Does Al or Kate know why radium glows in the dark?

. . . . 3. The reporters on this newspaper belongs to the Newspaper Guild.

. . . . 4. There are both tin and steel in a tin can.

. . . . 5. Disintegrating atoms of uranium gives off dangerous particles.

. . . . 6. With a magnifying glass, each of them have seen a fly's eyes.

. . . . 7. Everyone in the class was to give a report.

. . . . 8. There's two sides to that question.

. . . . 9. Have either Teresa or Mary ever told you what happened?

. . . . 10. Some of us has been studying electricity.

. . . . 11. The best game of the season was the last.

. . . . 12. Jill, along with Sharon and Larry, have hall duty first period.

. . . . 13. Where's those tickets I ordered?

. . . . 14. Neither juniors nor seniors are eligible.

. . . . 15. Bread and milk doesn't make a good supper.

. . . . 16. How was the fish and the dessert today?

. . . . 17. The cut of her clothes are always just right.

. . . . 18. Both Susan and Anthony play a good game.

. . . . 19. The colour of the drapes contrast with that of the furniture.

. . . . 20. Do either of them know how to swim?

Agreement of Pronoun and Antecedent

The antecedent of a pronoun is the word to which the pronoun refers and for which it stands.

A pronoun agrees with its antecedent in number.

EXAMPLES 1. Our pitcher was sure that he would win.
2. Each girl took her turn at bat.
3. A few of the students had brought their own lunches.
4. Several teachers expressed their opinions.

In the first two sentences above, the antecedents *pitcher* and *girl* are singular. Notice that the pronouns *he* and *her* (printed in red), which refer to these antecedents, are also singular. The pronouns, therefore, agree with their antecedents in number.

In sentences 3 and 4 the antecedents *few* and *teachers* are plural. The pronouns *their* and *their* (printed in red), which refer to *few* and *teachers*, are also plural. They therefore agree with their antecedents.

As you learned in your study of agreement between verb and subject, the following words are singular: *each, either, neither, one, everyone, everybody, no one, nobody, anyone, anybody, someone, somebody.* Use singular pronouns when referring to these words.

Note: In ordinary conversation we often hear *their* instead of *his* or *her* when referring to *everyone, everybody, anybody* because these words strongly suggest more than one person. However, in formal writing and in doing the exercises in this book, use the singular pronouns (*his, hers, its,* etc.) in referring to these words. In your own writing, you can, if you wish, avoid the problem of agreement with *everyone* by making the subject plural. For example, instead of saying *Everyone brought his lunch,* you could say *All brought their lunch.*

Two or more antecedents joined by and should be referred to by a plural pronoun.

EXAMPLE Rachel and Pat gave their speeches in class.

Two or more singular antecedents joined by or or nor should be referred to by a singular pronoun.

EXAMPLE Neither Rachel nor Pat gave her speech in class.

159

In the sentences in this exercise, the pronouns and their antecedents are printed in italics. Draw a line through each pronoun that does not agree with its antecedent and write the correct pronoun above it. (Add 10 points for each correctly marked sentence.)

1. If you see *either* of my sisters, ask *them* to call me.

2. Remember to correct the *pronouns* that do not agree with *their* antecedents.

3. Neither *student* has completed *their* assignment.

4. *Everyone* wore *their* costume to the party.

5. *Not one* of my friends asked *his* parents.

6. *Each* of the dogs was looking for *its* trainer.

7. *Anyone* who thought that deserved what *they* got.

8. *Neither* of them would lend me *their* book.

9. A *student* should accept *her* responsibilities.

10. *Nobody* in the class has done *their* assignment very well.

EXERCISE B   Fill the blank in each of the following sentences with a pronoun which will agree with its antecedent. Draw a line under the antecedent. (Add 10 points for each correct sentence.)

A. Everyone brought .. *his* .... skates.

B. Only one of the girls brought .. *her* .... tennis racquet.

1. Many of the parents voiced .... opinions.

2. No one wanted .... name mentioned in the paper.

3. Each student was given a locker for .... equipment.

4. If everyone had .... way, we'd never get anything done.

5. Both Mrs. Larson and Mr. Feldman took .... classes on a trip.

6. Everybody said what .... thought.

7. Neither wanted to have .... picture taken.

8. Some of the group expressed .... opinions quite frankly.

9. Both the carpenter and the welder finished .... work yesterday.

10. A person should be careful of .... English.

Chapter Review

EXERCISE A Circle the subject of each verb in parentheses; then select the correct verb within the parentheses and write it in the space at the left. (Add 5 points for each correct answer.)

Does A. (Does, Do) (anyone) have any ideas for the grade ten class party?

.... 1. There (is, are) several themes that have been suggested.

.... 2. If one of them (is, are) chosen today, we can start making plans.

.... 3. The best of the themes suggested (is, are) characters from movies.

.... 4. The members of the committee (has, have) chosen this idea.

.... 5. Bruce and Ted (is, are) making pioneer costumes.

.... 6. Either Patty or Lynn (wants, want) to go as Dorothy.

.... 7. Several students in my homeroom (is, are) dressing as munchkins.

.... 8. Even the faculty (is, are) designing their own costumes.

.... 9. The teachers in the science department (is, are) coming as monsters from science fiction movies.

.... 10. Everybody in the math department (is, are) dressing as a robot.

EXERCISE B Circle the antecedent(s) in each sentence. Then select the correct pronoun from the pair in parentheses and write it in the space provided. (Add 5 points for each correct answer.)

his A. (Everyone) there offered (his, their) help.

.... 1. Sue and Elaine bought (her, their) own tickets.

.... 2. She or Sally will lend you (her, their) books.

.... 3. One of the men forgot to bring (his, their) tools.

.... 4. The head of the detective team proposed (her, their) solution.

.... 5. Each new student has a guide assigned to (him, them).

.... 6. Both of the girls had (her, their) notes handy.

161

.... 7. Neither of the boys finished (his, their) job.

.... 8. All citizens should accept (his, their) responsibilities.

.... 9. Few boys on the team did (their, his) best.

.... 10. Anybody can pass this course if (he, they) will work.

EXERCISE C Write a plus (+) before each correct sentence; write a zero (0) before each sentence containing an error in agreement. Correct each error by crossing it out and writing the correct form above it. (Add 5 points for each correctly marked sentence.)

..+.. A. Neither of the boys played his best game.

..0.. B. One of the boys lost ~~their~~ *his* money.

.... 1. A person is always pleased when you laugh at their jokes.

.... 2. Neither of the children know how to swim.

.... 3. Each of Lois Marshall's roles is demanding.

.... 4. Ask Lisa and Francesca for their opinions.

.... 5. Only a brave person would risk their life in such a heavy sea.

.... 6. The trial of the three suspects has been postponed.

.... 7. Neither Lee nor Bob would reveal their plans.

.... 8. I think nobody could do this job by themselves.

.... 9. Some of the motorists want a change in the driving laws.

.... 10. Here's some ballots that have not been counted.

.... 11. Bread and cheese was a customary noon meal.

.... 12. Each of her grandparents live alone.

.... 13. One of her daughters looks exactly like her.

.... 14. Both women, when challenged, showed their true character.

.... 15. Every one of the games were close.

.... 16. Anybody can build their own boat with this kit.

.... 17. Do either Carmen or Norma have a driver's licence?

.... 18. The bottom of these cans is made of steel.

.... 19. Jill or Peg will bring her record player.

.... 20. We learned not to ask either of the nurses about her war experiences.

Cumulative Review

A In one of the paired items in columns A and B, punctuation and capitalization are correct. In the space to the right, write the letter (A or B) of the column containing the correct item. (Add 5 points for each correct answer.)

A	B	
1. Its almost midnight.	It's almost midnight.	....
2. On May 1, 1975, we moved.	On May 1, 1975 we moved	....
3. We'll win today's game.	We'll win todays game.	....
4. I live on Oak street.	I live on Oak Street.	....
5. I said she was wrong.	I said, "she was wrong."	....
6. a new baseball, bat	a new baseball bat	....
7. a clear, beautiful day	a clear beautiful day	....
8. the President of the club	the president of the club	....
9. I asked who it was.	I asked who it was?	....
10. They worshipped god.	They worshipped God.	....
11. in the early spring	in the early Spring	....
12. *To the Lighthouse*	*To The Lighthouse*	....
13. "Stop," he yelled!	"Stop!" he yelled.	....
14. Is his nickname "The Frog?"	Is his nickname "The Frog"?	....
15. She said, "I win."	She said, "I win".	....
16. a History course	a history course	....
17. my English teacher	my english teacher	....
18. I stumbled, and fell.	I stumbled and fell.	....
19. Who's turn is it?	Whose turn is it?	....
20. Who's pitching, Rebecca?	Who's pitching Rebecca?	....

B Correct all errors in the following passage: capital letters, punctuation, fragments, and run-on sentences. (Add 2 points for each correct answer. Each corrected fragment or run-on counts as one answer.)

CHOOSE YOUR CHEW

1   Please put your chewing gum into the wastebasket John says the

2   english teacher in the class and a dozen other students abruptly stop

3   chewing shift their gum, and try to look innocent. Yes gum-chewing
4   North Americas most popular habit is a frequent cause of strained
5   pupil-teacher relations in some schools it is forbidden. Although now
6   and then they may enjoy a stick themselves, high school teachers object
7   to gum-chewing in class. Teachers objections of course do not always
8   remove the rows of contented jaw-wagging faces. School custodians
9   furthermore frown upon gum, they are tired of cleaning it off desks,
10 chairs, and floors. Especially after its hardened.

11   The craze all started when Santa Anna the mexican dictator fled to
12 Staten island New York in 1875. Bringing with him a strange elastic
13 substance which he would break into pieces, put into his mouth, and
14 chew on Thomas Adams an amateur inventor asked Santa Anna about
15 this queer chewy substance. And learned that it was chicle a gum of the
16 sapodilla tree, a tree native to Mexico and guatemala. Adams tried first
17 to develop it as a rubber substitute but he failed in this attempt, then he
18 made the first chewing gum in America.

19   After getting his familys reaction to the product Adams put it on sale
20 in a local store. Because it sold well he invented a machine to manu-
21 facture it in stick form and he was soon shipping it all over North
22 America. As the gums success attracted other manufacturers various
23 flavours were tried out. Among them balsam pepsin, and Adams own
24 licorice, North Americas favourite flavour, however, has always been
25 mint.

Spelling: The Many Forms of *ad-* and *sub-*

How often have you misspelled such words as *accurate* and *support* because you neglected to write two *c*'s or two *p*'s? The knowledge you acquired in Lesson 74 concerning assimilation can help you to spell correctly such words as *accurate* and *support*. As you recall, *assimilation* is the tendency for a sound to become like the sound that immediately follows it. For example, you remember that when the prefix *in-* is added to the word *legal,* the *n* changes to an *l* and the word becomes *illegal.* The *n* is said to have been "assimilated."

The process of assimilation occurs in a great many words that contain the prefixes *ad-* (meaning "to, toward") or *sub-* (meaning "under, beneath"). The final consonant in each of these two prefixes tends to change and become the same as the beginning consonant of the root to which it is added.

Examine the words below, all of which contain an assimilated form of the *d* in *ad-*:

ad	+	cept	=	a ccept
ad	+	ford	=	a fford
ad	+	gravate	=	a ggravate
ad	+	leviate	=	a lleviate
ad	+	nounce	=	a nnounce
ad	+	ply	=	a pply
ad	+	rive	=	a rrive
ad	+	sert	=	a ssert
ad	+	tend	=	a ttend

As you see, *ad-* may change to *ac-, af-, ag-, al-, an-, ap-, ar-, as-,* or *at-*. If you learn to recognize the prefix in such words as those above, you will remember to include a double consonant where the prefix joins the root.

Now look at some words in which the *b* in the prefix *sub-* has become assimilated:

sub	+	cess	=	su ccess
sub	+	fix	=	su ffix
sub	+	pose	=	su ppose

EXERCISE A Combine the prefix *ad-* with each root to make a new word. Write the new word, correctly spelled, in the blank. (Add 5 points for each correct answer.)

EXAMPLE   ad + tract = *attract*

1. ad + cuse = ...

2. ad + proach = ...

3. ad + flict = ...

4. ad + tract = ...

5. ad + gressive = ...

6. ad + point = ...

7. ad + nulment = ...

8. ad + liance = ...

9. ad + rest = ... 15. ad + rayed = ...

10. ad + sume = ... 16. ad + cording = ...

11. ad + fection = ... 17. ad + fair = ...

12. ad + tempt = ... 18. ad + luring = ...

13. ad + nexation = ... 19. ad + cident = ...

14. ad + sist = ... 20. ad + prove = ...

EXERCISE B Combine the prefix *sub-* with each root below to make a new word. Write the new word, correctly spelled, in the blank. (Add 10 points for each correct answer.)

1. sub + fering = ... 6. sub + ceeding = ...

2. sub + press = ... 7. sub + focate = ...

3. sub + ported = ... 8. sub + cessful = ...

4. sub + ply = ... 9. sub + plant = ...

5. sub + fice = ... 10. sub + cumb = ...

EXERCISE C In the blanks, write five words (other than those taught in this lesson) in which the prefix *ad-* has become assimilated, and five words in which *sub-* has become assimilated. (Add 10 points for each correct answer.)

<table>
<tr><td align="center">*ad-*</td><td align="center">*sub-*</td></tr>
<tr><td>1. ....</td><td>1. ....</td></tr>
<tr><td>2. ....</td><td>2. ....</td></tr>
<tr><td>3. ....</td><td>3. ....</td></tr>
<tr><td>4. ....</td><td>4. ....</td></tr>
<tr><td>5. ....</td><td>5. ....</td></tr>
</table>

REVIEW EXERCISE In the blank in front of each word, write *in-*, *im-*, *il-*, or *ir-*, whichever form of the prefix *in-* is correct for that word. (Add 10 points for each correct answer.)

1. ....personal   5. ....mortal   8. ....active

2. ....legible   6. ....polite   9. ....mobile

3. ....efficient   7. ....regular   10. ....literate

4. ....responsible

Building Vocabulary: Words to Learn

adornment /ə dáurn mənt/ *n.* Anything that adds beauty and value to that to which it is attached, often in a mental or spiritual sense: *Honesty is among the chief adornments of a good character.*—**adorn**, *v.*

arduous /ár jū əs/ *adj.* Difficult because requiring hard, steady work to accomplish: *Tearing down a building is usually an arduous task. The climbers had chosen the most arduous route to the top of the mountain.*

beset /bi sét/ *v.* To attack from all sides: *Many difficulties beset the politician who tries to keep election promises. The poet's life was beset with grief.* Note that *beset* does not change when used with the helping verbs *to be* and *to have.*

intercept /ín tər sépt/ *v.* To catch something and keep it from getting where it is going: *The coast guard ship intercepted the smugglers before they could land.*

invincible /in vín sə bəl/ *adj.* Incapable of being conquered or overcome: *After winning eight straight games, the team seems invincible.*

isolate /í sə lāt/ *v.* To separate or keep by itself; to cut off from outside contact: *Heavy snowdrifts on the roads isolated the town for a week.*

query /kwír ē/ *v.* To ask questions; to question or cast doubt on the truth or accuracy of something: *Several committee members queried Wilma about her plans for the subscription campaign.*

sloth /slōth/ *n.* Great habitual laziness: *Mark said that he did not have time to do his homework, but the real reason was simply his usual sloth.*—**slothful**, *adj.*

slovenly /slúv ən lē/ *adj.* Sloppy in appearance or in manner of doing things: *The many erasures of the page showed it was done in a slovenly manner.*

succumb /sə kúm/ *v.* To give up or give in to; often, to die of something: *Twenty years ago, people often succumbed to pneumonia.*

EXERCISE Fill each blank with the word from this lesson that makes the best sense in the context. (Add 10 points for each correct answer.)

1. Tired of city life, the woman had sought to .... herself in a tiny cabin in the wilds of northern Labrador.

2. Only by the most .... efforts did the explorers succeed in fording the raging river.

3. Mr. Winstanley finally .... when offered a piece of pumpkin pie with whipped cream, and that was the end of his diet.

4. Shakespeare's genius would have been the .... of any age.

5. I'm sorry to have to .... your conclusions, but I believe you've made a mistake somewhere.

6. Karen's .... is so great that we have given up expecting her to be of any help in our project.

7. Napoleon must have seemed .... to the frightened people of Europe before he began his disastrous invasion of Russia.

8. Fortunately, the Allies .... the message to the Axis troops in Normandy.

9. How can you live in such a(n) . . . .-looking room, with the bed unmade and dirty clothes lying on the floor?

10. With her pockets full of money, the girl was . . . . by many temptations.

REVIEW EXERCISE In the space at the left, write the letter of the best meaning for the italicized word. (Add 5 points for each correct answer in the first group and 10 points for each correct answer in the second group.)

.... 1. *profound* interest   a. disease spread by contact

.... 2. a *rational* plan   b. to speak strongly against

.... 3. an efficient *administrator*   c. to speak in favour of

.... 4. *inadequate* help   d. deep, serious

.... 5. dangerous *contagion*   e. not enough

.... 6. *denounce* a criminal   f. reasonable or logical

.... 7. overcome by *pessimism*   g. reverent respect

.... 8. *advocate* a plan   h. a manager

.... 9. *piety* toward parents   i. to grieve deeply for

.... 10. *lament* a past mistake   j. gloomy lack of hope

To the left of each sentence, write the letter of the word that could best fill the blank.

.... 11. It was hardly ____ to make faces at that police officer.
a. grotesque   b. prudent   c. placid

.... 12. A small ____ stands in the way of the bill's passage.
a. elocution   b. pretext   c. faction

.... 13. After several failures, we decided the problem was ____.
a. insoluble   b. inflexible   c. incompetent

.... 14. A bully may ____ at someone in order to be frightening.
a. sulk   b. bicker   c. bluster

.... 15. Phyllis said the restaurant's food was ____ and sent it back.
a. immaterial   b. valid   c. unpalatable

CHAPTER NINE

Using Verbs Correctly

As you study the verbs printed in red in the sentences below, notice how the basic forms (or principal parts) of the verb *see* are used to express various times.

PRINCIPAL PARTS OF THE VERB *see*

Present	*Present Participle*	*Past*	*Past Participle*
see	seeing	saw	(have) seen

1. I see the point now.   (present)
2. He is seeing double.   (present)
3. Yesterday she saw the captain.   (past)
4. I had seen Gwen before then.   (past)
5. She will see a circus tomorrow.   (future)

It is important to remember that the past participle of a verb must always have a helper: *have seen, has seen, had seen, was seen.* The present participle (a fourth principal part of the verb) ends in *-ing* and is used with forms of *to be* (*am, is, are—was, were—been*): *were seeing, will be seeing, has been seeing.* By learning the principal parts of verbs and their uses, you can avoid serious mistakes with verb forms (such as "I seen" or "I have saw").

LESSON 86

Regular and Irregular Verbs

Regular Verbs   Most verbs form their past and past participle forms by adding *-d* or *-ed* to the present form. Such verbs are called *regular verbs.*

PRESENT	PAST	PAST PARTICIPLE
believe	believed	(have) believed
risk	risked	(have) risked

Because the *-d* or *-ed* is sometimes difficult to hear and pronounce, you may carelessly omit this important verb ending in your writing. Avoid the error by remembering that the *-d* or *-ed* is used for every tense except the present and future.

NONSTANDARD	Last week Fran *ask* me to her party.
STANDARD	Last week Fran asked me to her party.
NONSTANDARD	Grandmother was *use* to hard work.
STANDARD	Grandmother was used to hard work.

169

Irregular Verbs   Many verbs that you use often are not regular. Because they do not form their past and past participle forms by adding -d or -ed to the present, they are called *irregular verbs*. To use them correctly, you must know their principal parts.

Memorize the principal parts of the following common irregular verbs. In repeating the principal parts to yourself, always say *have* with the past participle.

PRESENT	PAST	PAST PARTICIPLE
begin	began	(have) begun
come	came	(have) come
do	did	(have) done
drink	drank	(have) drunk
give	gave	(have) given
go	went	(have) gone
ride	rode	(have) ridden

EXERCISE   Fill the blank in each of the following sentences with the correct past form of the verb given before the sentence. (Add 5 points for each correct answer.)

ride   1. The rodeo champion had safely . . . . a bull.

suppose   2. We were . . . . to read the next chapter.

come   3. Alicia had finally . . . . home.

go   4. Has Gwen already . . . . to the laboratory?

ask   5. Yesterday the dentist . . . . me to return Monday.

see   6. Last night we . . . . both pictures twice.

give   7. Flo . . . . me the book last night.

do   8. Benita . . . . all she could to help.

ride   9. She has . . . . every horse in the corral.

drink   10. Roger asked if I had . . . . the last bottle of soda.

begin   11. I . . . . to think you weren't here.

give   12. Have they . . . . anything to the rummage sale?

come   13. Perry and Alice . . . . to see you yesterday.

see   14. Has anyone ever . . . . a dodo?

go   15. Aunt Ev and Uncle Leo have never . . . . there.

drink   16. Pearl . . . . her coffee in great haste.

begin   17. We had . . . . to wonder what was wrong.

do   18. Gary has . . . . more than his share.

see   19. I had already . . . . the principal.

come   20. At last the lawyer . . . . to the point.

170

More Irregular Verbs

Memorize the principal parts of the following irregular verbs. In repeating them to yourself, always say *have* with the past participle.

PRESENT	PAST	PAST PARTICIPLE
break	broke	(have) broken
ring	rang	(have) rung
run	ran	(have) run
speak	spoke	(have) spoken
swim	swam	(have) swum
take	took	(have) taken
throw	threw	(have) thrown
write	wrote	(have) written

EXERCISE A   Fill the blank in each of the following sentences with a correct form of the verb given before the sentence. (Add 5 points for each correct answer.)

write   1. Had Jane .... any poetry before she studied medicine?

speak   2. "I have ....!" Melissa shouted, ending the argument.

throw   3. The bowler had .... a strike.

take   4. Had they .... her prisoner?

write   5. Before 1450 books were .... by hand in Europe.

break   6. Was your watch .... in the scuffle?

run   7. Suzie and Crystal .... all the way to the bus.

swim   8. I wish I'd .... out to the raft after you did.

throw   9. We had .... away the garbage.

run   10. Stan had just .... 73 m for a touchdown.

take   11. Barbara Ann Scott must have .... pride in her skating ability.

ring   12. The clerk .... up fifty cents on the cash register.

swim   13. Yesterday Brie .... twenty lengths of the pool.

ring   14. I didn't know the bell had ....

break   15. Dad has never .... 90 on the golf course.

speak   16. Silence reigned; not one word was ....

swim	17. Helen had never . . . . in salt water.
take	18. Melodie . . . . the initiative and apologized.
write	19. Dale . . . . up the laboratory experiment last night.
speak	20. Peter Gzowski . . . . to the author of the book before the show went on the air.

EXERCISE B   This exercise covers verbs in this lesson and in Lesson 86. There are ten incorrect verbs. Cross out the incorrect verb and write the correct verb form above it. (Add 10 points for each correct answer.)

MODERN DRAGONS

1   Yesterday afternoon our English teacher told us about the occurrence

2   of dragons in literature. I was taken aback when she said that dragons

3   actually do exist today. Before the bell rung, she gave us our assignment.

4   By Friday we were to turn in compositions we had wrote on the Komodo

5   dragon.

6   I went to the library immediately after school and begun work on my

7   report. Komodo dragons have existed since prehistoric times. No one

8   knows how they come to the Indonesian island of Komodo long ago.

9   Some scientists think the dragons might have swam to the island from

10   the continent, island hopping along the way. This might have gave rise to

11   the legends about sea monsters. These creatures grow up to 3m long

12   and weigh up to 135 kg. Animals unlucky enough to have ran into

13   Komodo dragons have served as food. One hit with these dragons'

14   massive tails has throwed many an animal several metres. One bite

15   from their powerful jaws has broke many a creature, including humans,

16   in two. Komodos, are, however, their own worst enemy. Hungry

17   dragons, hemmed in by civilization, have took to eating members of

18   their own species.

The Irregular Verbs LIE and LAY

In order to use *lie* and *lay* correctly, you must understand the difference in meaning between them and memorize their principal parts.

The verb lie means to recline, to rest, or to be in place.

EXAMPLES   On Sundays I lie around reading the papers.
The key lies under the doormat.

The verb lay means to put or to place something.

EXAMPLE   Please lay the newspaper on the table in the hall.

Be able to write the principal parts of the two verbs from memory.

PRESENT	PRESENT PARTICIPLE	PAST	PAST PARTICIPLE
lie (to recline or rest)	(is) lying	lay	(have) lain
lay (to put something)	(is) laying	laid	(have) laid

If you are not sure whether to use *lie* or *lay,* ask yourself whether your intended meaning is "to recline (to be in place)" or "to put something." If it is "to recline," use a form of the verb *lie.* If it is "to put something," use a form of the verb *lay.* As a double check, notice whether the verb has a direct object. *Lie* never has an object. *Lay* usually does.

Next, ask yourself the *time* of the verb and select the principal part of the verb to express this: present, present participle, past, or past participle.

PROBLEM: We (lay, laid) our papers on your desk yesterday.
Meaning: place or put. The verb is *lay.*
Principal part: past. The past form of *lay* is *laid.*
Correct: We laid our papers on your desk.

PROBLEM: The dog is (lying, laying) on the porch.
Meaning: recline. The verb is *lie.*
Principal part: present participle. The present participle of *lie* is *lying.*
Correct: The dog is lying on the porch.

EXERCISE   Solve each of the following *lie-lay* problems by filling in the blanks thoughtfully. (Add 4 points for each correct answer.)

A. *Problem:* I must have (lain, laid) there an hour.

Meaning? ..... *recline* ..... Which verb? ..... *lie* .....
Principal part? *past participle* Verb form? ..... *lain* .....
Correct: I must have ..... *lain* ..... there an hour.

173

B. *Problem:* She (lay, laid) the ice cubes on the hot stove.

Meaning? *to put something* Which verb? *lay*

Principal part? *past* Verb form? *laid*

Correct: She *laid* the ice cubes on the hot stove.

1. *Problem:* The cattle were (lying, laying) in the shade.

Meaning? .... Which verb? ....

Principal part? .... Verb form? ....

Correct: The cattle were .... in the shade.

2. *Problem:* These boulders have (lain, laid) here for centuries.

Meaning? .... Which verb? ....

Principal part? .... Verb form? ....

Correct: These boulders have .... here for centuries.

3. *Problem:* I could not (lie, lay) still any longer.

Meaning? .... Which verb? ....

Principal part? .... Verb form? ....

Correct: I could not .... still any longer.

4. *Problem:* Which rug (lies, lays) here?

Meaning? .... Which verb? ....

Principal part? .... Verb form? ....

Correct: Which rug .... here?

5. *Problem:* (Lying, Laying) her fork down, she looked up.

Meaning? .... Which verb? ....

Principal part? .... Verb form? ....

Correct: .... her fork down, she looked up.

More Practice with LIE and LAY

EXERCISE A The forms of *lie* and *lay* are printed below. Refer to them as you do the following exercise. Write in the blanks below each problem sentence the information asked for. (Add 10 points for each correct line.)

PRESENT	PRESENT PARTICIPLE	PAST	PAST PARTICIPLE
lie (to *recline* or *rest*)	(is) lying	lay	(have) lain
lay (to *put* something)	(is) laying	laid	(have) laid

A. When we came in, we (lay, laid) our coats on a chair.

meaning *put*   prin. part. *past*   correct form *laid*

1. A heavy mist (lay, laid) in the valley.

meaning.........   prin. part..........   correct form.........

2. Before Mother went to work, she (lay, laid) my carfare on the table.

meaning.........   prin. part..........   correct form.........

3. The saucepan (lies, lays) under the stove.

meaning.........   prin. part..........   correct form.........

4. You have (lain, laid) here long enough.

meaning.........   prin. part..........   correct form.........

5. Someone had (lain, laid) the dishes on the chair.

meaning.........   prin. part..........   correct form.........

6. Just (lying, laying) around the house is boring.

meaning.........   prin. part..........   correct form.........

7. His work has (lain, laid) untouched for days.

meaning.........   prin. part..........   correct form.........

8. Would the baby rather (lie, lay) on her back?

meaning.........   prin. part..........   correct form.........

9. The old tractor is (lying, laying) behind the barn.

meaning.........   prin. part..........   correct form.........

10. The movers (lay, laid) the new rug on the stairs.

meaning.........   prin. part..........   correct form.........

EXERCISE B Underline the correct one of the two verbs in parentheses. Although you are not asked to write the meaning or the time or tense of each verb, you should determine it carefully before deciding which form is correct. (Add 4 points for each correct answer.)

1. I couldn't (lie, lay) down the biography of Norman Bethune until I'd read the last page.

2. Has the dog been (lying, laying) in the mud?

3. Jean (lay, laid) her books on the floor.

4. Hundreds of dollars were (lying, laying) on the counter.

5. They had (lain, laid) a board under each wheel.

6. The ambulance attendants (lay, laid) him gently on a stretcher.

7. Allison Harbour (lies, lays) 5 km east of here.

8. Your pencil case is (lying, laying) over there.

9. Our chicken (lay, laid) two eggs this morning.

10. Robert had (lain, laid) his books on my lunch bag.

Write the correct form of *lie* or *lay* in each blank.

11. I told my dog to . . . . down. He obeyed and . . . . down near the stove. He has been . . . . there for an hour.

12. When I entered, I noticed the tackle box . . . . on the floor. Olivia must have . . . . the box there yesterday.

13. You will find those clothes . . . . in the hamper, where I . . . . them last week. They have . . . . there for days.

14. A few moments ago I . . . . the exhausted cat on the porch. She has been . . . . very quietly. With your permission, I will . . . . her in a corner of the warm kitchen.

15. I will . . . . down on that sofa and read the magazine that is . . . . on the table. After I have read it, I will . . . . it down where I found it. The magazine will be . . . . there when you are ready to read it.

The Irregular Verbs SIT and SET

The verb sit means to be in or to take a sitting position.

EXAMPLES Let's **sit** down here on the front steps.
How long has the lamp been **sitting** there?

The verb set means to put or to place something.

EXAMPLES Let's **set** the flower pot on the bottom step.
After **setting** the lamp on the table, the man went out.

Notice that *sit* rarely has an object while *set* usually does.

PRESENT	PRESENT PARTICIPLE	PAST	PAST PARTICIPLE
sit (in a sitting position)	(is) sitting	sat	(have) sat
set (to put something)	(is) setting	set	(have) set

EXERCISE In the first space at the right tell whether the intended meaning of the verb is *to be or stay in a sitting position* or *to place or put something*. In the second space write the correct one of the two verbs in parentheses. (Add 4 points for each correctly marked sentence.)

	Meaning	Verb
A. I was (sitting, setting) the flowers on the window ledge.	*put*	*setting*
B. (Sitting, Setting) in the den, Mother called that it was Mrs. Martin.	*sit*	*sitting*
1. "Won't you (sit, set) here?" I said to Mrs. Martin.		
2. She (sat, set) down and began talking about Newton's laws of motion.		
3. "(Sit, Set) in this chair, Jo," she told me.		
4. "Now (sit, set) that chair out of the way," she went on.		
5. I (sat, set) down as instructed.		
6. She showed me how to (sit, set) an object in motion by propulsion.		
7. "As you (sit, set) here," she said, "lift both feet and kick them out quickly."		

177

8. I did so, and the chair I was (sitting, setting) in moved backward.   . . . .

9. (Sit, Set) the lamp there.   . . . .

10. Why are you (sitting, setting) here?   . . . .

11. Was he (sitting, setting) by her?   . . . .

12. Please (sit, set) the box here.   . . . .

13. Lucy has (sat, set) the groceries there.   . . . .

14. Aunt Beth has (sat, set) in that chair every day for years.   . . . .

15. I was (sitting, setting) perfectly still.   . . . .

16. She asked the pupils to (sit, set) down.   . . . .

17. While we waited for her, we (sat, set) near the window.   . . . .

18. Who (sat, set) this cup here?   . . . .

19. Just (sit, set) still, please.   . . . .

20. I was (sitting, setting) up late.   . . . .

21. Who (sat, set) at my desk while I was gone?   . . . .

22. Her house (sits, sets) by the side of the road.   . . . .

23. She always (sits, sets) her pocketbook on the table.   . . . .

24. (Sitting, Setting) next to her, I enjoyed her conversation.   . . . .

25. Did you notice where I (sat, set) my books?   . . . .

The Verbs RISE and RAISE

The verb rise means to go up, to get up, or to come up.

EXAMPLE   When the fog rises, the sun will shine.

The verb raise means to lift something.

EXAMPLE   It's time to raise the curtain.

Notice that *rise* never has an object while *raise* often does.

PRESENT	PRESENT PARTICIPLE	PAST	PAST PARTICIPLE
rise (to go up)	(is) rising	rose	(have) risen
raise (to lift)	(is) raising	raised	(have) raised

Of the two verbs, only *rise* is irregular. *Raise* is perfectly regular, since it forms its past and past participle by adding *-d* to the present.

EXERCISE   In the first space at the right tell whether the intended meaning of the verb is *to go up* or *to lift*. In the second space, write the correct one of the two verbs in parentheses. (Add 10 points for each correctly marked sentence.)

	Meaning	*Verb*
A. The smoke is (rising, raising).	*go up*	*rising*
B. The workers will have to (rise, raise) the house 10 cm.	*lift*	*raise*
1. The river has been (rising, raising) all night.		
2. The movers (rose, raised) the piano with ropes and a pulley.		
3. Before reaching the mountains, our plane (rose, raised) to 6000 m.		
4. The crowd (rose, raised) their hero to their shoulders.		
5. When the speaker sat down, Mr. Segal (rose, raised) to his feet.		
6. She was (rising, raising) to answer as the bell rang.		
7. The model plane (rose, raised) a short distance and then dropped.		

8. I (rose, raised) the car with a jack. . . . .

9. Her income has gradually (risen, raised). . . . .

10. She has (risen, raised) as high in her profession as a person can go. . . . .

REVIEW EXERCISE Underline the correct one of the two verbs in parentheses. (Add 5 points for each correct answer.)

1. I was daydreaming as I (sat, set) in English class, waiting for the teacher to arrive.

2. I (began, begun) to imagine my rosy future.

3. I saw myself (sitting, setting) at a desk in the Legislative Building.

4. Papers (laying, lying) on the desk awaited my signature.

5. Reporters were (sitting, setting) around asking me questions.

6. "Now that I've (drank, drunk) my coffee, I'll speak," I said.

7. "I'll just (lay, lie) all my cards on the table," I continued.

8. I told them that I had (wrote, written) a speech for the Assembly.

9. Then I leaned back and (give, gave) them a summary of my speech.

10. "When I (came, come) here last February," I announced, "I had some new ideas about what government can do for education."

11. The reporters (began, begun) to show more interest.

12. (Rising, Raising) to my feet, I continued the news conference.

13. "Now, I (saw, seen) long ago the need for new laws," I said.

14. I (use, used) my powers of persuasion when I presented my program.

15. "All courses should be (taken, took) by choice, not by requirement."

16. "School officials have not (ask, asked) students for ideas for courses often enough," I stated.

17. "They have not (saw, seen) the need for students to take an active part in planning their education," I added.

18. "Students who have been (gave, given) responsibility can act with maturity," I continued.

19. "I have only (began, begun) to fight for educational reform," I shouted.

20. Suddenly a loud bell (rang, rung), the teacher arrived, and my daydream ended.

Consistency of Tense

Do not change needlessly from one tense to another.

When you are writing a composition, especially a story, you must be careful to keep your verbs consistent in tense. If your story is told in the past tense, you should, as much as possible, keep your verbs in the past tense. It may, of course, be necessary to shift the tense, but do not do so unless you have a good reason.

NONSTANDARD After Gerald *caught* the long pass, he *races* to the twenty-yard line. (mixed tenses—present with past)

STANDARD After Gerald <u>caught</u> the long pass, he **raced** to the twenty-yard line. (consistent tenses—all past)

NONSTANDARD Thor, my toy bulldog, *takes* Blair by surprise and *nipped* the back of her right leg. (mixed tenses—past with present)

STANDARD Thor, my toy bulldog, <u>takes</u> Blair by surprise and **nips** the back of her right leg. (consistent tenses—all present)

STANDARD Thor, my toy bulldog, **took** Blair by surprise and <u>nipped</u> the back of her right leg. (consistent tenses—all past)

EXERCISE A The following story contains examples of mixed tenses. Read the selection through and decide whether it should be in present or past time. Then make the tenses consistent by crossing out each incorrect verb and writing the correct form above it. (Add 10 points for each correct answer.)

SNAKES, ANYONE?

1   Last Saturday, Jack invites Sue to view his live snake collection.
2   Although she did not like snakes, she decides to accept his invitation,
3   just to satisfy her curiosity. So off she went! The snakes were housed in
4   glass cages in the empty half of Jack's garage. When Sue sees Jack
5   handling the snakes, she admires his skill and quickly recovered from her
6   initial dislike. In fact, she even decides to join him on a snake hunt.
7   After an hour of hunting in the wooded city park, Jack had captured a
8   half-dozen harmless snakes and turns them loose in the car. Since Sue
9   was now an enthusiast, she enjoys riding with them. On the way back, at
10   stoplights, it was great fun to watch the expressions of people in other
11   cars when they saw the live snakes curled around the rearview mirror

12 and crawling across the dashboard. Some persons scream; others
13 pointed; most stare with open mouths. Jack and Sue smiled and waved
14 and then drive on to the snake farm.

EXERCISE B Decide whether the following story should be in present or past time. Then make the tenses consistent by crossing out each incorrect verb and writing the correct form above it. (Add 10 points for each correct answer.)

RENDEZVOUS AT OLD FORT WILLIAM

1   Last summer, we went to Old Fort William in Thunder Bay, On-
2   tario. Built in 1803, Fort William is the North West Company's inland
3   headquarters for its fur trade business. When we arrived, Dad parks
4   the car and we drove to the fort in a horse-drawn wagon. We pause
5   at the fort's main gate and stared at the massive palisade and all the
6   buildings. Once inside, we are amazed at the hustle and bustle. Our
7   guide explains to us that we were witnessing the re-enactment of the
8   Great Rendezvous. Apparently, when the fort was first built, a thous-
9   and or more Nor'Westers converge by canoe, bateau, and schooner
10 at the fort every summer for hectic transactions, serious meetings and
11 noisy celebrations. Now, nearly two hundred years later, we watch
12 canoes arrive and depart, fur packs weighed, graded and stored, and
13 skilled tradesmen perform ancient crafts. We study Ojibwa arts,
14 listened to voyageur songs and tales and visited the farm animals.
15 Then we go to the "Cantine Salope", the historic restaurant, and
16 sampled homemade bread—still warm from the brick oven, thick
17 pea soup, and decide between several tempting desserts. The day is
18 over far too soon for my liking, but Mom and Dad promised we could
19 go back again soon.

Chapter Review

EXERCISE A   Select the correct one of the verbs in parentheses and write it in the blank at the right. (Add 5 points for each correct answer.)

1. The McCabes had (rode, ridden) in the car twelve hours.   1. ....

2. Yesterday he (came, come) in wearing purple socks.   2. ....

3. They have all (went, gone) to see the play.   3. ....

4. She often (sat, set) up all night working.   4. ....

5. Had he (wrote, written) two symphonies by 1853?   5. ....

6. The team (did, done) its best to win.   6. ....

7. We (saw, seen) many blueberry stands along the road.   7. ....

8. The architect (laid, lay) her plans on the table.   8. ....

9. Pat had (laid, lain) down to take a quick nap.   9. ....

10. The fireworks (began, begun) shortly after dark.   10. ....

11. I was (laying, lying) down when you phoned.   11. ....

12. Please go into the living room and (sit, set) down. 12. ....

13. Where have the girls (went, gone)?   13. ....

14. She's (rode, ridden) her bike to school regularly.   14. ....

15. The bell hasn't (rang, rung).   15. ....

16. I just (lay, laid) a new floor in the kitchen.   16. ....

17. By four o'clock the sun had (risen, raised).   17. ....

18. When the rain started, we (ran, run) for cover.   18. ....

19. We (saw, seen) Gina at the game.   19. ....

20. All day the temperature (rose, raised) steadily.   20. ....

EXERCISE B   If a sentence below contains no error in verb usage, write C, for *correct,* in the blank at the right. If a sentence contains an incorrect verb form, cross it out and write the correct form in the blank. (Add 10 points for each correctly marked sentence.)

1. Have you drank all the lemonade?   1. ....

2. The teacher give me a second chance.   2. ....

3. Algebra class has not yet begun.   3. ....

183

4. Has Mrs. Katakura spoke to you about the tour?   4. . . . .

5. Has Lori or Don threw curve balls?   5. . . . .

6. My watch was laying on the diving board.   6. . . . .

7. Perhaps they saw us when we did it.   7. . . . .

8. Yesterday Livvie swum across the lake.   8. . . . .

9. You could have took the girls with you.   9. . . . .

10. I was suppose to mow the lawn.   10. . . . .

EXERCISE C The following story contains needless changes in tense. Read it through and decide whether it should be in present or past time. Then make the tenses consistent by crossing out each incorrect verb and writing the correct form above it. (Add 10 points for each correct answer.)

1 The topic of sports programs was brought up at the school meeting last

2 Thursday. As expected, tempers flare as the topic is discussed. Neither

3 side wanted to listen to the other side. Both were sure the opposing side

4 had nothing to say and is merely acting out of ignorance.

5 Friday, students at St. Laurent High School talk about what happens

6 at the meeting. Sylvia Polombo proposes an idea for calming tempers.

7 It would show how people could work together for the benefit of all.

8 St. Laurent High School had tennis courts but no swimming pool.

9 Overland High School had a swimming pool but no tennis courts. Sylvia

10 suggests that the two schools combine their afterschool gym programs

11 so that both groups of students could have the benefit of both facilities.

12 The students adopt the proposal and presented it to the principal. Mr.

13 Byrd confer with the principal of Overland High School. At the next

14 school meeting, he told those present about the students' idea. Influ-

15 enced by the spirit of co-operation that was shown by the students, the

16 group settles down to work out a peaceful solution to the sports issue.

184

Cumulative Review

A In each of the following sentences a complement is italicized. In the space at the right name the complement, using abbreviations: *s.c.* for subject complement; *d.o.,* direct object; *i.o.,* indirect object. (Add 10 points for each correct answer.)

A. I put the baby *bird* back in its nest.   A. *d.o.*

1. Woodpeckers make their *nests* in a hollow tree.   1. . . . .

2. That dangling bag of twigs must be an oriole's *nest.*   2. . . . .

3. The lazy cowbird uses the *homes* of other birds.   3. . . . .

4. Have you ever seen a three-story bird's *nest?*   4. . . . .

5. Lend *me* your camera for a moment.   5. . . . .

6. A snapshot of the parrot should be *colourful.*   6. . . . .

7. Jo's parrot speaks both *French and English.*   7. . . . .

8. Crows and parrots seem unusually *intelligent.*   8. . . . .

9. A Chinese delicacy is *bird's nest soup.*   9. . . . .

10. Give *Jo* a book about birds for her birthday.   10. . . . .

B If a sentence contains an error in agreement of subject and verb or of pronoun and antecedent, cross out the incorrect word and write the correct word in the blank at the left. If a sentence is correct, write *C* (for *correct*) in the blank. (Add 5 points for each correctly marked sentence.)

. . . . 1. Was Sally or Barb the first to give a party?

. . . . 2. Nitrogen and phosphorus in the soil is necessary for a healthy lawn.

. . . . 3. Every one of the rats was either killed or captured.

. . . . 4. Neither of the kittens have green eyes.

. . . . 5. The cries of a lemur sounds like the howling of a wolf.

. . . . 6. Neither of these medicines are habit-forming.

. . . . 7. One of the lanterns on the jetty has gone out.

. . . . 8. Is *oodles* and *jiffy* considered colloquial?

. . . . 9. Before any person is hired, they must pass a test.

. . . . 10. Where's your brother and sister?

. . . . 11. Do either of these candidates appeal to you?

. . . . 12. When a person is criticized, they should not be angry.

185

.... 13. Everybody wanted to express their opinion.

.... 14. Both parts of the test were easy.

.... 15. If anyone is late, they must have a good excuse.

.... 16. I wrote to one of my friends, but they did not reply.

.... 17. Each of them cooked their own supper.

.... 18. Has Sue or Karen telephoned you?

.... 19. Both Elliot and Alice buy their books at Larsen's.

.... 20. One of the drivers lost control of their car.

C Insert capital letters and punctuation where needed. Correct all sentence fragments and run-on sentences. (Add 2 points for each correct answer.)

A CURE FOR HALLOWEEN

1   At the Ritz theatre last friday, I told Jim the following true story.

2 While waiting for the feature *monsters at large* to begin.

3   Late halloween night nobody disturbed the peace at the home of the

4 Cliftons, who live at 2224 Tewsley place. Earlier, children had rung the

5 doorbell every few minutes. And yelled Trick or treat! Finally Frank

6 and Steven two sons of dr. and mrs. Clifton decided to discourage the

7 would-be pranksters. By playing a trick on them with a 2 m metal

8 monster. One that could walk and talk about eight o'clock, when a group

9 of students from delwood elementary school arrived. The monster

10 clanked its way to the door. An eerie record that Steven had bought at

11 the hudson novelty company began to play, its noise seemed to come

12 from the monsters moving lips. Help cried the groups leader Lets get out

13 of here After that, only a few curious children dared to ring the Cliftons

14 doorbell, eventually fear conquered curiosity and by nine o'clock the

15 doorbell was silent.

Spelling: How to Spell the /k/ Sound

The sound /k/ at the beginning of a word can be spelled with either the letter *k* or the letter *c*. How can you decide which letter to use? Look at the two lists below, and see if you can determine any patterns regarding the choice of *k* or *c*. What letters follow the *k* or *c*?

1	2
kit	cart
king	cabin
kidnap	comb
kindergarten	confess
killing	cube
keep	current
kernel	club
keyhole	climate
kerosene	crest
kerchief	cranberry

In list *1*, the second letter in each word is either an *i* or an *e*. The beginning *k* in the words in list *2* is followed by *a, o, u, l,* or *r.*

The sound /k/ is nearly always (see exceptions below) spelled *k* at the beginning of a word if the second letter in the word is *i* or *e*. Otherwise the /k/ sound is spelled with *c*.

EXCEPTIONS The exceptions to the rule are almost all words borrowed from foreign languages. Although you may use many of these words infrequently, it is interesting to know how to spell them correctly and from what languages they come.

kangaroo	(native Australian)	kola	(West African)
kapok	(Javanese)	kosher	(Hebrew)
kale	(Scottish)	kowtow	(Chinese)
kayak	(Eskimo)	kudu	(Hottentot)
koala	(native Australian)	kumquat	(Chinese)

EXERCISE A Complete each word by writing *k* or *c* in the blank. Follow the rule you have learned. (Add 5 points for each correct answer.)

1. ....idney

2. ....ommerce

3. ....left

4. ....eel

5. ....obweb

6. ....eyboard

7. ....ufflink

8. ....itchen

187

9. ....andle   15. ....imono

10. ....larinet   16. ....obra

11. ....ettle   17. ....riminal

12. ....indliness   18. ....ennel

13. ....een   19. ....adet

14. ....ushion   20. ....rest

EXERCISE B Use your dictionary to find five words (not taught in this lesson) that illustrate the use of the letter *k* for the beginning /k/ sound, and five that use the letter *c* for the /k/ sound. Write them in the columns below.

1. k ....   1. c ....

2. k ....   2. c ....

3. k ....   3. c ....

4. k ....   4. c ....

5. k ....   5. c ....

EXERCISE C Give a brief definition for any five of the "exception" words given in this lesson. First write the word, and then next to it, the definition. (Use a dictionary where necessary.)

1. ....

2. ....

3. ....

4. ....

5. ....

EXERCISE D Be prepared to write from dictation the words taught in this lesson. (Add 2 points for each correctly spelled word.)

REVIEW EXERCISE Use your knowledge of assimilation to correctly combine each prefix and word part to make a new word. Write the new word in the blank. (Add 10 points for each correctly spelled word.)

1. sub + cess = ...   6. ad + gressive = ...

2. ad + proach = ...   7. sub + focate = ...

3. ad + ford = ...   8. ad + nounce = ...

4. sub + press = ...   9. sub + ceeding = ...

5. ad + liance = ...   10. ad + cident = ...

Building Vocabulary: The Total Context

You can often form a good idea of a word's meaning from a very brief context—a sentence or two showing how the word is used. With many important words, however, you must consider a larger context.

To understand the word *democracy*, for example, you need some knowledge of political ideas and their history in North America and Europe. To understand the word *utopian*, you should know that it comes from the title of a famous book. *Utopia*, by Thomas Moore—a description of a perfect (but perhaps impractical) government. Here are some ways in which you can get at the total context of important words like *democracy*, so that you can understand such words fully and use them accurately.

1. In a dictionary, find the meaning of any root words from which the word is formed. Many English words are formed from Latin or Greek roots that carry over their basic meanings into English.

2. Use an encyclopedia to check on matters of history that may have contributed to the meaning of the word.

3. Check references to literature in an encyclopedia or a reference book like the *Oxford Companion to English Literature.*

Notice how the suggestions above are applied in explaining the meanings of the following useful words.

august /au gúst/ *adj.* Majestic, noble, and awe-inspiring: *The people were silent in the august presence of the monarch.* The Latin word *augustus,* from which *august* comes, was used as a title by the Roman emperors, the most powerful and the most honoured rulers of the ancient world.

bountiful /bóun tə fəl/ *adj.* Extremely generous; abundant: *Thanksgiving Day dinner is the most bountiful meal of the year.* The word comes from the noun *bounty,* which means both great generosity and the kind of gift which would express generosity. *Bounty* might be used of the gifts monarchs or wealthy nobles would give or of the generous spirit in which they would be expected to give them.

discriminate /dis krím ə nāt/ *v.* To notice accurately the differences between two things; also, to make an unfair difference, to treat someone unfairly (*discriminate against*). The word's meaning depends on the preposition. With *between* or *among* it suggests a desirable quality, as when professional tasters *discriminate* among the dozens of different kinds of coffee from which they

must choose. More commonly, with *against, discriminate* suggests a bad quality, as *to discriminate against someone because of that person's race or religion.*

eccentric /ek sén trik/ *adj.* Out of the ordinary, odd, peculiar in behaviour, ideas, etc. The word comes from the Greek words *ek* (out of) and *kentron* (centre) and means literally *off centre.* Hence, in geometry, *eccentric* circles are circles that overlap but have different centres. An *eccentric* gear or wheel is mounted *off centre* so that it does not go around with a circular movement.

gesture /jés chər/ *n.* A movement of the hands that carries meaning of some kind: *With a sweeping gesture, the umpire sent the player from the game. Gesture* can also mean any large action done more for effect than for the sake of achieving some goal: *When Jane competed for a scholarship, she hoped the gesture would please her parents, even if she didn't obtain one.*

imperious /im pír ē əs/ *adj.* Haughty, commanding. The word is connected with the Latin *imperator,* which at first meant a commanding general, later the all-powerful

189

Roman *emperor;* hence, the word literally means *like an emperor: With an imperious nod, the general silenced his soldiers.*

indignation /ín dig nắ shən/ *n.* Anger aroused by a mean or unworthy action. The word is made up of the prefix *in-* (*not*) and a form of the word *dignity:* we feel *indignation* for something that is beneath the *dignity,* or sense of worth, of the person who does it.—**indignant,** *adj.*

mediocre /mế dē ố kər/ *adj.* Ordinary. *Mediocre* goes back to the same Latin word as *middle;* a *mediocre* book or movie is one that is "right in the middle," neither good nor bad, not outstanding in any way.

perspective /pər spék tiv/ *n.* The true relationship of objects, events, ideas, etc., or the ability to view them in this way: *By studying history, one gains perspective on the meaning of current events.* In painting, *perspective* is the art of depicting objects on a flat surface so that they look as they would in reality, seen in depth.

radiant /rắ dē ənt/ *adj.* Coming in straight lines, or rays, as light and heat do, from a central source; hence, often, very happy, because we think of happiness as lighting up a person in the same way: *After winning the tennis tournament, Joan was simply radiant.* The word comes from the Latin *radius,* the spoke of a wheel, an accurate picture of the way light travels outward from the sun or any other source.—**radiate,** *v.*

EXERCISE   In the light of the definitions above, study the context in which each italicized word is used. Circle *C* (correct) for any word that is used correctly and appropriately. Circle *I* (incorrect) for any word that is used incorrectly or inappropriately. (Add 10 points for each correct answer.)

C   I   1. Some universities actually *discriminate* against athletes.

C   I   2. An *eccentric* person is just like everyone else.

C   I   3. Skilful public speakers emphasize their ideas with *gestures.*

C   I   4. Stand back so that you can see the painting in *perspective.*

C   I   5. A pot-bellied stove is a good example of *radiant* heating.

C   I   6. A *mediocre* performance on a test usually earns a good mark.

C   I   7. The queen's *august* bearing impressed all who met her.

C   I   8. Public *indignation* drove the mayor back to private life.

C   I   9. The *bountiful* river irrigates the entire valley.

C   I   10. Napoleon was perhaps the most *imperious* ruler of all time.

CHAPTER TEN

Using Pronouns Correctly

Notice in the following examples that a few pronouns change their form according to the way they are used in a sentence. *I, he, she, we,* and *they* (used as subjects) change to *me, him, her, us,* and *them* (when used as objects).

SUBJECT OF VERB	VERB	OBJECT OF VERB
I		me
he		him
she	like (s)	her
we		us
they		them

The grammar term used to name the relation of a pronoun to other words in the sentence is *case.* The pronouns used as subjects are said to be in the *nominative* case; the pronouns used as objects are said to be in the *objective* case. In order to use pronouns correctly, you must know the forms of the pronouns in these two cases. Say the lists to yourself this way:

NOMINATIVE CASE   I, he, she, we, they
OBJECTIVE CASE   me, him, her, us, them

When you have memorized the case forms, you should learn when to use the nominative forms and when to use the objective forms.

LESSON 97

Uses of the Nominative Case: Subject

The subject of a verb is in the nominative case.

This rule means that the following pronouns are used as subjects of a verb: *I, he, she, we, they.* (The pronouns *you* and *it,* whether used as subject or object, have the same form.)

	Subject	Verb
EXAMPLES	1. Janet and I	have been travelling.
	2. Janet and he (she)	have been travelling.
	3. Janet and we	have been travelling.
	4. Janet and they	have been travelling.
	5. We girls	have been travelling.

Note: In sentences like number 5 that contain common expressions such as *we girls, we boys, us girls, us boys,* do not be misled by the words following the pronoun. Drop these words (*girls, boys*) from the sentences, and determine the correct pronoun in the usual way. Never use an objective pronoun as the subject of a verb.

NONSTANDARD   *Us* girls have been travelling.
STANDARD   **We** girls have been travelling.

EXERCISE   In the spaces provided, write the subject and the verb in each of the following sentences. Notice that the pronouns used as subjects are nominative pronouns. Most of the subjects are compound. (Add 5 points for each correct numbered item.)

	Subject	*Verb*
A. Mary and he often quarrel.	*Mary, he*	*quarrel*
1. Jo and she save dimes and pennies.		
2. We girls caught a few dogfish.		
3. Can Ed or she operate this edger?		
4. We girls swam in the deep water.		
5. He and I then built a raft.		
6. Are she and I partners?		
7. We and they met in the finals.		
8. Did you and she have sodas?		
9. Karen and I had sundaes.		
10. Do you and she speak French?		
11. My parents and they are friends.		
12. Have you and he been absent?		
13. You and we will work together.		
14. The coach and she disagreed.		
15. Maybe you and I will be chosen.		
16. Have Dennis and they already gone?		
17. Can Sue and I have the football?		
18. Stan and he look like brothers.		
19. Did you and she have mumps?		
20. We boys ate fried grasshoppers!		

Uses of the Nominative Case: Subject Complement

A subject complement is in the nominative case.

A complement is a word which completes the meaning of a verb. It is the third part of a three-part sentence base. (The first two parts of a sentence base are, of course, the subject and the verb.)

	Subject	Verb	Complement
EXAMPLES	This	is	she
	The leader	was	he
	These people	could be	they

A pronoun used as a subject complement almost always follows a form of the verb *to be: am, are, is, was, were,* and verbs ending in *be* or *been* (*may be, could be, have been,* etc.). When a pronoun is used as a subject complement, it refers to the same person as the subject.

EXAMPLES   This is **she**   (*She* and *this* mean the same person.)

The leader was **he**   (*He* and *leader* mean the same person.)

EXERCISE   In the space provided, write the subject complement in each of the following sentences. Notice that the pronouns used as subject complements are nominative pronouns. Some of the complements are compound. (Add 10 points for each correct sentence.)

Subj. Comp.

A. The guests of honour are Ted and she.   *Ted, she*

1. It was probably they.

2. That is she.

3. I thought you were he.

4. That may be she.

5. It could not have been she.

6. The winner will be either Bill or he.

7. What would you have done if you had been they?

8. My best friends are Richard and she.

9. It would have been either Phyllis or she.

10. It was we girls.

Uses of the Objective Case: Object of the Verb

The object of a verb is in the objective case.

The following pronouns are used as objects of verbs: *me, him, her, us, them.*
(*You* and *it,* as you know, have the same form whether they are used as
subjects or objects.)

		Objects
EXAMPLES	He challenged	Cliff and me.
	I have seen	Walter and him.
	Did you invite	Frances or her?
	Will he include	you and them?
	They sent	us girls the prize.

Note: Indirect objects, as well as direct objects, are in the objective case. In
the last sentence, *prize* is the direct object; *us* is the indirect object. (The noun
girls is an appositive.)

EXERCISE In the first space at the right of each sentence write the verb. In the
second space write the correct pronoun from the pair in parentheses. (Add 10 points
for each correctly marked sentence.)

	Verb	*Pronoun*
A. Larry surprised Carlo and (me, I).	*surprised*	*me*
1. I will ask my mother and (she, her).		
2. You can believe Anne and (I, me).		
3. Did anyone tell Dorothy and (she, her)?		
4. I met Sue and (he, him) in Halifax.		
5. Will you take (we, us) girls with you?		
6. Do you remember Ella and (they, them)?		
7. I was expecting Harold and (she, her).		
8. You could help (we, us) boys.		
9. I recognized you and (them, they).		
10. Did she mean Nan or (me, I)?		

Uses of the Objective Case: Object of a Preposition

The object of a preposition is in the objective case.

A prepositional phrase begins with a preposition. The final word in a prepositional phrase is the object of the preposition which begins the phrase.

Object	*Object*	*Object*
EXAMPLES at **him**	in **them**	from **us**

The objective forms of the personal pronouns are used as objects of prepositions: *me, him, her, us, them.*

EXAMPLE   The rider was coming <u>toward Jim and me</u> (**him, her, us, them**).

WORDS COMMONLY USED AS PREPOSITIONS

about	before	by	like	to
above	behind	concerning	near	toward
across	below	down	of	under
after	beneath	during	off	up
against	beside	except	on	upon
among	between	for	over	with
around	beyond	from	past	within
at	but (meaning *except*)	in	through	without

Note: When any of these words are used as adverbs, they will not have an object.

EXERCISE   Write the preposition in each of the following sentences in the first space at the right. In the second space write the correct pronoun from the pair in parentheses. (Add 10 points for each correctly marked sentence.)

	Prep.	*Pronoun*
1. Bill sat behind Nadine and (I, me).	. . . .	. . . .
2. Will you go with Dad and (me, I)?	. . . .	. . . .
3. The dog was between Al and (her, she).	. . . .	. . . .
4. There were letters for Lucy and (he, him).	. . . .	. . . .
5. No one but you and (her, she) saw the play.	. . . .	. . . .
6. I played against Alicia and (they, them).	. . . .	. . . .
7. The work falls to you and (we, us).	. . . .	. . . .

195

8. Who was talking to you and (they, them)? . . . .

9. Come with Gretchen and (I, me). . . . .

10. It was about Beth and (she, her). . . . .

Now that you have learned some uses of both nominative and objective pronouns, you are ready for more practice in selecting the correct pronoun in a sentence. First, determine how the pronoun is used. If it is used as the subject of a verb or a subject complement, select a pronoun in the nominative case. If it is used as the object of a verb or preposition, select a pronoun in the objective case.

Most errors in pronoun usage occur when the pronoun is part of a compound subject or object. An easy way to select the correct form is to say the sentence aloud, omitting the first two words in the compound construction. In most sentences, your ear will tell you the correct pronoun.

EXAMPLES   Bob and (he, him) called.   (*He* called. Bob and *he* called.)
Ask Betty and (she, her).   (Ask *her*.   Ask Betty and *her*.)

REVIEW EXERCISE   Four uses of the nominative and objective pronouns are listed below with abbreviations opposite them. In the first space at the right of each of the following sentences, write the proper abbreviation to indicate in which of these four ways the pronoun is used in the sentence. In the second space write the correct one of the two pronouns in parentheses. (Add 10 points for each correctly marked sentence.)

NOMINATIVE USES	OBJECTIVE USES
subj. = subject of verb	*o.v.* = object (direct or indirect) of verb
s.c. = subject complement	*o.p.* = object of preposition

	Use	*Pronoun*
A. Jan and (I, me) borrowed a lantern.	*subj.*	*I*
1. (We, Us) adventurers explored the old cave.	. . . .	. . . .
2. Marvin gave Joe and (I, me) some advice.	. . . .	. . . .
3. Her brother and (she, her) sang ballads.	. . . .	. . . .
4. That must be (they, them) now.	. . . .	. . . .
5. Between you and (I, me), we were a hit.	. . . .	. . . .
6. The principal saw Diane and (we, us).	. . . .	. . . .
7. You and (she, her) make a good team.	. . . .	. . . .
8. Have Jane and (he, him) gone shopping?	. . . .	. . . .
9. It was certainly (they, them).	. . . .	. . . .
10. It's up to Sue and (she, her).	. . . .	. . . .

196

Pronoun Practice

EXERCISE A   The four uses of pronouns are listed below with abbreviations opposite them. In the first space at the right of each of the following sentences, write the proper abbreviation to indicate in which of these four ways the italicized pronoun is used in the sentence. In the second space put a plus (+) if the pronoun is correct. If the pronoun is incorrect, cross it out and write the correct form in the space. (Add 10 points for each correctly marked sentence.)

NOMINATIVE USES	OBJECTIVE USES
subj. = subject of verb	*o.v.* = object (direct or indirect) of verb
s.c. = subject complement	*o.p.* = object of preposition

		Use	*Pronoun*
A.	Have you or ~~her~~ ever heard of Hob Creek?	*subj.*	*she*
B.	Someone mentioned the creek to *us* girls.	*o.p.*	*+*
1.	It must have been *him* and Paul.		
2.	A few of *us* girls decided to fish there.		
3.	Jo and *me* could see the fish.		
4.	I quickly called Myra and *she*.		
5.	"You and *she* drop your hooks here!" I yelled.		
6.	*Us* girls saw two fish approach our hooks.		
7.	They really surprised Jo and *I*.		
8.	Instead of biting, they stared at *we* girls.		
9.	To Jo and *I* they seemed to say, "Suckers!"		
10.	Then they swished their tails and haughtily swam away from *us*.		

EXERCISE B   Write the correct pronoun in the blank before each sentence. (Add 5 points for each correct answer.)

....   1. Did you hear Sally and (I, me)?

....   2. We need you and (her, she) for our softball team.

....   3. Don and (he, him) are always working in the laboratory.

....   4. Have you and (they, them) ordered the ice cream?

....   5. The test seemed hard to Lou and (he, him).

....   6. What marks did you and (her, she) get in English?

.... 7. Valerie and (I, me) thought it was easy.

.... 8. Liz and (she, her) are going to take French next year.

.... 9. Larry and (I, me) would rather take Latin.

.... 10. Every law affects you and (I, me).

.... 11. The lawyer and (him, he) have arrived.

.... 12. The camp bus left Mary and (them, they) behind.

.... 13. This should be an easy course for you and (she, her).

.... 14. You and (me, I) are not old enough to drive.

.... 15. Did you see Nancy and (he, him) at the karate meet?

.... 16. At least, I thought it was (they, them).

.... 17. Janet and (her, she) were repairing their bicycles.

.... 18. You and (I, me) will play against Anne and (she, her).

.... 19. She thought that (we, us) girls had been absent.

.... 20. I'll call for you and (they, them).

EXERCISE C Write sentences using the words below as instructed. (Add 10 points for each correct sentence.)

subj. = subject of verb   o.v. = object of verb
s.c. = subject complement   o.p. = object of preposition

A. Carol and he (s.c.):   *That must be Carol and he now.*

1. we students (subj.): ....

2. us students (o.p.): ....

3. Michael and they (subj.): ....

4. Michael and they (s.c.): ....

5. you and I (subj.): ....

6. you and me (o.v.): ....

7. you and me (o.p.): ....

8. Scott or he (subj.): ....

9. Scott or him (o.v.): ....

10. Scott or him (o.p.): ....

Pronouns After THAN and AS

After than and as introducing an incomplete construction, use the form of the pronoun you would use if the construction were complete.

Study the following examples of pronouns used after *than* and *as:*

EXAMPLES   The boys were as scared as <u>we</u>. (= as we were)
He helped John more <u>than I</u>. (= than I helped John)
He helped John more <u>than me</u>. (= than he helped me)

You can see that the words *than* and *as* introduce incomplete constructions. In order to tell what pronoun to use after *than* and *as,* you must complete the sentence in your mind. The words in parentheses show how the sentences may be completed. Notice that in the second and third sentences either *I* or *me* may be correct, depending on your intended meaning.

EXERCISE   In the space after each sentence, write the words you would use to complete the incomplete construction. Begin with *than* or *as.* Select the correct pronoun from those given. Which pronoun you choose will sometimes depend on how you complete the construction. (Add 10 points for each correct sentence.)

A. Sarah likes her more than (I, me) = *than she likes me.*

B. Is he as popular as (she, her) = *as she is?*

1. I can't swim as well as (she, her) = ...

2. Ms. Weldelkin said Carl did better than (he, him) = ...

3. These pants fit you better than (I, me) = ...

4. Mr. Clark praised us more than (they, them) = ...

5. He paid Ben more than (I, me) = ...

6. You are not so heavy as (he, him) = ...

7. I expect more of Loretta than (she, her) = ...

8. They play tennis better than (we, us) = ...

9. I wish you would work as hard as (she, her) = ...

10. I can carve turkey better than (she, her) = ...

REVIEW EXERCISE   In the space before each sentence write a plus sign (+) if the italicized pronoun is correct. If it is incorrect, write a zero (0), cross out the incorrect pronoun, and write the correct form above it. (Add 4 points for each correctly marked sentence.)

..+. A. She writes better reports than *I*.

..0. B. Are you telling Bob and ~~I~~ *me* the truth?

.... 1. She fries eggs better than *me*.

.... 2. Should Mark and *I* display our paintings?

.... 3. He discussed the solution with Pete and *she*.

.... 4. Mike's a better Ping-Pong player than *him*.

.... 5. Does your cousin remember Polly and *me*?

.... 6. You can count on *us* boys.

.... 7. The fastest runners were *us* three.

.... 8. She was even more stubborn than *I*.

.... 9. Did you get a letter from Marian and *her*?

.... 10. I phoned Helen and *she* last night.

.... 11. They went out with Jimmy and *him*.

.... 12. Are the tickets for both you and *I*?

.... 13. You and *I* had better go to the library this afternoon.

.... 14. Those slacks are getting too short for you and *him*.

.... 15. No, *him* and *me* are getting too tall for the slacks.

.... 16. Are you going to the game with Diane or *she*?

.... 17. Mrs. Leibowitz invited Joanne and *me*.

.... 18. You and *me* had better get that lawn mowed.

.... 19. In science Beth sits in front of Pete and *I*.

.... 20. Was it *them*?

.... 21. We helped Fred and *he* with the lesson.

.... 22. Mr. Lawrence thought that *we* three were guilty.

.... 23. Annette taught Ann and *I* a French folk song.

.... 24. After Ginny and *I* came the other guests.

.... 25. I can decorate the tree better than *him*.

Chapter Review

In the proper columns below, list the forms of the pronouns that change according to how they are used.

NOMINATIVE	OBJECTIVE
. . . .	. . . .
. . . .	. . . .
. . . .	. . . .
. . . .	. . . .
. . . .	. . . .

EXERCISE A In the first space at the right of each sentence tell whether the pronoun in parentheses is used as (1) subject of verb; (2) subject complement; (3) object of verb; (4) object of preposition. Use the abbreviations *subj., s.c., o.v.,* and *o.p.* In the second space write the case of the pronoun required by its use: *nom.* or *obj.* In the third space write the correct pronoun. (Add 10 points for each correctly marked sentence.)

	Use	*Case*	*Pronoun*
A. Sue and (her, she) built a trailer.	*subj.*	*nom.*	*she*
1. (They, Them) and Max saw June yesterday.	. . . .	. . . .	. . . .
2. It couldn't have been (her, she).	. . . .	. . . .	. . . .
3. Who was nominated by Leslie and (him, he)?	. . . .	. . . .	. . . .
4. Julio and (she, her) went to Ingonish.	. . . .	. . . .	. . . .
5. They elected Peg and (I, me).	. . . .	. . . .	. . . .
6. Are Phil and (he, him) ready?	. . . .	. . . .	. . . .
7. Did Anne and (she, her) get home?	. . . .	. . . .	. . . .
8. Mother drove Janice and (they, them).	. . . .	. . . .	. . . .
9. Were you talking to Alex and (we, us)?	. . . .	. . . .	. . . .
10. Was that (she, her)?	. . . .	. . . .	. . . .

EXERCISE B If a sentence below is correct, write a plus sign (+) in the space provided. If it is incorrect, write a zero (0), cross out the incorrect pronoun, and write the correct form above it. (Add 4 points for each correctly marked sentence.)

+ A. She and her sister volunteered.

0 B. Sarah can play tennis better than ~~me~~. *I*

.... 1. Have you or he ever seen a squirting cucumber?

.... 2. Tell Richard and I what *reciprocal* means.

.... 3. Us boys were in the middle of the lake when the storm hit.

.... 4. Can you or they think of a better way to raise money?

.... 5. Miss Savalas kept Dick and me in her office.

.... 6. Has she invited he and Laura?

.... 7. The girls have to ride with him and Mrs. Holmes.

.... 8. Who packed this lunch for her and Sarah?

.... 9. Are you sure it wasn't them and Thelma?

.... 10. No, her and Vic were at the movies.

.... 11. That picture didn't appeal to Vera or me.

.... 12. Her and Carol will be at camp for two months.

.... 13. No, she and Bill went alone.

.... 14. She can skate faster than either you or he.

.... 15. Who's going sailing with Paula and I?

.... 16. He told Toni and I the whole story.

.... 17. No one spoke except him and Bob.

.... 18. It was the best movie that Yvonne or we had ever seen.

.... 19. It was them, all right.

.... 20. The play was written by Mr. Goldman and her.

.... 21. Mr. Edelman wanted Ned and I.

.... 22. My sister looks like my father and I.

.... 23. He and Mother went shopping.

.... 24. The teacher told Nancy and I about the term paper.

.... 25. Karen arrived later than him.

Cumulative Review

A Choose the correct word in parentheses and write it in the space provided. (Add 5 points for each correct answer.)

.... 1. Each of us (has, have) various ways of analysing character.

.... 2. According to Joe, if you want to analyse someone's character, ask (them, him) for a sample of handwriting.

.... 3. Yesterday Helene (give, gave) Joe a long note.

.... 4. Of course, Joe immediately (lay, laid) her note on his desk and examined her handwriting.

.... 5. "One of your *o*'s (are, is) looped," he mumbled.

.... 6. "A few of your *t*'s (are, is) crossed high," he added.

.... 7. Helene was (setting, sitting) on the edge of her chair.

.... 8. She grew curious and (asks, asked) Joe for his analysis.

.... 9. Joe said, "I (saw, seen) aggressiveness and secretiveness in your handwriting."

.... 10. "I shouldn't have (wrote, written) that note!" she sighed.

.... 11. "We have only (began, begun) to analyse," Fran said.

.... 12. Helene stared at us and then quickly (departs, departed).

.... 13. Fran (rose, raised) from her chair.

.... 14. "Have I ever (spoke, spoken) to you about dreams?"

.... 15. Then Fran sat down, (lay, laid) back against the wall, and proceeded to lecture us.

.... 16. "A man dreamed that he (did, done) a great favour."

.... 17. "Dreamers reveal (his, their) subconscious desires."

.... 18. "Neither handwriting nor a dream (reveal, reveals) the true character of a person," I bluntly interrupted.

.... 19. "(Sit, Set) still," I said, "and listen while I enlighten you with words of wisdom."

.... 20. "A person's countenance, attire, gait, and laughter (shows, show) what that person is."

Add capital letters and punctuation. Remove fragments and run-on sentences. (Add 1 point for each correct answer.)

1   Have you ever heard of Katimavik I asked Diane, my friend.

2   No she replied, what is it a town.

3   Well, I said. Katimavik is described as an action-learning challenge for

4   young Canadians. My sister who has just finished High School decided

5   to apply for the nine-month program Katimavik is financed by the

6   Federal Government. And its aim is to provide participants with the

7   means and resources and the support to make a contribution. To

8   Canada.

9   Terrific exclaimed Diane, tell me more.

10   I continued, my sister will be in a group with ten others and shell be

11   assigned to three different three-month projects and the projects might

12   be. Environmental clean-up. Trail cutting. Reforestation, construction.

13   Construction. Are you sure, asked Diane.

14   Oh yes I answered. Just because shes a girl doesnt mean shell have an

15   easier time of it than a boy. Anyway, shell also be involved in restoration

16   of historical sites and many more projects She might also work with

17   senior citizens, with the handicapped. Or with children. In day care

18   centres. one of the projects will be in a francophone environment. In

19   order that the participants learn french. My sister will be travelling.

20   Across Canada shell live with local families and meet people from all

21   over the nation. At each project living conditions will be different. But

22   most are simple and basic.Emphasizing self-sufficiency the group will do

23   its own cooking and cleaning.

24   Boy said Diane this program certainly sounds difficult. Is your sister

25   really excited about it.

26   Of course. If she enjoys it Ill think of applying, later, you have to be

27   between seventeen and twenty-one. When Im finished school, itll be fun

28   to spend some time involved in katimavik.

Usage: Unnecessary Words and Letters

The words *of, here,* and *there* sometimes slip into our speech and writing where they do not belong.

had of, off of

NONSTANDARD   If I *had of thought* about it, I would have told you.
STANDARD   If I had thought about it, I would have told you.

NONSTANDARD   He took the jacket *off of* the hanger.
STANDARD   He took the jacket off the hanger.

off of for **from**

NONSTANDARD   I got this pen *off of* Jane.
STANDARD   I got this pen from Jane.

this here, that there

NONSTANDARD   *This here* question has me stumped.
STANDARD   This question has me stumped.

NONSTANDARD   *That there* notebook is mine.
STANDARD   That notebook is mine.

EXERCISE A   If a sentence is correct, mark it plus (+); if it is incorrect, mark it zero (0). Cross out the incorrect word, and write the correct word above it. If the word is unnecessary, simply cross it out. (Add 10 points for each correctly marked sentence.)

.... 1. It is forbidden to dive off of the dock.

.... 2. Does this here wallet belong to you?

.... 3. The motor has been running well.

.... 4. That there remark was very annoying.

.... 5. Reubin fell off of the bridge.

.... 6. I wish you had of warned me.

.... 7. We bought our tickets off of the seller at the gate.

.... 8. That girl over there is my cousin.

.... 9. This here book is exciting.

.... 10. You can get dance tickets off of any senior.

Do not add an s to words ending in where.

NONSTANDARD   Some*wheres* around here is a restaurant.
STANDARD   Some*where* around here is a restaurant.

Do not add an s to way unless it is plural.

EXERCISE B   Cross out each error below and write your correction in the blank at the right. If a sentence has no usage error, write *C* (for *correct*) in the blank. (Add 5 points for each correct answer.)

1. That fire must be somewhere near here!   . . . .

2. "I can't find *gnat* anywheres in my dictionary."   . . . .

3. You hadn't ought to put salt in the sugar bowl.   . . . .

4. Kate always walks a short ways with me.   . . . .

5. He makes friends everywheres he goes.   . . . .

6. Paul seldom behaves as good as he should.   . . . .

7. We hadn't ought to eat so much.   . . . .

8. It's quite a ways to Victoria.   . . . .

9. I'll bring my record player to Linda's when I go.   . . . .

10. She'll go anywheres the crowd goes.   . . . .

Write in the blank the letter of the correct form (*a* or *b*).

11. a. This here animal is a hare.   b. This animal is a hare.   . . . .

12. a. It fell off of the bed.   b. It fell off the bed.   . . . .

13. a. We looked everywhere.   b. We looked everywheres.   . . . .

14. a. Had he ought to go?   b. Ought he to go?   . . . .

15. a. You sing well.   b. You sing good.   . . . .

16. a. He wishes you had told him.   b. He wishes you had of told him.   . . . .

17. a. That there lunch is for you.   b. That lunch is for you.   . . . .

18. a. It must be somewheres.   b. It must be somewhere.   . . . .

19. a. I made this here sweater for you.   b. I made this sweater for you.   . . . .

20. a. An Olympic champion lives somewhere around here.   b. An Olympic champion lives somewheres around here.   . . . .

Spelling: Always Write *u* after *q*

When you hear the sound /kw/ in a word, you can be sure that it is spelled *qu*. In the English language, the letter *q* is *always* followed by a *u*. Here are some common words containing the sound /kw/:

*qu*iet   fre*qu*ent

*qu*ote   ade*qu*ate

In a few words, all of which are borrowed from French, the letters *qu* have the sound /k/. You must simply memorize such words. Here are some you should know how to spell. Look at them, say them to yourself, and write them.

bou*qu*et   uni*qu*e

cro*qu*et   physi*qu*e

con*qu*er   mysti*qu*e

REMEMBER   Always spell /kw/ with *qu*.

EXERCISE A   In the blank next to each word below, indicate whether the letters *qu* represent the sound /kw/ or the sound /k/. (Add 10 points for each correct answer.)

EXAMPLE   acquaint   ...*kw*...

1. quality   .../.../...   6. equipped   .../.../...

2. picturesque   .../.../...   7. liquor   .../.../...

3. quota   .../.../...   8. quite   .../.../...

4. acquire   .../.../...   9. equal   .../.../...

5. etiquette   .../.../...   10. conqueror   .../.../...

EXERCISE B   Write *qu* plus a vowel to complete each word correctly. Listen for the vowel sound that comes after the *qu*. Use the chart "Vowel Sounds and Their Common Spellings" on the inside of the back cover, if you wish. If you need to do so, consult a dictionary. The definitions in parentheses will help you think of the words. (Add 10 points for each correctly spelled word.)

1. ......z   (a brief test)

2. conse......nce   (result)

3. anti......   (very old)

4. ......et   (silent)

5. obli......   (slanting)

6. ......rantine   (isolation because of contagious disease)

7. delin......nt   (in violation of the law)

8. co......tte   (a flirt)

9. ......tation   (someone else's words)

10. con......red   (defeated)

EXERCISE C Study all the words taught in this lesson, and be ready to write them from dictation. (Add 4 points for each correctly spelled word.)

REVIEW EXERCISE   Complete each word by writing *k* or *c*, whichever is correct, in the blank. (Add 4 points for each correct answer.)

1. ....idney

2. ....ube

3. ....onfess

4. ....ettle

5. ....andle

6. ....een

7. ....ommerce

8. ....ennel

9. ....obra

10. ....angaroo

11. ....eyboard

12. ....riminal

13. ....limate

14. ....imono

15. ....adet

16. ....ernel

17. ....ranberry

18. ....erosene

19. ....larinet

20. ....lub

21. ....ale

22. ....attle

23. ....iss

24. ....ocoa

25. ....ream

208

Building Vocabulary: Words to Learn

abject /áb jekt/ *adj.* Brought low in spirit, general condition; contemptible: *The abject poverty of the London slums in the nineteenth century was almost beyond belief.*

allude /ə lūd/ *v.* To refer to something indirectly; to mention without describing fully: *When the man asked if I had been brought up in a barn, he was alluding to my failure to shut the door.*—**allusion**, *n.*

anticipate /an tís ə pāt/ *v.* To look forward to or expect; to do ahead of time: *Priscilla anticipated the outing with pleasure. The waitress had anticipated our order.*—**anticipation**, *n.*

compulsory /kəm púl sər ē/ *adj.* Necessary or required because accompanied by force or the threat of force: *School attendance is usually compulsory until the age of sixteen.*

cringe /krinj/ *v.* To crouch or draw back in fear: *The dog cringed when its owner approached it with a rolled-up newspaper.*

definitive /di fín ə tiv/ *adj.* Final and not likely to be replaced: *The Prime Minister has made a definitive statement on taxes.*

phenomenal /fi nóm ə nəl/ *adj.* Highly unusual: *The weight lifter's phenomenal strength was incredible.*

recur /ri kúr/ *v.* To happen, or occur, again; to come to mind again: *The same objections recur every time this question comes up. As Jeff waited for the race to begin, all his old uneasiness recurred to him.*

seditious /si dish' əs/ *adj.* Inciting public disorder or rebellion against the government: *The British considered the writing of Thomas Paine to be seditious.*

stamina /stám ə nə/ *n.* The strength and vigour needed in any long-continuing activity; endurance: *Long-distance running requires greater stamina than tennis.*

EXERCISE Fill each blank with the word from this lesson that makes the best sense in the context. (Add 10 points for each correct answer.)

1. After a(n) . . . . run of bad luck and injuries, the team has at last won its first game of the season.

2. If extracurricular activities were made . . . ., we probably would not enjoy them as much. Part of their attraction is that we are free to choose what activities to go out for—or to do nothing at all.

3. The protesters were charged with . . . . activities, but were soon freed because of insufficient evidence.

4. Ms. Potemkin explained that in the poem the poet . . . . to Artemis, the goddess of the moon in Greek mythology, when he speaks of the Queen of the Night.

5. Mountain climbing probably requires greater . . . . than any other sport.

6. A few years ago, many people were horrified by the . . . . . . conditions mental patients were forced to live under.

7. Before the contest Thelma insisted that she did not . . . . any difficulty in breaking the school athletic record.

8. The pleasant things of the day . . . . to me as I try to go to sleep at night.

9. If you insist on a(n) . . . . answer immediately, then the answer is "no."

10. The thief . . . . pitifully when the detective seized him by the shoulder and told him he was under arrest.

REVIEW EXERCISE In the space to the left, write the letter of the best meaning for the italicized word. (Add 4 points for each correct answer.)

. . . . 1. *compassion* for those suffering
. . . . 2. a *glamorous* profession
. . . . 3. children often *sulk*
. . . . 4. an *inflexible* will
. . . . 5. *atrocious* behaviour
. . . . 6. *subsist* on bread and water
. . . . 7. *bicker* over money
. . . . 8. *arduous* duties
. . . . 9. *isolate* from reality
. . . . 10. *eccentric* behaviour

a. to quarrel in a petty way
b. barely to live
c. firm, unyielding
d. odd, peculiar
e. to cut off from contact
f. pity with desire to help
g. requiring hard work
h. savage, wicked
i. to be cross
j. attractive but deceptive

Circle *T* for a true statement or *F* for a false one. Your answer will depend on the meaning of the italicized word.

T F 11. You would probably still be hungry after a *bountiful* meal.

T F 12. A *mediocre* player would not be likely to make the school team.

T F 13. A person falsely accused of cheating would feel *indignation*.

T F 14. A *slovenly* appearance makes a good impression on an employer.

T F 15. An *intercepted* message would probably be delivered promptly.

T F 16. A person with good *elocution* is easy to understand.

T F 17. The earthquake and fire were a terrible *cataclysm*.

T F 18. We do not expect great *rectitude* in a rabbi or minister.

T F 19. A *discreet* person might be trusted with a secret.

T F 20. Most businesses prefer *incompetent* employees.

T F 21. A large city offers a wide choice of *cultural* activities.

T F 22. To *allege* a fact is to offer proof that it is true.

T F 23. We *condescend* to people we treat as equal.

T F 24. A football team that often loses would be called *invincible*.

T F 25. A person who has *succumbed* to a disease will soon recover.

CHAPTER ELEVEN

Sentence Combining

This chapter of ENGLISH WORKSHOP will help you combine short, choppy sentences into longer, smoother sentences. By combining sentences in a variety of ways, you will gain experience in joining closely related ideas, in showing logical relationships, and in adding interest to your writing style.

LESSON 108

Combining Sentences with Adjectives, Adverbs, and Prepositional Phrases

Combine two or more short, choppy sentences by taking adjectives, adverbs, and prepositional phrases from one sentence and placing them in another.

EXAMPLES The golfer missed the ball.
The golfer was nervous.

The <u>nervous</u> golfer missed the ball. (The adjective *nervous* combines with the first sentence.)

The actor spoke the lines.
The actor spoke clearly.

The actor spoke the lines <u>clearly</u>. (The adverb *clearly* combines with the first sentence.)

The artist drew a sketch.
The artist drew with a pencil.

The artist drew a sketch <u>with a pencil</u>. (The prepositional phrase *with a pencil* combines with the first sentence.)

You can often combine sentences in different ways.

EXAMPLES The sun shone on the runners.
The sun was bright and hot.
The sun shone during the race.

During the race the bright, hot sun shone on the runners.
or
The sun, bright and hot, shone on the runners during the race. (Notice how the positions of the adjectives *bright* and *hot* and the prepositional phrase *during the race* can change.)

211

As you combine sentences, notice that the placement of adjectives, adverbs, and prepositional phrases can affect the meaning of what you write.

EXAMPLE   On the way <u>to the bank</u> we saw a parade.

We saw a parade on the way <u>to the bank</u>. (The meanings of the two sentences are different.)

Before you complete the following exercise, you may want to review the use of commas with adjectives and introductory words and phrases.

EXERCISE On the lines provided, combine each of the following sets of sentences into one sentence by using adjectives, adverbs, or prepositional phrases. You may leave out any unnecessary words. (Correct answers may vary. Add 20 points for each correct sentence.)

1. The Hopi are Indians and live in Arizona.

   They are Pueblo Indians. ....

   ....

   ....

2. Hopi villages contain many buildings called pueblos.

   The buildings are square. ....

   ....

   ....

3. The Hopi have lived in pueblos.

   They have lived in them for more than eight hundred years. ....

   ....

   ....

4. The Hopi grow, spin, and weave cotton into cloth.

   The cotton is from their farms.

   The cloth is beautiful. ....

   ....

   ....

5. A woman rules a Hopi clan.

   She is elderly.

   She rules by tradition. ....

   ....

   ....

Combining Sentences Through Co-ordination

Combine related elements of two or more sentences by using the conjunction *and, but,* or *or.*

EXAMPLES   Mom entered the contest.
Dad entered the contest.

Mom <u>and</u> Dad entered the contest.   (*And* joins the two subjects.)

Our team played hard.
Our team still lost the game.

Our team played hard <u>but</u> still lost the game.   (*But* joins the two verbs.)

You must keep up your grades.
You will lose the scholarship.

You must keep up your grades, <u>or</u> you will lose the scholarship.   (*Or* joins the two sentences.)

While sentences can often be combined through the use of conjunctions, a careful writer will never string together ideas that belong in separate sentences. Joining unequal or unrelated ideas in a single sentence results in *weak co-ordination*.

STRONG CO-ORDINATION   The principal told a joke and the students laughed.   (*And* joins two related ideas.)

WEAK CO-ORDINATION   The band plays well and needs new uniforms.   (*And* joins two unrelated ideas.)

Before you begin this exercise, you may want to review agreement of compound subjects and verbs and the use of commas in compound sentences.

EXERCISE   On the lines provided, combine each of the following pairs of sentences into one sentence by using conjunctions. Be sure that subject and verb agree in number in the combined sentence. Add commas where necessary. (Correct answers may vary. Add 10 points for each correct answer.)

1. Good diet is important for physical fitness.

   Regular exercise is important for physical fitness. . . . .

   . . . .

   . . . .

2. You must exercise your muscles.

   They will begin to weaken. . . . .

   . . . .

   . . . .

3. Food is essential for your body.
   Oxygen is essential for your body. ....

   ....

   ....

4. Your body can store food.
   It cannot store oxygen. ....

   ....

   ....

5. Exercise makes the lungs more efficient.
   It strengthens the heart. ....

   ....

   ....

6. Swimming is an excellent form of exercise.
   Jogging is an excellent form of exercise. ....

   ....

   ....

7. Cycling every day conditions the body.
   Walking every day conditions the body. ....

   ....

   ....

8. Moderate exercise does not cause fatigue.
   Moderate exercise does not damage the heart. ....

   ....

   ....

9. Exercise helps you do more.
   Exercise helps you feel less tired. ....

   ....

   ....

10. Begin an exercise program slowly.
    You could hurt yourself. ....

    ....

    ....

Combining with Appositive Phrases and Participial Phrases

Appositive Phrases

An **appositive phrase** is a group of words which explains or identifies a noun or pronoun. It is set off from the rest of a sentence by commas.

EXAMPLE   We talked with Mrs. Peters, <u>the editor in chief.</u>

You can combine short, related sentences by using an appositive phrase.

EXAMPLE   Mary won the school tournament.
She is an excellent tennis player.
Mary, <u>an excellent tennis player,</u> won the school tournament. (appositive phrase: *an excellent tennis player*)

EXERCISE A   Combine each of the following pairs of sentences into one sentence by using an appositive phrase. Add commas where necessary. (Correct answers may vary. Add 20 points for each correct sentence.)

A. Blues music is usually sad in tone.

The music is a distinctly American art form. *Blues music, a distinctly American art form, is usually sad in tone.*

1. W. C. Handy published "The Memphis Blues" in 1913.

He was one of the first blues musicians. . . . .

. . . .

2. Handy also wrote "The St. Louis Blues."

It is perhaps the most famous blues song. . . . .

. . . .

3. Louis Armstrong was an innovative trumpeter.

He was a famous blues instrumentalist. . . . .

. . . .

4. Bessie Smith's blues compositions made her famous during the 1920's.

They were simple songs full of power and beauty. . . . .

. . . .

5. B. B. King continues the blues tradition.

He is a contemporary singer and composer. . . . .

. . . .

Participial Phrases

A **participial phrase** is a group of words which begins with a participle*
and is used as an adjective to modify a noun or pronoun.

EXAMPLE   Edgar wrote a poem *describing a beautiful sunset.*

You can combine short, related sentences by using a participial phrase.

EXAMPLE   Frank eluded the tacklers.
He crossed the goal line.

Eluding the tacklers, Frank crossed the goal line.   (participial phrase:
eluding the tacklers)

When it comes at the beginning of a sentence, a participial phrase is followed
by a comma.

EXERCISE B   Combine each of the following pairs of sentences into one sentence
by using a participial phrase. Add commas where necessary. (Correct answers may
vary. Add 20 points for each correct sentence.)

A. Many blues songs describe disappointments in love.
They are popular. *Many blues songs describing disappointments in love are popular.*

1. Blues music includes odd notes.
The notes are deliberately played out of tune. . . . .

. . . .

2. Traditional blues lyrics consist of stanzas.
The stanzas contain three lines each. . . . .

. . . .

3. "The Memphis Blues" was written for a political campaign.
This song made blues music popular. . . . .

. . . .

4. Blues music has strongly influenced many American composers.
These composers include George Gershwin. . . . .

. . . .

5. Today there are many rock songs.
These songs reflect the influence of the blues. . . . .

. . . .

*A *present participle* is a verb form ending in *-ing*. A *past participle* is most often formed by adding *-ed* to the verb.

Combining Sentences with Adjective Clauses

An **adjective clause** is a subordinate clause used as an adjective to modify a noun or pronoun. An adjective clause usually begins with a relative pronoun: *who, whom, whose, which,* or *that.*

EXAMPLE   The referee pointed to the player who had committed the foul.

You can often combine two related sentences by changing one of the sentences into an adjective clause and by adding a relative pronoun.

EXAMPLES   Ask the clerk.
           The clerk is behind the counter.
           Ask the clerk who is behind the counter.
           We saw the meteor shower.
           The newspaper had predicted the shower.
           We saw the meteor shower, which the newspaper had predicted.   (Notice which unnecessary words are left out of the combined sentence.)

Use commas to set off adjective clauses unless the clause answers the question "Which one?" and is therefore essential to the meaning of the sentence.

NONESSENTIAL   My bike, which is a ten-speed, has a light frame.   (commas needed)

ESSENTIAL   The driver who ran the stop sign received a ticket.   (no commas)

EXERCISE A   On the lines provided, combine each of the following pairs of sentences by changing one of the sentences into an adjective clause. Add commas where necessary. (Correct answers may vary. Add 10 points for each correct sentence.)

A. The sinking of the *Empress of Ireland* was a disaster.

In this disaster more than one thousand people died. *The sinking of the Empress of Ireland was a disaster in which more than one thousand people died.*

1. The ship was bound for London.

The ship set sail from Quebec on May 28, 1914. ....

....

....

2. The ship was travelling downstream.

The ship suddenly encountered a wispy fog near the mouth of the St.

Lawrence River. ....

....

....

3. The captain of the *Empress* spotted the lights of another ship.
   The ship was passing nearby. . . . .

   . . . .

   . . . .

4. The captain decided to change direction.
   He had miscalculated the position of the other ship. . . . .

   . . . .

   . . . .

5. Tragically, the other ship changed its direction also.
   This ship was called the *Storstad.* . . . .

   . . . .

   . . . .

6. The freighter *Storstad* knifed into the *Empress of Ireland.*
   The *Storstad* could not stop its momentum. . . . .

   . . . .

   . . . .

7. The collision almost split the *Empress.*
   The ship sank within fifteen minutes. . . . .

   . . . .

   . . . .

8. On board the *Empress of Ireland* were many people.
   They acted with great heroism. . . . .

   . . . .

   . . . .

9. A passenger rescued a young girl by carrying her on his back.
   She could not swim. . . . .

   . . . .

   . . . .

10. One man had also survived the sinking of the ocean liner *Titanic.*
    He was pulled from the water. . . . .

    . . . .

    . . . .

Combining Sentences with Adverb Clauses

An **adverb clause** is a subordinate clause used as an adverb.

EXAMPLE   We cheered <u>when the team won</u>.   (tells *when* we cheered)

You can often combine sentences by changing one of the sentences into an adverb clause and by adding one of the following subordinating conjunctions:

after	as if	before	than	when	wherever
although	as though	if	unless	whenever	while
as	because	since	until	where	

EXAMPLES   We were sleeping.
          The storm arrived.

<u>While we were sleeping</u>, the storm arrived.   (The sentence *We were sleeping* has been rewritten as an adverb clause, *while we were sleeping.*)

They will continue trying.
They succeed.

They will continue trying <u>until they succeed</u>.   (The sentence *They succeed* has been rewritten as an adverb clause, *until they succeed.*)

Often you may vary the style of your sentences by placing an adverb clause either *in front of* or *after* the main clause.

EXAMPLES   We all went swimming because the day was so hot.
          Because the day was so hot, we all went swimming.
          (Note the use of the comma after an introductory adverb clause.)

EXERCISE   On the lines provided, combine each of the following pairs of sentences by changing one sentence into an adverb clause. Choose appropriate subordinating conjunctions from the list on this page. Add commas where necessary. (Correct answers may vary. Add 10 points for each correct sentence.)

1. The comedian entertained the audience.

   The stagehands changed the sets. . . . .

   . . . .

   . . . .

2. The assignment was difficult.

   Jules was able to finish in time. . . . .

   . . . .

   . . . .

3. Rosa does well in her audition.
   She may receive a part in the play. ....

   ....

   ....

4. The athletes began to practise the plays.
   The coach assigned the various positions. ....

   ....

   ....

5. Paul learned his routine well.
   He coached the other members of the team. ....

   ....

   ....

6. A hush fell upon the study hall.
   The teacher walked into the room. ....

   ....

   ....

7. Carla's group will not play at the dance.
   The student government votes money to pay them. ....

   ....

   ....

8. Lucy did her homework in the afternoon.
   She wanted to go to the fair in the evening. ....

   ....

   ....

9. Francisco was the best artist.
   We asked him to draw the mural. ....

   ....

   ....

10. We could not leave on the field trip.
    The buses came. ....

    ....

    ....

Combining Sentences with Noun Clauses

A **noun clause** is a subordinate clause used as a noun.

EXAMPLE   This gift is <u>what I wanted</u>.

You can often combine sentences by changing one of the sentences into a noun clause and by using one of these connecting words: *that, what, whatever, where, who, whoever, whom, whomever, why.*

EXAMPLES   You pick someone.
This person will win the nomination.
<u>Whoever you pick</u> will win the nomination. (The word *someone* in the first sentence has been dropped, and the connecting word has been added to form the noun clause *Whoever you pick.*)

EXERCISE   On the lines provided, combine each of the following pairs of sentences into one sentence. If necessary, choose appropriate introductory words from the list given above. (Correct answers may vary. Add 10 points for each correct sentence.)

A. We now realize something about the Beatles.

The Beatles changed the course of popular music. *We now realize that the Beatles changed the course of popular music.*

B. Many teen-agers prefer rock music to all other music.

This preference disturbs some adults. *That many teen-agers prefer rock music to all other music disturbs some adults.*

1. The singer told us something about the auditorium.

The auditorium was filled to capacity. . . . .

. . . .

. . . .

2. Someone will win the trophy.

He will have the best batting average in the league. . . . .

. . . .

. . . .

3. Why had the referee made that call?

The coach wanted to know. . . . .

. . . .

. . . .

4. We had put the car keys somewhere.
   We could not remember. . . . .

   . . . .

   . . . .

5. The golfer's ball had gone somewhere.
   The golfer could not discover where. . . . .

   . . . .

   . . . .

6. The actor told us something.
   It was something we wanted to hear. . . . .

   . . . .

   . . . .

7. A person will buy this car.
   That person will have to fix it. . . . .

   . . . .

   . . . .

8. Give the record to someone.
   You decide upon the person. . . . .

   . . . .

   . . . .

9. Solar cells work somehow.
   How they work is baffling to me. . . . .

   . . . .

   . . . .

10. The scene should include a car chase.
    The director insisted. . . . .

    . . . .

    . . . .

Review of Sentence Combining

EXERCISE   Rewrite each of the following groups of sentences by combining choppy sentences into longer, smoother sentences. Use the lines provided. (Correct answers may vary.)

A. Stonehenge is in southern England.

Stonehenge is the ruins of a monument.

The monument is from the Stone Age.

People used this monument.

They used it for performing religious rites.

They used it for observing the stars.

The monument contains a great circle of stone columns.

The columns have a mass of more than 40 tonnes.

The columns rise 7 m above the ground.

. . . .

. . . .

. . . .

. . . .

. . . .

. . . .

. . . .

. . . .

. . . .

. . . .

B. Alice Munro is an award-winning author.

She is the daughter of a fox-farmer.

She was born in Wingham, Ontario.

She started writing at the age of eleven.

Munro's stories are based on her own upbringing.

Her stories are full of an emotional intensity.

In one book, the stories are about Del Jordan.

Del Jordan is a young girl.

She is growing up and trying to understand the people around her.

C. Franck Klusky was a Polish medium.

He claimed a special ability.

He said that he could make people and animals appear out of the air.

One of his apparitions left handprints in a bowl of wax.

The apparition then disappeared.

The handprints were smaller than the hands of any of the witnesses.

These witnesses were present during this strange event.

Review of Sentence Combining, Continued

EXERCISE Rewrite each of the following paragraphs by combining choppy sentences into longer, smoother sentences. Use the lines provided. (Correct answers may vary.)

A. The Book of Remembrance is a record. It contains the names of 66 651 Canadians. These Canadians lost their lives. They died during the First World War. The book was placed in the Peace Tower in Ottawa. It was placed in a room called the Memorial Chamber. It was placed there in 1926. The book rests on an altar stone. The stone was a gift of the British Government. The walls and floor of the chamber are of stone and marble. The marble and stone are from Belgium and France. There is also a second book. It contains 44 000 names. These people died in the Second World War. Both books are lettered. The lettering is beautiful. Guards perform a ritual. The ritual happens daily. A page is turned in each book.

. . . .

. . . .

. . . .

. . . .

. . . .

. . . .

. . . .

. . . .

B. Nicholas Cugnot was a French artillery captain. He invented the automobile in 1770. It was the first successful automobile. The contraption was ugly. It had three wheels. The wheels were wooden. It resembled a large tricycle. A boiler produced steam. The boiler was coal-fired. The boiler was in front. The steam pushed two pistons. The pistons were on either side of the front wheel. The automobile moved at the speed of 4 km/h. This speed included time for stopping. The machine stopped every few hundred meters and regained steam pressure. The machine slipped on wet roads. The machine had steering problems. Cugnot's success inspired other daring inventors.

....
....
....
....
....
....
....
....
....
....
....
....

CHAPTER TWELVE

Composition

As you develop the writing skills discussed in this chapter, you will have a chance to apply what you have learned from the other chapters in this book. Your knowledge of grammar, punctuation, capitalization, and standard usage should help you write clear, correct sentences. Clarity and correctness are basic to good writing.

Even more important, however, is the ability to make what you say interesting and effective. If you will follow the directions in this chapter to the best of your ability, you should learn to choose interesting words, make vivid comparisons, and organize and develop your ideas effectively. In short, you should be able to improve your writing.

LESSON 116

Choosing Effective Nouns and Verbs

Your assignment in this lesson will be to write a story. In stories your choice of nouns and verbs is especially important. Writers of uninteresting stories often use many vague nouns and weak (usually linking) verbs to talk *about* settings, characters, and actions. Writers of good stories use vivid nouns and strong action verbs to make the readers *see* the settings and the characters' actions.

As you read and compare the following groups of sentences, notice especially the difference that vivid nouns and action verbs make in presenting (1) a setting, (2) characters, and (3) an action.

1

DULL   The road ended at a lawn with shrubs and I could see the outline of the Grange. A dim light showed in a room. Save for the cry of owls and the croaking of frogs, the place was quiet.

VIVID   The avenue presently opened out upon a lawn with overgrown shrubberies and in the half darkness I could see the outline of the Grange itself, a rambling, dilapidated building. A dim light struggled through the casement of a window in a tower room. Save for the melancholy cry of a row of owls sitting on the roof, and croaking of the frogs in the moat which ran around the grounds, the place was soundless.[1]

—STEPHEN LEACOCK

[1] From *Laugh With Leacock* by Stephen Leacock reprinted by permission of The Canadian Publishers, McClelland and Stewart Limited, Toronto.

DULL   People who had been pleasant became sad. Douglas tried but could not eat the food, nor could Tom and Dad. People just did not like the food.

VIVID   Smiling people stopped smiling. Douglas chewed one bite of food for three minutes. He saw Tom and Dad do the same. People swashed the food together, making roads and patterns, drawing pictures in the gravy, forming castles of the potatoes, secretly passing meat chunks to the dog.[1]

3

DULL   The signal from the pitcher was clear. I was ready to catch a ball at least two feet outside the plate, but when he threw the ball, I was surprised.

VIVID   He called that he was going to throw a fast-breaking curve and warned me to expect the ball at least two feet outside the plate. Then he wound up and let it go, and that ball came whistling right down the groove for the center of the plate.[2]

Vivid, specific nouns and verbs are better than vague ones.

Notice the specific words (in italics) that can be substituted for the following very general nouns and verbs.

1. say—*whisper, mumble, shriek, bark, grunt, bluster*
2. move—*flit, drift, rush, shuffle, slide, jog, sway*
3. music—*jazz, waltz, lullaby, psalm, polka, ditty*

A vivid, specific verb is usually better than an ordinary verb modified by an adverb.

In the following pairs, notice that the single verb at the right is more effective than the verb-adverb combination at the left. It describes the action more forcefully.

VERB-ADVERB	VERB
1. looked steadily	stared
2. walked slowly, carelessly	strolled
3. cried loudly	howled
4. cooked noisily	sizzled

A vivid, specific noun is usually better than an ordinary noun modified by an adjective.

---

[1] From *Dandelion Wine* by Ray Bradbury. Published by Curtis Publishing Co.
[2] From *Farewell to Sport* by Paul Gallico. Copyright 1938, renewed 1966 by Paul Gallico. Reprinted by permission of Alfred A. Knopf, Inc.

Again, notice that the single noun at the right is more effective than the adjective-noun pair. It calls up a single, precise picture.

NOUN-ADJECTIVE	NOUN
1. flat-bottomed, clumsy rowboat	scow
2. large, unruly crowd	mob
3. rapid, rushing river	torrent
4. sharp, short answer	retort

EXERCISE A List at least five specific words that could be substituted for each vague word below.

1. eat: ....

2. a message: ....

3. go: ....

4. a building: ....

5. take: ....

EXERCISE B For each of the word groups in the left-hand column, write a single noun or verb which will give the same meaning more effectively.

1. *walking* lightly and rapidly   ....

2. *walking* stealthily, hesitatingly   ....

3. a stingy, selfish, greedy *person*   ....

4. *said* quietly and softly   ....

5. a huge, oval *grandstand*   ....

EXERCISE C On a separate sheet of paper, rewrite each of the following sentences, replacing ineffective words with more vivid ones.

1. The young man raised the window, took a worn, brightly coloured square of cloth from his pocket, and moved it vigorously back and forth.

2. She put up her hands, took the ball out of the hands of the intended receiver, and went across the goal line.

3. Cars were going rapidly past us and noisily going around the sharp turn beyond.

4. Jimmy swam noisily into midstream, and then he called frantically that a big fish was after him.

5. A group of jet planes passed rapidly and noisily overhead and went quickly out of sight.

WRITING ASSIGNMENT   Write a story of at least 150 words about an experience you had that would be interesting to others. As you plan and write your story, keep the following principles in mind:

1. *Limit your story to a single incident.* For example, you might choose to write about what you did at camp, but since you could not present in 150 words all your experiences, you would need to limit your story to only one experience—such as taking an overnight canoe trip or winning a swimming meet.

2. *Decide upon your purpose.* Decide upon the one effect (amusement, fright, surprise) that you want your story to have on the readers. Then select those facts and details that will help you achieve your purpose.

3. *Begin with action, and end before you risk losing the readers' interest.* Avoid a dull, rambling introduction. Start with action. End your story as soon as you have presented its climax. As you proofread your story, strike out all unnecessary details.

4. *Carefully choose vivid, specific nouns and verbs.*

The following list of topics may remind you of experiences that you would enjoy writing about.

1. The time I played the hero
2. A blabbermouth keeps a secret
3. Searching for a ghost
4. Just good luck?
5. A dog chooses me
6. My kid brother at the zoo
7. Nobody laughed
8. A false alarm
9. My first long-distance bike race (hike, trip)
10. Temporary defeat meant final victory
11. Was my face red!
12. The day I appeared on TV
13. I should have listened to my parents
14. A few seconds make a big difference
15. Laws should be obeyed
16. I'll never be the same again
17. The funniest sight I ever saw
18. I had to take the blame
19. The time I took charge
20. The game (or match) I helped to win
21. Spending my first allowance
22. The longest hour of my life
23. My secret ambition
24. Overcoming a handicap
25. Someone who influenced me

Using Comparisons

Your writing can be made more interesting by the use of comparisons. For instance, when you are describing a thing or an action, you can often make it clearer and more arresting by comparing it to something else. Such a comparison is called a *figure of speech*. You may make comparisons in two ways, either by saying something is or acts *like* something else or by saying it *is* something else.

Read the following comparisons and notice how effective they are.

1. Like some prehistoric dragon belching smoke and fire, the rocket rises from the launching tower.
2. She is as inconsiderate as an alarm clock.
3. It is as vulnerable as a newborn turtle, searching for its way to the sea.
4. It all seemed blurred, unreal, like a picture in the newspaper.
5. A flock of pigeons that fly below have the look, in the dull light, of wastepaper blown by the wind.
6. The climber came quickly and heavily down the slope, swaying from side to side like a puppet dancing at the end of a string.
7. The child moved as quickly and excitedly as a kitten playing with a rubber ball.
8. The vendor's stand is an oasis during the dry summer months.
9. I would have about as much chance as an icicle in July.
10. The girl's eyes were like two small chips of blue tile.

EXERCISE A Make effective comparisons by filling the blanks in the following sentences. Compare yours with those written by other students in your class.

1. She stared at me like ....

   ....

2. The clown had large feet, shaped like ....

   ....

3. He seemed as confused as ....

   ....

4. The cars climbing the distant hill looked smaller than ....

   ....

5. Falling water in the sunlight was like ....

   ....

6. The twins were as close as ....

....

7. To the frightened boy the moving shadows were ....

....

8. The heavy fog was ....

....

9. The sailboats skimmed the water more lightly than ....

....

10. To press his clammy hand was like ....

....

EXERCISE B Comparisons of all kinds are made with words—sometimes a single word, sometimes a phrase, a clause, or an entire sentence. In the passage below, put parentheses around the part or parts of each sentence that express a comparison of any kind. Be ready to discuss the passage, showing what the comparisons mean.

Again there came a shifting in the scenes. It looked as if some unseen hands were spreading a sheet above these flocculent clouds—a thin and vapoury sheet that came from the north and gradually covered the whole roof of the sky. Stars and moon disappeared; but not, so far, the light of the moon; it merely became diffused—the way the light from an electric bulb becomes diffused when you enclose it in a frosted globe. And then, as the sheet of vapour above began to thicken, the light on the snow became dim and dimmer, till the whole of the landscape lay in gloom. The sheet still seemed to be coming, coming from the north. But no longer did it travel away to the south. It was as if it had brought up against an obstacle there, as if it were being held in place. And since there was more and more of it pressing up—it seemed rather to be pushed now—it telescoped together and threw itself into folds, till at last the whole sky looked like an enormous system of parallel clothes-lines over all of which one great, soft, and loose cloth were flung, so that fold after fold would hang down between all the neighbouring pairs of lines; and between two folds there would be a sharply converging, upward crease. It being night, this arrangement, common in grey daylight, would not have shown at all, had it not been for the moon above. As it was, every one of the infolds showed an increasingly lighter grey the higher it folded up, and like huge, black udders the outfolds were hanging down.[1]

—FREDERICK PHILIP GROVE

WRITING ASSIGNMENT Describe in about 150 words a scene or an event with which you are familiar. Present interesting details. By using several com-

[1] Frederick Philip Grove. "Skies and Scares" from *Over Prairie Trails*. By permission of Mr. A.L. Grove. Toronto, Ontario.

parisons and vivid verbs and nouns, make your readers *see* the colour and the action of the scene.

As you plan and write your description, follow these steps:

1. Begin by listing all the actions, colours, and sounds that you may use in your description. Then cross from the list any details that you decide not to include.

2. Arrange your material in a clear, logical order—which did you notice first, second, third?

3. Like a photographer setting up a camera, select a definite position from which to view the scene or event. If you wish to move and describe what you see as you go, do so, but let your readers know your movements.

Here are some suggested topics for this assignment:

1. Watching a sunrise
2. Standing on a mountaintop
3. Riding across the desert
4. The high school locker room
5. A visit to the zoo
6. A crowd at the beach
7. Watching a parade
8. A thrilling sight
9. An audience at the theatre
10. Fans in the stadium
11. A supermarket on Saturday
12. A destructive storm
13. The corner drugstore
14. An automobile accident
15. Your room at midnight

WRITING ASSIGNMENT You have learned two ways to make your writing interesting: (1) by selecting nouns and verbs carefully; (2) by using comparisons. In this assignment show how effectively you can do these two things.

Write another story or another description. Your story may be an experience of your own, one you learned about from someone else, or one you imagined. Here is a good chance to try your hand at mystery or science fiction, if you wish. If you prefer to write a description again, you may make it either full of action or mostly stationary like a word picture of a place you are fond of. Whether you write a story or a description, make your writing interesting by using vivid words and fresh comparisons. The following lists may suggest a topic for your composition.

STORIES

1. My invention changed the world
2. A fight nobody won
3. My first trip into space
4. The night I stayed in Transylvania
5. Was it a person, a beast, or a ghost?

6. My talking horse (dog, cat)
7. The teacher read my mind
8. I dashed to the rescue
9. I solve a mystery
10. Who was to blame?
11. I always learn the hard way
12. My first experience as a millionaire

DESCRIPTIONS

1. My school in the year 2000
2. Night sounds at camp
3. Cloud formations
4. A sight I'll never forget
5. An impressive painting
6. The moods of the ocean
7. The inside of a clock (television, radio)
8. A striking window display
9. The inside of an abandoned house
10. Diary entries of an explorer from Mars after seeing a baseball game
11. A lake after a shower
12. The beach in early fall
13. A cat readying to strike
14. The crowd at a baseball game
15. A table set for Thanksgiving
16. The smells from a bakery
17. A crowded amusement park
18. The view from a high mountain
19. The view from the top of a tall building
20. The town after a hurricane

What Is a Paragraph?

A paragraph is a group of closely related sentences developing one topic.

A paragraph may be short or long but it must always stick to just one topic. Writers usually state this topic in the first sentence of a paragraph and then develop it in the remaining sentences. If a sentence is not closely related to the topic, a writer will eliminate it from the paragraph.

The following paragraph begins by stating the author's delight and excitement at an Indian bazaar. The paragraph then gives details which explain her delight.

AN INDIAN BAZAAR

To me an Indian bazaar is a source of endless delight and excitement. It is usually a series of plain wooden stalls on which are piled, with unconscious artistry, brightly colored fruits, vegetables, spices, gleaming silver jewelry, brilliant silks and cottons or charming, grotesque painted wooden toys. The vendors who can't afford a stall sit on the sidewalk outside the market, their baskets stacked behind them, their wives in vivid cotton saris crouching in the shade, and in front of them are spread carpets of scarlet chillies drying in the sun, small hills of saffron, turmeric, coriander, ginger, cinnamon—all the magical names from the old days of the spice trade with the Indies. With a worn stone mortar and pestle the vendor or his wife will grind your spices for you, blending them according to your particular taste, and weigh them in tiny brass scales strung on twine and balanced delicately in one hand. In all transactions you receive a pleasantly individual attention—nothing is standardized.[1]

All of the sentences in this paragraph are closely related to the topic, the excitement of an Indian bazaar. If the author had decided to end the paragraph with a sentence like "Shopping in a supermarket is easier," the paragraph would have gone off in an entirely different direction, introducing a new topic that has nothing to do with the other sentences.

EXERCISE In the space provided, write *P* for any sentence group that is a paragraph and *X* for any sentence group that does not contain a series of sentences developing one topic.

1. . . . . Because people do not pick up after themselves, Jim and I must do it for them. The cart, however, can hold only so much litter. Jim likes sweeping the sidewalk more than picking up bottles. I wish more companies would sell soft drinks in returnable glass bottles. Actually, I do not complain as much as I could.

[1] "Return to India" by Santha Rama Rau. Copyright © 1960 by Santha Rama Rau. Reprinted by permission of William Morris Agency, Inc., on behalf of the author.

2. . . . . Trying to leave school a few minutes early for a game is not simple. You must be very careful not to do anything wrong, or else your teacher will ask you to clean the blackboards. Also, you must be sure that you have not made a date to meet someone right after school. Finally, you must secure your principal's permission to leave before class is officially dismissed.

3. . . . . Rita told us how she eats an ice-cream cone. First she licks off the edges of ice cream that might drip. Then she smooths the remaining ice cream until it is shaped into a point. After she has eaten the ice cream down to the level of the cone, she bites off a little portion of the cone around the entire edge. When only a bit of the cone is left, she pops all of it into her mouth.

4. . . . . Most people enjoy a good adventure film. *The Three Musketeers* is an example of a good adventure film. Why, however, do people enjoy science-fiction films? Perhaps they are fascinated by outer space. Some people would probably travel into space if they were given the chance. Is there a recent movie about outer space that has not attracted millions of viewers?

Writing the Paragraph: The Topic Sentence

The sentence which states the topic of the paragraph is called the <u>topic</u> <u>sentence</u>. **The other sentences in the paragraph develop the idea expressed by the topic sentence.**

Read the following paragraph. The topic sentence is italicized. Note how it is developed by the other sentences, each of which adds information concerning the idea expressed in the topic sentence.

AN ASTRONAUT'S TRAINING

The boys' training at the Cape was not so much arduous as tedious. It was sedentary, even. It involved no flying. Some days they would be briefed on launch procedures. Or they would drive out to the launching base and go inside an old converted rat-shack hangar, Hangar S, and sit all day in a simulator known as the "procedures trainer," which on the inside was a replica of the capsule they would ride in during flight. Or technically they sat in there all day; in fact, they were lying down. It was as if you took a chair and pushed it over backward so that its back was on the floor and then sat in it.[1]

A Paragraph Outline   The simple organization of the preceding paragraph can be shown by a brief outline.

TOPIC   The boredom of an astronaut's training
1. No flying
2. Briefing on procedures
3. Spending day in hangar
4. Sitting all day in training capsule

Before you write a paragraph, jot down a simple outline like this. Following such an outline as you write will make your paragraph clear, and your readers will find it easy to follow your ideas.

EXERCISE   Underline the topic sentence in each of the following paragraphs. Then in the space provided make an outline of the subtopics of the paragraph, using the outline form shown above.

1. I never call a stupid fellow a "birdbrain" because I know that birds are intelligent. In my backyard I have seen a sparrow pick up a stale crust of bread, fly to the birdbath, and dip the crust into the water in order to soften the food for her young. Across the street is a blue jay that has as much sense as the sparrow. The jay watches a squirrel find nuts, patiently waits until he

---

[1] From *The Right Stuff* by Tom Wolfe. Copyright © 1979 by Tom Wolfe. Reprinted by permission of Farrar, Straus & Giroux, Inc., and International Creative Management.

cracks and starts eating them, and then dives down and snatches a good meal. I remember reading about a sea gull that used similar tactics. Wanting to eat a clam but unable to break its shell, the gull placed the clam behind a parked convertible and dived menacingly at the driver. Finally the annoyed driver backed up, obligingly smashed the clam, and thus provided a tasty meal for the wise bird. Like an attentive parent, a female sparrow carefully prepares food for her young; like a shrewd thief, a jay steals from an honest laborer; like an intelligent human, a gull solves a problem by making use of past experience. Certainly *birdbrain* is not a synonym for *crackbrain*.

TOPIC: . . . .

1. . . . .

2. . . . .

3. . . . .

2. The changes worked in fine-looking, cleareyed youngsters who adopt the ring as a profession are sometimes shocking to observe. You see them at the start fresh and unmarked, and you live through their gradual disintegration. The knotted ears and the smashed noses are the least of their injuries. Their lips begin to thicken, and their eyes seem to sink deeper and deeper into the cavernous ridges above them, ridges that are thickened and scarred from battle. Many of them acquire little nervous tics. Their voices change to husky, half-intelligible whispers. Some of them go blind. Their walk is affected. Worst of all, sometimes they cannot remember, or they say queer things. The industry laughs and says, "Don't pay attention to him. He's punchy!"[1]

TOPIC: . . . .

1. . . . .   6. . . . .

2. . . . .   7. . . . .

3. . . . .   8. . . . .

4. . . . .   9. . . . .

5. . . . .   10. . . . .

WRITING ASSIGNMENT   Write a well-organized paragraph of about 100 words explaining a topic. Before writing, make a paragraph outline like the ones you have been making in this lesson. Hand in your outline with your paragraph.

[1] From *Farewell to Sport* by Paul Gallico. Copyright 1938, renewed 1966 by Paul Gallico. Reprinted by permission of Alfred A. Knopf, Inc.

As in any composition assignment, write about a subject with which you are familiar. If you need help, one of the following topic sentences may suggest an idea.

SUGGESTED TOPIC SENTENCES

1. It is great fun to fish (hike, ski) at sunrise.
2. I know what the joys of mountain climbing are.
3. As a weather-watcher, I never make cocksure predictions.
4. Each of my friends has at least one characteristic that amuses me.
5. Every pet has a distinctive personality.
6. The changes in a teen-ager growing up are sometimes surprising.
7. I have observed the changes that take place when an amateur ballplayer becomes a professional.
8. The duties of an editor of a school publication are varied.
9. I have learned how to live on an allowance.
10. A good sport knows how to lose and how to win.
11. History is my favourite subject for three reasons.
12. I understand why a person brags.

Strong Topic Sentences

A strong topic sentence has a carefully stated and limited topic.

A strong topic sentence prepares the reader for what will follow in the paragraph. It gives the reader clear direction.

Weak topic sentences do not focus on a single limited topic; they do not tell the reader what to expect in a paragraph. Strong topic sentences do the opposite; they focus the reader's attention on a single, clearly limited topic, which can be developed in a paragraph. For example, compare weak and strong topic sentences for the following paragraph outline:

TOPIC   The delights of acquiring new friends
1. Talking to new people
2. Learning how other people live
3. Introducing new friends to old friends
4. Helping new friends adjust
5. Being someone new friends can rely upon

WEAK TOPIC SENTENCES   1. It's fun to acquire new friends.
2. Acquiring friends is delightful.

STRONG TOPIC SENTENCES   1. Acquiring new friends is an opportunity for personal growth.
2. New friends can often become a greater source of joy than old friends.

EXERCISE   After each of the following paragraph outlines, write a strong topic sentence for a paragraph based on the outline.

A. TOPIC   Caring for tropical fish

1. Outfitting the tank
2. Keeping the tank clean
3. Choosing different species of fish
4. Studying the habits of the fish

Topic sentence: ....

....

B. TOPIC: Building a tree house

1. Choosing the right tree
2. Finding the right place for the house
3. Locating scrap wood
4. Gathering additional materials

Topic sentence: ....
....

C. TOPIC: My first-grade classroom
       1. Participating in activities
       2. Acquiring friends
       3. Paying attention to the teacher
       4. Obeying rules

Topic sentence: ....
....

D. TOPIC: Swimming in a pool
       1. Obeying the lifeguard
       2. Diving
       3. Using inner tubes and rafts
       4. Swimming long distances
       5. Playing games

Topic sentence: ....
....

E. TOPIC: The benefits of a sports program
       1. Keeping in good physical shape
       2. Uplifting the emotions
       3. Improving co-ordination skills
       4. Learning teamwork
       5. Learning from victory or defeat

Topic sentence: ....
....

Writing the Paragraph: Sticking to the Topic

Every sentence in a paragraph should be closely related to the topic.

As you read the following paragraph, observe that the topic is stated in the first sentence and that each of the following sentences is closely related in meaning to the topic.

The promotion department of a radio station is responsible for promoting the station's name and for developing positive public relations. At a small radio station, promotion is shared among all staff, with the station's manager and advertising sales people doing most of the work. Many large stations have a promotion director whose job is to assess public attitudes toward the station and promote a favourable relationship with the community. Stations also try to foster good community relations by making time available free for the broadcast of public service announcements from various social agencies, service organizations and citizens' groups.[1]

Any idea that does not support the topic or that is only vaguely related to it—such as the idea that some wrestlers fight only to please the spectators or that some professional football players earn more money than senators—would, if included, disrupt the unity of the paragraph above. You can write unified paragraphs if you will (1) begin with the topic, (2) stick to it, and (3) eliminate any unrelated idea.

EXERCISE A   Four paragraph outlines are given below. In each outline there are two or more unrelated ideas which should not be included in the paragraph. In the space provided after each outline, write a topic sentence. Then draw a line through any unrelated ideas, leaving a good paragraph outline, but with the topic sentence below the list of ideas.

A. Developing a good news story
   Interview people involved   ~~Friends at the news office~~
   Organize material   Research background information
   ~~Wear the right clothes~~   Check sources
Topic sentence: *The careful reporter follows several steps to develop a story.*

1. Benefits of exercise
   Better muscle tone   Improved co-ordination
   Limber body   Inexpensive activity
   Difficult exercises   Increased rate of concentration

[1]From *Reading Writing and Radio* by Winston G. Schell and Marston E. Woollings. Copyright © 1977. Reprinted by permission of Academic Press Canada.

Topic sentence: ....

....

2. Values of a course in public speaking

Increased self-confidence	A hard course
The teacher of the course	Improved ability to plan a talk
	Course liked by Jack
Improved pronunciation	Easy homework assignments

Topic sentence: ....

....

3. Ways to earn money

Delivering newspapers	Saving money
Mowing lawns	Baby-sitting
Asking parents for more allowance	Washing cars
	Doing volunteer work

Topic sentence: ....

....

EXERCISE B   Each of the following paragraphs contains one or more sentences which are not closely related to the topic of the paragraph, which is expressed in the first sentence. Draw a line through these unrelated sentences.

1. *It was opening night and I was scared.* I peeked out from behind the curtains and saw the full auditorium. The curtains were a deep purple colour and in need of repair. So vividly did my fright heighten my ability to see that I was able to pick out faces I knew from the back row. My aunt and uncle told me last week they would come to the show. My left leg started spasming and my hands became clammy. I knew that at the moment the houselights dimmed and the orchestra started playing I would be all right. Until then I would go through this opening night ritual of sheer fear.

2. *One of the things I like about fishing is the surprises you get when you pull in your line.* I particularly remember one experience while on holiday in Florida. I sat dozing with my back braced against a gently swaying palm and occasionally catching a pompano. Dad and Mother had gone shopping. In the midst of my daydreaming, I finally noticed that my line, bit by bit, was running out into the blue water of the tropical Atlantic. There were several fishing boats in the distance. Calmly I started to reel in. The line felt exactly as if I had a 5 kg rock tied to the hook. When at last I managed to pull in my catch, I found a baby octopus clinging to the end of my line!

3. *It is more fun to go swimming in the ocean surf than in a lake.* The water in a lake is usually still and offers no opposition to you as you swim. The water in the ocean, however, is always tumbling over in great breakers which try to

knock you down and swirl you around. Swimming in a river is likely to be hard because of the current. Otherwise it is very much like swimming in a lake. In the ocean you must be constantly on guard, ready to dive under the waves or fight through them. In a lake you have only to keep afloat. If the fun of constant excitement is what you want, the ocean is the place for you.

WRITING ASSIGNMENT   Write a paragraph giving advice. The advice may be on any subject with which you believe you have had enough experience to set yourself up as an adviser. The list below may be helpful.

Your purpose in this assignment is to write a good paragraph without letting any unrelated ideas get into it. Make an outline first. This is the surest way to keep out unrelated ideas. Begin your paragraph with a topic sentence. Make sure that every other sentence is closely related to the topic sentence. You may give your paragraph to several classmates to find out whether they can spot any unrelated ideas.

SUGGESTED PARAGRAPH TOPICS

1. To a younger brother (sister)
2. To a new ninth-grader
3. To a teacher
4. To a new student in junior high
5. To a beginner in tennis (any sport)
6. On playing first base (any position, any sport)
7. To parents
8. On make-up
9. On eating between meals
10. On sunbathing
11. On learning to play the violin (any instrument)
12. On selecting an outfit
13. On buying a camera
14. On appropriate school clothes
15. On dating
16. On going steady
17. On getting a job
18. On buying a bike

Writing the Paragraph:
Developing the Topic Sentence

Experienced writers sometimes put the topic sentence in the middle or at the end of the paragraph. Sometimes they omit it entirely. But you will do well always to put your topic sentence first. Writing it first will help you to keep the other sentences closely related to it. Furthermore, you will naturally proceed to *develop* in your paragraph the idea in the topic sentence.

Developing an idea is different from merely restating it. In a good paragraph the sentences *add* specific information that makes the topic sentence more meaningful.

A paragraph may be developed by specific details, examples, reasons, or incidents which support the topic sentence.

1. Use details to develop a paragraph. Specific details make a paragraph interesting and full of meaning. Generalizations, however, usually make the topic dull and unconvincing. Compare the two paragraphs below.

GENERAL   *A photograph can acquire a specific meaning from the position of the camera.* Few moviegoers realize that when a character appears on the screen, they can be made to 'like' or 'dislike' him according to the distance of the shot and the camera angle. Motion-picture directors use several techniques like this to add meaning to their films.

SPECIFIC   *A photograph can acquire a specific meaning from the position of the camera.* This is a fact that few moviegoers are aware of. A character appears on the screen, and in spite of the fact that he is respectably dressed, the audience identify him as someone that they don't like. The reason is that the camera is shooting from a position five or ten metres above floor level. The camera has expressed for the audience a mental "looking down". On the other hand, the same person shot at eye level appears friendly. He is seen as an equal and a friend, because the camera angle suggests that he is of normal size. When the camera shoots upwards towards the person, he takes on a greater dignity and respect. A close-up of a person causes people to react quickly to him: a liking for or a dislike of the person is almost immediate. A long shot of a person creates a mental distance, and the viewers do not judge him as quickly. These are the techniques used by motion picture directors to give their shots added meaning. To understand a movie, you must not become too absorbed in the pictures themselves; you must be alert to the meaning that the director puts into each shot.[1]

2. Use examples to develop a paragraph. An example is a definite reference to a specific thing. If you were writing a criticism of the equipment

[1]From *Mass Media and You* by Austin Repath. Copyright © 1966. Reprinted by permission of Academic Press Canada.

245

in your school, you might refer to such things as broken window shades, carved-up desks, and worn-out blackboards. The writer of the following paragraph is commenting on a kind of television comedy that, he suggests, has been overworked. He develops his point humorously with slightly exaggerated *examples* of scenes that recur on many family comedy programs.

FATHER IN TV COMEDIES

A never-failing source of fun is Father's efforts to do minor repairs in the home. He cannot change a fuse without blowing out the lights in the entire neighborhood. If he puts a washer in the kitchen faucet, the shower in the bathroom explodes, flooding the house. There are endless hours of glee in his attempts with a paintbrush, which usually end on a hilarious note as Father falls headfirst into a can of paint. Junior usually comes to the rescue here with an ingenious invention of his own for paint removal, thus proving that his experiments with the chemistry set have not been in vain. The fact that the remover also removes Father's hair and skin is only incidental.[1]

3. Give reasons to develop a paragraph. Whenever you are presenting an opinion or one side of an argument, you give reasons to support or explain your point. Notice that the writer of the following paragraph gives several reasons for his opinion.

THE PLEASURES OF THE McMICHAEL COLLECTION

The McMichael Canadian Collection in Kleinburg, Ontario is an interesting spot to visit for several reasons. The thirty gallery rooms are constructed from hand-hewn timbers and native stone and the entire complex stands on the crest of the Humber River Valley. Along the walls are displayed works by Lawren Harris, Tom Thomson, Clarence Gagnon, Emily Carr and David Milne, to name only a few. Superb carvings and paintings by native Indian and Inuit artists are on show as well. After a tour of the Collection, it is relaxing to sit and enjoy tea in the pine-panelled dining room. Finally, the Gallery Shop contains many fine gifts and crafts that can be purchased.

4. Use incidents from your experience to develop a paragraph. Sometimes a topic sentence can be most effectively developed by telling a brief story, an incident, or an anecdote. As you read the following paragraph, notice that the writer uses a story not merely as an interesting incident but as convincing evidence to prove the topic stated in the first sentence.

CHIMPANZEE COMMUNICATION

Since both chimpanzees and baboons are well known for their intelligence, it is not really surprising that to some extent individuals of the two species are able to communicate with each other. One day, for example, a female baboon passed very close to

---

[1] From "Out on a Limb with Father" by Michael Pine. From *Literary Cavalcade*, © 1956. Reprinted by permission of Scholastic Magazines, Inc.

Mr. Worzle (a chimpanzee) and seemed to startle him slightly. He raised his arm and gave a soft threat bark, at which she instantly crouched and presented submissively. Mr. Worzle then reached his hand toward her rump and almost certainly touched her in reassurance. At any rate her posture became relaxed and she sat quite close to him. We have seen many other incidents of this sort.[1]

EXERCISE A First, underline the topic sentence of each paragraph below. Then give the method used to develop the topic: *details, examples, reasons,* or an *incident.*

1. Although exercise should be an important part of all our lives, there are times when exercise can be overdone or badly managed. If you aren't feeling well, your body is trying to tell you something and you should not exercise at all. At the very least, modify your program. You should never exercise after a severe illness, without word from your doctor. You should avoid exercising under dangerous conditions. Icy surfaces, lung-biting cold or excessive heat and humidity can be damaging to the body. Never exercise with improper equipment. Finally, avoid sudden, violent exercise, especially as you grow older.

Developed by ....

2. Believe it or else: aerosol sprays are the deadly product X. The propellant gases they release may be a time bomb. Harmless in the air we breathe, these gases slowly rise miles above the earth where years later they apparently attack the ozone, the layer of the upper atmosphere that protects us from the sun's most lethal ultraviolet rays. Without that ozone shield, man could not survive.[2]

Developed by ....

3. Canada certainly has its share of curious rules and regulations. Did you know that in Moose Jaw, Saskatchewan there was a by-law requiring pedestrians to walk on the right side of the sidewalk? Etobicoke, Ontario had a by-law regarding the maximum temperature allowable for bath water. The residents of Lakefield, Ontario felt compelled to restrict birds from singing for more than a half hour between 8 a.m. and 10 p.m. From 10 p.m. to 8 am. warbling was restricted to 15 minutes. Section 331 of the Canadian Criminal Code states that it is illegal to send a telegram or letter threatening a bird. Several cities and towns still have by-laws on the books regarding the care and feeding of horses.

Developed by ....

[1] From *In the Shadow of Man* by Jane van Lawick-Goodall. Reprinted by permission of Houghton Mifflin Company and Collins Publishers.
[2] From "Not With a Bang, But With a Psssssst!" in *New Times* Magazine, March 7, 1975. Reprinted by permission of the publisher.

4. In spite of the exercise of every caution in avoiding inferences and reporting only what is seen and experienced, we all remain prone to error, since the making of inferences is a quick, almost automatic process. We may watch a car weaving as it goes down the road and say, "Look at that *drunken driver*," although what we *see* is only *the irregular motion of the car*. The writer once saw a man leave a one-dollar tip at a lunch counter and hurry out. Just as the writer was wondering why anyone would leave so generous a tip in so modest an establishment, the waitress came, picked up the dollar, put it in the cash register as she punched up ninety cents, and put a dime in her pocket. In other words, the writer's description to himself of the event, "a one-dollar tip," turned out to be not a report but an inference.[1]

Developed by ....

EXERCISE B Each of the following topic sentences may be developed by at least one of the methods described in this lesson. Decide which method you would use to develop the topic, and write it on the *final* line. Then, on the lines below each sentence, list the details, examples, or reasons, or write a note summarizing a story which you would use to develop the topic.

1. I have several ambitions in life, not just one. ....

....

....

....

Developed by ....

2. Sometimes .... is very annoying. ....

....

....

....

Developed by ....

3. Homework should not be assigned over a vacation. ....

....

....

....

....

Developed by ....

[1] From *Language in Thought and Action* by S. I. Hayakawa. Reprinted by permission of Harcourt Brace Jovanovich, Inc., and George Allen & Unwin Ltd.

4. I prefer life in the country (city) to life in the city (country). . . . .

. . . .

. . . .

. . . .

. . . .

Developed by . . . .

WRITING ASSIGNMENT   From the four paragraphs outlined above, choose the one you think you could develop best. Write the topic sentence first. Then develop the topic, using the material from your outline. Write 100–150 words.

WRITING ASSIGNMENT   Use one of the following as a topic sentence and develop it, using at least 100 words. In parentheses are suggested ways to develop the ideas. By answering these questions, you can make your paragraph specific and interesting. If you wish, you may change the wording of the sentence you choose.

1. Observing the faces of people while walking down the street can be an interesting experience. (*Details:* What can you tell about the people you see? What do you imagine each person does? Have you ever been proven wrong in your judgment?)
2. At times I act as though I am superstitious. (*Examples:* When do you act superstitious? Exactly what do you do? Can you present three particularly interesting actions?)
3. Everyone should have a hobby. (*Reasons:* Why is a hobby desirable? In what ways does it contribute to a person's happiness?)
4. I have difficulty making friends with other people's pets. (*Incident:* Which one of your experiences can best illustrate this statement? What did you do to make friends? How did the pet respond?)
5. If people keep calm during a severe storm (tornado, hurricane, blizzard), they can avoid getting hurt. (*Incident:* What is an incident that can prove the topic? How did a calm person avoid injuries in a particular storm? What exactly happened?)
6. I don't (do) like diving. (*Reasons:* What thoughts flash across your mind as you stand on the end of a diving board? What do you dislike (like) about diving: the height of the board, the apparent solidity of the water, hitting the cold water?)
7. A television set is an idiot box. (*Reasons:* Why exactly is a television set an idiot box? Why would only an idiot watch certain programs? Why do you think some television characters behave like idiots?)
8. A television set is a wonderful teaching machine. (*Reasons:* Why is television a better teacher than a lecturer or a textbook? Why do television fans learn more in front of television sets than they do in classrooms? Why do they remember what they learn?)
9. Homesickness can be a miserable illness. (*Story:* What do you remember about one of your most severe attacks of homesickness? How was it a miserable experience? What happened? What did you think, feel, do?)

10. Almost anything can be a miracle. (*Examples:* What are a half-dozen things that could be considered miracles? Could such things as a sunrise or a flower be looked upon as a miracle? Do any other "ordinary" occurrences at times appear especially wonderful?)

WRITING ASSIGNMENT   Choose one of the following topic sentences, make an outline, and then write a unified, interesting, well-developed paragraph of at least 100 words.

1. Doubting your own ability can be a serious handicap.
2. I prefer swimming in a lake to swimming in the ocean.
3. Although you may not know it, I am really a wonderful person.
4. In the near future a solution will have to be found to the problem of feeding all the hungry people in the world.
5. I think it is very important (not very important) for Canada to build up its military strength.
6. Many people have recurring dreams that trouble them.
7. If I ever write books, they will be tales of science fiction (adventure, romance, etc.).
8. A cartoon can often make a point quicker than an essay.
9. I never have trouble writing, but once the writing becomes an assignment, my mind becomes blocked.
10. One day I would like (not like) to throw my hat into the political arena.

Arranging Ideas in a Paragraph

Achieve coherence in a paragraph by arranging details in chronological order, spatial order, or order of importance.

Paragraphs in which sentences flow smoothly and naturally from one to another are said to have *coherence*. One of the best ways to achieve coherence is through a clear arrangement of ideas.

When you are writing about how to make or do something, such as how to build a campfire or how to somersault, organize the steps of the process in the order in which they must be carried out. This is called *chronological,* or *time, order.* Chronological order is also useful in story writing. The following example of chronological order is a brief story about an after-dinner walk. Words which help indicate chronological order are underlined.

A SUNSET IN ETHIOPIA

<u>After our meal</u> we went for a stroll across the plateau. The day was already drawing to a close as we sat down upon a ledge of rock near the lip of the western precipice. From where we sat, as though perched high upon a cloud, we looked out into a gigantic void. <u>As we sat,</u> the sun sank fast, and the heavens in the western sky began to glow. It was a coppery fire <u>at first,</u> the orange streaked with aquamarine; but <u>rapidly</u> the firmament expanded into an explosion of red and orange that burst across the sky sending tongues of flame through the feathery clouds to the very limits of the heavens. <u>When the flames had reached their zenith,</u> a great quantity of storks came flying from the south. <u>Then,</u> gathering together, they flew off into the setting sun, leaving us alone in peace to contemplate. The sun died beyond the hills; and the fire withdrew.[1]

It is sometimes useful to describe something or to tell a story by organizing details according to their position in space: to the left, to the right, behind, in front, etc. The following paragraph shows how *spatial order* can help achieve coherence.

THE STUDY

I worked at a commodious green-topped table placed directly <u>in front of the west window</u> which looked out over the prairie. <u>In the corner at my right</u> were all my books, in shelves I had made and painted myself. <u>On the blank wall at my left</u> the dark, old-fashioned wallpaper was covered by a large map of ancient Rome, the work of some German scholar. Cleric had ordered it for me when he was sending for books from abroad. <u>Over the bookcase</u> hung a photograph of the Tragic Theater at Pompeii, which he had given me from his collection. When I sat at work I half-faced a deep, upholstered chair which stood at the end of my table, its high back against the wall.[2]

[1] From *Sanamu: Adventures in Search of African Art* by Robert Dick-Read. Copyright © 1964 by Robert Dick-Read. Reprinted by permission of Curtis Brown Ltd. and A. P. Watt & Son Ltd.
[2] From *My Ántonia* by Willa Cather. Copyright 1918, 1926, 1946 by Willa Sibert Cather; copyright 1954 by Edith Lewis. Reprinted by permission of Houghton Mifflin Company.

When a paragraph states reasons, they may be arranged in logical order: from the least to the most important reason or from the most to the least important reason. Reasons arranged in their order of importance are easier for the reader to follow.

In the following paragraph, the author lists the destructive effects of acid rain, from the least important effect (holes in nylon stockings) to the most important effect (the death of freshwater fish).

ACID RAIN

Acid rain is very destructive. It eats holes in nylon stockings and corrodes stone and metal buildings. Many beautiful statues the world over have been severely damaged by the fallout of acid pollutants. Acid rain also threatens many types of living things, particularly fish in freshwater lakes. In many lakes throughout our country, bass and trout have vanished. Restocking the lakes with new fish has been largely useless.

Occasionally a writer may arrange details by more than one method. For example, a paragraph about tornadoes may focus on the creation of tornadoes (chronological) and the shape of tornadoes (spatial).

EXERCISE In the space provided, write C (for chronological), S (for spatial), or I (for order of importance) to show which method is best for developing each topic. Choose only one method for each topic.

1. . . . . History of the Panama Canal
2. . . . . Why everyone should wear seat belts
3. . . . . Steps in baking a cake
4. . . . . A baseball stadium
5. . . . . Redecorating a room
6. . . . . The inside of a space station
7. . . . . The qualities of a friend
8. . . . . Cleaning out the garage
9. . . . . The advantages of a vegetarian diet
10. . . . . A school activity
11. . . . . How to fix a desk lamp
12. . . . . Plans for the future
13. . . . . Drawing a map
14. . . . . A chemistry experiment
15. . . . . The reasons for electing a candidate
16. . . . . A favourite painting
17. . . . . How to play basketball
18. . . . . Why we play basketball
19. . . . . Where we play basketball
20. . . . . How to prepare for a test

WRITING ASSIGNMENT Write one paragraph using one of the topics in the preceding exercise or a topic of your own choice. Arrange the details, examples, or reasons in your paragraph chronologically, spatially, or in order of importance.

Using Transitional Devices

Transitional devices are connecting words or phrases that show the relationship between details, examples, or reasons in a paragraph.

Transitional devices help to connect sentences and to show the arrangement of a paragraph. The following list contains some of the most common transitional devices.

TO SHOW CHRONOLOGICAL ARRANGEMENT:

After	Following
At the same time	Later
At first	Soon
Finally	Then

TO SHOW SPATIAL ARRANGEMENT:

Above	On top of
Below	Opposite from
Close by	To the right (*or* left)
Next to	Up to

TO SHOW ORDER OF IMPORTANCE:

First (second, third, *etc.*)	Moreover
Furthermore	To begin with
In addition	

In the following paragraph transitional devices are underlined. The author uses them to arrange the details of his paragraph chronologically.

A KITTEN AT PLAY

A kitten is playing with its classical plaything, a ball of wool. Invariably it begins by pawing at the object, first gently and inquiringly with outstretched forearm and inwardly flexed paw. Then, with extended claws, it draws the ball toward itself, pushes it away again, or jumps a few steps backward, crouching. It lies low, raises its head with tense expression, glaring at the plaything. Then its head drops so suddenly that you expect its chin to bump the floor. The hind feet perform peculiar, alternately treading and clawing movements as though the kitten were seeking a firm hold from which to spring. Suddenly it bounds in a great semicircle and lands on its toy with stiff forepaws, pressed closely together. It will even bite it, if the game has reached a pitch of some intensity. Again it pushes the ball, and this time it rolls under a cupboard which stands too close to the floor for the kitten to get underneath. With an elegant "practiced" movement, it reaches with one arm into the space and fishes its plaything out again. It is at once clear to anyone who has ever watched a cat catching a mouse, that our kitten, which we have reared apart from its mother, is performing all those highly specialized movements which aid the cat in the hunting of its most important prey—the mouse. In the wild state, this constitutes its "daily bread."[1]

WRITING ASSIGNMENT   Use the following paragraph outline or one of your own to write a paragraph in which transitional devices help connect the sentences. Underline the transitional devices in the paragraph you write.

TOPIC   Preparing for a long-distance run
1. Selecting proper equipment
2. Eating the right foods
3. Choosing a course
4. Stretching muscles

[1] From "On Feline Play" in *Man Meets Dog* by Konrad Lorenz. Copyright 1953 by Konrad Lorenz. Reprinted by permission of Houghton Mifflin Company, and Konrad Lorenz.

Writing a Narrative Paragraph

The narrative paragraph tells "what happened."

The narrative paragraph tells a brief story or ancedote. It focuses on a single event, such as a visit to the dentist or an interesting dream. Often a narrative paragraph can illustrate a topic such as a parent's kindness or a friend's absent-mindedness. Details in the paragraph are usually arranged in chronological order.

In the following example of a narrative paragraph, the author tells the story of a large meteor's fall to earth. Notice that the author includes specific details of place and time.

METEOR

Details of Place and Time

Transitional Device

One of the most spectacular falls occurred in Norton County, Kansas, in 1948. It was a sunny February day with a blue sky overhead. At about five in the afternoon in the small town of Jennings, eleven-year-old Creta Carter was taking the family laundry down from a clothesline in her backyard. Suddenly a brilliant ball of fire blossomed out in the clear sky, flashing directly across her field of view. Several denotations of sound followed rapidly one upon another like a cannonade, and the fireball turned into a red streak followed by an angry boiling cloud. The air was filled with hissing sounds. Undismayed by frightening apparitions, Creta calmly watched the smoking mass fall and marked the place where it disappeared behind the town's largest building. Although the ball of fire was bright enough to be seen for hundreds of miles, Creta was one of the few people to have her face tipped up to the sky at exactly the instant when the object burst into flames.[1]

Before you write a narrative paragraph, make an outline of the events you wish to narrate. List each step in chronological order. The following outline could serve for the model paragraph.

TOPIC The fall of a meteor
1. Sunny February day, five in the afternoon
2. Creta Carter in her backyard
3. Ball of fire in the sky
4. Cannonlike sounds
5. A red streak
6. Hissing sounds
7. Disappearance of the meteor behind a building

[1] From *Earth's Aura* by Louise B. Young, Copyright © 1977 by Louise B. Young. Reprinted by permission of Alfred A. Knopf, Inc.

WRITING ASSIGNMENT Using one of the following topics or one of your own, write a narrative paragraph. Prepare an outline in chronological order before you begin to write.

A moment of good luck
Teamwork and the success it brings
My first experience with _____
A lesson I learned the hard way
People are not always what they seem

Writing a Descriptive Paragraph

A descriptive paragraph tells what something looks, sounds, feels, tastes, or smells like.

A descriptive paragraph usually focuses on a single object or scene and depends upon a close observation of details. To convey impressions vividly, a descriptive paragraph uses words that appeal to the reader's senses. For example, on a hot day, the sidewalk *glitters* (sight), the insects *hiss* (sound), the chrome on a car *scorches* the fingers (touch), and so on. Effective nouns and verbs are the most important aspect of a descriptive paragraph.

The following paragraph describes a turtle as it moves along the ground. Notice the close observation of details, the vivid verbs and nouns, and the appeal to the senses. Notice, too, that the writer arranges details in spatial order, which is often the best organization for a descriptive paragraph.

THE TURTLE

Appeal to Senses

Close Observation of Details

Vivid Verbs

Concrete Nouns

The sun lay on the grass and warmed it, and in the shade under the grass the insects moved, ants and ant lions to set traps for them, grasshoppers to jump into the air and flick their yellow wings for a second, sow bugs like little armadillos, plodding restlessly on many tender feet. And over the grass at the roadside a land turtle crawled, turning aside for nothing, dragging his high-domed shell over the grass. His hard legs and yellow-nailed feet threshed slowly through the grass, not really walking, but boosting and dragging his shell along. The barley beards slid off his shell, and the clover burrs fell on him and rolled to the ground. His horny beak was partly open, and his fierce, humorous eyes stared straight ahead. He came over the grass leaving a beaten trail behind him, and the hill, which was the highway embankment, reared up ahead of him.[1]

Before you write a descriptive paragraph, make an outline of the scene or object you wish to describe. Arrange details in the outline in spatial order. The following outline could serve for the model paragraph.

TOPIC   A turtle moving in the grass
1. The sun's warmth
2. Insects under the grass
3. Turtle moving over the grass
4. Trail behind, embankment ahead

[1] From *The Grapes of Wrath* by John Steinbeck. Copyright 1939; © renewed 1967 by John Steinbeck. Reprinted by permission of Viking Penguin Inc., McIntosh and Otis, Inc., and Curtis Brown Ltd.

WRITING ASSIGNMENT Using one of the topics below or a topic of your own, write a descriptive paragraph. Prepare an outline before you begin to write. Be sure to include vivid nouns and verbs that appeal to the senses. Organize the description spatially.

A favourite room at home
A sunset
A scary place
A local meeting spot
The appearance of an unusual person

Writing an Expository Paragraph That Gives Information

An expository paragraph may give information about something by presenting facts, examples, or reasons.

You have already learned the principles of organizing an expository paragraph. It should state its topic clearly, it should be arranged in logical order, and it should contain transitional devices to join sentences and to make the arrangement clear.

The following expository paragraph gives information about tsunamis (tsōō-nä′mē), or tidal waves. Notice that the writer develops the paragraph by means of examples.

TSUNAMIS

Topic Sentence   Tsunamis have an extraordinary range.[1] In 1833, for example, when volcanic explosions destroyed Krakatoa, an island between Java and Sumatra, seismic waves traveled all around the world.[2] A 1946 earthquake in the Aleutian trench caused a wave that did great damage when it hit the Hawaiian Islands some 2,200 miles away.[3] The wave that followed the 1964 Good Friday Alaska quake wrought considerable destruction on the Oregon and northern California coasts, including the death of a family camping overnight on an Oregon beach.*

Examples (1–3)

The following topic outline could serve for the model paragraph.

TOPIC The range of tsunamis
1. Waves from 1833 Krakatoa explosion
2. Wave from Aleutian trench to Hawaiian Islands
3. Wave after 1964 Alaska quake

WRITING ASSIGNMENT Use the following list of information to write an expository paragraph. Begin your paragraph with a topic sentence. Arrange the information in logical order. (Be sure to use complete sentences.)

Five planets visible to the naked eye: Mars, Venus, Mercury, Saturn, Jupiter
The order of these planets, by distance from the Sun: Mercury (closest), Venus, Mars, Jupiter, Saturn
The brightest of these planets: Venus
The smallest of these planets: Mercury
The largest of these planets: Jupiter
The least bright of these planets: Saturn
The planet most often thought to support life: Mars

*Excerpt from *More Misinformation* by Tom Burnam. (Lippincott/Crowell). Copyright © 1980 by Tom Burnam. Reprinted by permission of Harper & Row, Publishers Inc.

WRITING ASSIGNMENT   Using one of the lists provided, write an expository paragraph that conveys information. Before you begin to write, you must prepare a topic outline based on the lists. Be sure to state your topic in a topic sentence, to arrange facts or examples in a logical order, and to use transitional devices wherever necessary. If you wish, you may prepare your own list to work with.

A. Basketball
   1. dribbling
   2. the tip-off
   3. passing
   4. shooting
   5. the lay-up
   6. the dunk

B. Television
   1. schedule
   2. personalities
   3. different kinds of shows
   4. commercials
   5. reruns

Writing an Expository Paragraph That Explains

An expository paragraph may explain a process, or how something works.

When you tell someone how to sharpen a knife or how to prepare a recipe, you are explaining a process. To write an effective explanation of a process, you must be sure to include all the essential steps in their correct order. Transitional expressions, such as *first, next,* and *finally,* help to make this order clear.

Steps in an explanation of a process are most often arranged in chronological order.

The following paragraph explains the process of baking cornbread in a Dutch oven. Its steps are arranged chronologically.

BAKING CORNBREAD

Steps
Arranged
in Chrono-
logical
Order
(1–7)

Dutch ovens were usually used for baking bread and biscuits, but they could also be used for baking cakes and potatoes, roasting meats, and heating soup and stew. Here's how to bake cornbread in one. [1]Preheat the oven and the lid on the coals. [2]Then carefully grease the whole inside of the oven with a piece of pork rind. [3]Mix up the batter by combining two cups of cornmeal, one cup of flour, one cup of buttermilk, and a spoonful of salt and soda. [4]Sprinkle a handful of cornmeal on the sides and bottom inside the oven so the bread won't stick, and then pour the batter in, making sure the oven is level so the bread will be the same thickness all around. [5]Using some tongs, place the lid on the oven and cover it with hot coals. [6]The bread will be ready in fifteen to twenty minutes depending on how hot the coals are. [7]It can be slid out by removing the lid and tipping the oven, or it can be cut right in the oven and taken out with a fork or large spoon.*

WRITING ASSIGNMENT Using the following list of information, write an expository paragraph that explains a process. Begin your paragraph with a topic sentence. Arrange the information in a logical order.

Honey is made from nectar, which bees gather from different plants and flowers.
Honey is taken from the hive by beekeepers.
Bees store honey in wax cells in the hive.
Nectar changes into honey through enzyme action in the bodies of bees.
The honey ripens in the hive and thickens because of evaporation.

*Excerpt from *The Foxfire Book* edited by Eliot Wigginton. Copyright © 1968, 1970, 1971, 1972 by The Foxfire Fund, Inc. Reprinted by permission of Doubleday & Company, Inc.

WRITING ASSIGNMENT Using one of the topics below or one of your own, write an expository paragraph that explains a process. Before you begin to write, prepare a topic outline. Be sure that your paragraph contains a strong topic sentence, organizes its steps in logical order, and contains transitional expressions where necessary.

How to fix a flat tire
How to keep score in tennis
How to fly a kite
How to repot plants
How to carve a pumpkin for Halloween

Paragraphing and Outlining a Composition

A paragraph is a series of sentences developing one topic. A composition is a series of paragraphs developing one central idea. For example, the paragraph on page 259 develops the topic that tsunamis, or tidal waves, travel great distances. If the writer wishes to discuss how people can protect themselves from tsunamis or what current research shows about these killer waves, he would use these ideas as topics for other paragraphs.

Dividing a composition into paragraphs makes it much easier to read. Readers know that a new paragraph means some kind of change in the content. When the writer starts a new paragraph, the readers, in effect, are being told that a different phase of the central idea is about to be discussed. In general, begin a new paragraph when you introduce a new topic.

An outline is an important aid in writing any composition. The outline of a composition lists in order the main topics, which are usually the topics of the paragraphs. These are preceded by Roman numerals. Subtopics, preceded by capital letters, are the supporting details that you use in developing a paragraph.

EXAMPLE   *Central Idea:* Tornadoes have violent winds which trigger freak accidents and cause much destruction.·

    I. Violent winds
      A. Break measuring instruments
      B. Probably whirl at speeds of over 750 km/h
      C. Create an area of low pressure, almost a vacuum
   II. Freakish accidents
      A. Straws pushed through wooden posts
      B. A baby carried 5 km without serious harm
      C. Whole house lifted 9 m
  III. Destructive force
      A. Property destroyed
      B. People killed

EXERCISE   As you read the following composition, decide what the central idea is and study the plan of its development. Then fill in the blanks below, giving the central idea, the main topics, and the subtopics of the outline.

WINDSHIELD WASHER

Handy windshield squirt-washers can be made easily from empty plastic bottles of the type used for spray deodorants. Use two of these sprayers—one containing water for muddy windshields and the other a window-cleaning solution—for cutting through oily film.

Remove the nozzles of the sprayers by giving them a slight twisting pull. Wash out the containers and the nozzles before refilling. Replace the nozzles securely, cap tightly with original stoppers, and label with waterproof tape.

When the windshield needs cleaning, squirt water or cleaner solution on the glass and let your windshield wipers do the rest. For best results, the plastic bottle should be made to give a squirting rather than a spraying action by tilting the nozzle slightly lower than the rest of the bottle.[1]

Central Idea: ....

   I. ....

      A. ....

      B. ....

   II. ....

      A. ....

      B. ....

      C. ....

      D. ....

 III. ....

      A. ....

      B. ....

WRITING ASSIGNMENT Write a composition of 3 or 4 paragraphs, expressing your ideas on one of the subjects in the list below or, if you wish, on a subject of your own. First write what the central idea of your composition will be. Then make an outline by paragraphs like the one you made in the preceding exercise. The outline is to be handed in with your composition. Be sure you have a topic sentence in each paragraph and that each paragraph sticks to its topic.

Your purpose in this composition is to show how well you can organize ideas. In other words, do not tell a story.

SUGGESTED COMPOSITION TOPICS

1. How to build birdhouses
2. How to have a healthy dog
3. Types of singers
4. Teen-age eating habits
5. Three ways to make friends
6. How to be different
7. How to get high grades
8. Planning a party
9. How to avoid boredom
10. Types of teen-age activities

[1] "Windshield Washer" by Alex H. Kizer, Jr., in *1001 How-to Ideas.* Reprinted by permission of *Science and Mechanics.*

SUGARING-OFF FESTIVITIES

1. Mention the words maple sugar to Canadians, and everyone immediately conjures up romantic visions out of the past. How easy it is to picture pioneers in their horse-drawn sleighs stopping in the snowy forests. Imagine them gathering around huge iron kettles hung over roaring fires as a thick, heavy cloud laden with the sweet, intoxicating aroma of maple syrup settles about the trees. Is there anything that reminds people so vividly of pioneer days and Canadian heritage as do thoughts of maple sugar? Ah, but people would be wrong if they were to believe these visions belong exclusively to the past. While the production of maple sugar products has changed in some ways over the years, the romantic spirit of old-time sugaring-off festivities has not been lost.

2. The technique of making maple syrup was discovered by the Indians. When the early settlers arrived in North America, they learned from the Indians how to use maple syrup for all their sugar supplies. With their European utensils, the settlers developed new techniques for more efficient syrup production. They realized, for example, that tapping with an axe, as the Indians had, caused considerable damage to the trees. Today, sugar bush operators drill holes with a special wood-boring bit. The operators know, too, that they must drill new holes each year, a few centimetres from the previous year's holes. This way the tree stays healthy while producing the maximum amount of sap. Once the sap had been collected, the Indians would drop hot stones into a wooden trough to boil the sap, and the settlers used a copper or iron kettle over an open fire. Now sugar bush operators have an evaporator building that houses a complicated system of siphons and pans. Today, as well, syrup producers place a disinfectant tablet into each drilled hole, in order to prevent the growth of mould and to ensure that the sap will run for a longer time and will always be clean and fresh, unlike the maple syrup produced by the Indians and the settlers, which was strong and smoky in flavour, dark in colour, and contained many impurities.

3. These and other changes reflect the operator's increased knowledge of sanitation and forestry. While this knowledge adds to the efficiency of syrup production, very little has interfered with the original pioneer-feeling of the whole procedure. The sap is still collected outside, on a warm day under a late winter sun. Families can still go on outings to the woods, taking advantage of the inexpensive tours offered at many sugar bush farms. There they can still

enjoy hot sap, syrup, and toffee as they learn about the history of syrup production. And although it comes from large evaporator houses rather than an open kettle, the winter air is still heavy with the heady aroma of maple syrup.

In the space to the left, write the letter of the words that best complete each statement. (Add 10 points for each correct answer.)

.... 1. The primary purpose of the author is (a) to tell a story, (b) to describe a process, (c) to write vivid description.

.... 2. The central idea of the composition is that (a) maple sugar recalls the past, (b) many changes have been made in syrup production, (c) the romantic feeling of sugaring-off has not changed.

.... 3. Paragraph 1 is developed by (a) reasons, (b) examples, (c) facts.

.... 4. Paragraph 1 (a) sets forth the main idea of the composition, (b) gives the author's personal feelings about maple syrup, (c) explains why people like maple products.

.... 5. Paragraph 2 is developed by (a) facts, (b) examples, (c) incident.

.... 6. In paragraph 2 the topic is (a) stated in the first sentence, (b) given in the last sentence, (c) not stated but clearly implied.

.... 7. A good topic sentence covering paragraph 2 would be (a) Since the Indians first started producing maple syrup, several innovations have been introduced. (b) The early settlers enjoyed maple syrup. (c) Maple trees now remain healthier.

.... 8. Paragraph 3 is developed by a combination of (a) examples and incidents, (b) facts and incidents, (c) facts and examples.

.... 9. The purpose of paragraph 3 is to (a) make a last point, (b) summarize the composition, (c) suggest topics not yet covered in the composition.

.... 10. In general this article is developed by (a) reasons, (b) facts, (c) examples, (d) incidents.

WRITING ASSIGNMENT Your assignment is to write a composition setting forth an opinion or idea. First set forth your opinion or idea; then strive to convince your readers of the truth of your opinion by vividly describing an event that illustrates or supports your idea.

266

Choose one of the following sentences (or use a sentence of your own), and use it as the central idea for your composition. Write a short introductory paragraph stating the central idea and explaining its exact meaning. Then prove your point by giving a vivid account of an event that is interesting, specific, and pertinent. Finally, write a short concluding paragraph that restates in an emphatic way your central idea.

COMPOSITION TOPICS

1. Basketball (football, tennis) is full of surprises.
2. High school is full of disappointments.
3. I am a firm believer in children's liberation.
4. Common sense is as important as book learning.
5. Television is not really a wasteland.
6. A person in love is tolerant, not blind.
7. Sitting at a desk in school all day makes me feel roped in.
8. Lucky breaks are the keys to success.
9. In reality, luck is pluck.
10. Backseat drivers cause more accidents than they prevent.
11. At times all of us are players acting parts as though the world were a stage.
12. An apparent calamity can turn out to be a real blessing.
13. I know that experience is the best teacher.
14. Chivalry is not dead.
15. A childhood experience can explain an irrational fear.
16. It pays to listen after the bell rings!
17. Prejudice is ignorance.
18. Never do today what you can put off until tomorrow.
19. Some times it is better to run than to fight.
20. The punishment should fit the crime.

REVIEW EXERCISE B Carefully read the following composition so that you can correctly fill in the blanks that follow. Observe especially the way that the author organizes and develops his ideas.

MOVIE STUNTS

1. When we see a movie, we are often amazed at the dangerous feats that stuntmen perform so realistically. Although there is a great deal of risk involved, stuntmen have devised tricks over the years that make their work easier. Three stunts that have been made safer are (1) falls, (2) fires, and (3) shootings.

2. Sometimes stuntmen must fall 20 or 30 metres through the air before they hit ground. They devise a soft landing-place, which they call a rig. Usually, the rig is a pile of boxes covered in mattresses. The rig can't be too soft, though, or the stuntman would fly back up into the air. This all happens out of camera range, but sometimes directors want the real effect of a body landing. Then the stuntman buries a large bag in the ground, covering it lightly with earth. Whatever the rig looks like, it is important

that the stuntman falls on his back, absorbing the impact with all of his body. Otherwise, he can be fatally injured.

3. While falls probably allow the most room for error, getting set on fire is not a carefree stunt either. Fire-retardant clothes must be worn. These are painted with a special glue that is quick to burn and results in bright flames which show up well on film. Sometimes stuntmen wear false hair to keep their own from burning. If the entire body is to go up in flame and the actor is not recognizable, stuntmen will wear a fire-suit and oxygen mask. However the stunt is done, the fire is always put out extremely quickly.

4. Falls and fires are now relatively safe, but would you want a loaded gun pointed at your chest? In early films, real guns were actually fired in the vicinity of the actor. Now there are two different methods of 'killing' with bullets. Sometimes a small, sticky ball of red 'blood' is fired from an airgun. It breaks open on contact and blood appears to come from a bullet-hole. On other occasions, the stuntman wears a small explosive under his clothes which he can fire himself. It makes a loud noise and blows a hole in his clothes. While there are many other fascinating stunts being performed everyday in the movies, falls, fires, and shootings have always provided great excitement for the audience and the stuntmen.

In your own words, complete the following statements about the article you have just read. (Add 10 points for each statement supported by the article.)

1. The first paragraph is not a presentation of the first main point in the author's outline, but it does serve to ....

....

2. The first sentence is closely related to the title because of the repetition of ....

3. The central idea of the composition is ....

4. The author's main points are ....

....

5. The topic of paragraph 2 is stated in its .... sentence.

6. The method used to develop this topic is (examples, reasons, story).

....

7. The author makes a good transition (bridges the gaps between ideas) by referring to .... and .... at the start of paragraph 3.

8. The author develops this topic by using ....

9. What links paragraph 4 to the rest of the composition? . . . .
. . . .

10. The topic of paragraph 4 is . . . .

Now on a separate sheet of paper, write an outline of "Movie Stunts." You should find three main topics and at least two subtopics for each main topic.

WRITING ASSIGNMENT   Your assignment is to write a composition (about 4 paragraphs), using the technique shown in "Movie Stunts." First decide upon your central idea. Then write an outline of the main points you will cover. In the first paragraph of your composition, state your central idea, repeat the key words or ideas of the title, and list the main points of your outline. Then develop each main point into a paragraph by using specific facts, reasons, or examples. Discuss your first main point in the second paragraph, the second point in the third paragraph, and so on. Bridge the gaps between paragraphs by referring to preceding key words or ideas. In your final paragraph write a strong last sentence that emphatically restates your central theme.

COMPOSITION TOPICS

1. Why people love science fiction
2. Why you are your dog's best friend
3. Why baseball is more popular than ever before
4. Why fads attract teen-agers
5. Why we keep making and breaking resolutions
6. Why television will never completely replace the movies
7. Why people study history
8. Why I shall always be an optimist (*or* a pessimist)
9. Why my friends like me
10. Why a sense of humour is often helpful

Letter Writing: The Form of the Friendly Letter

A friendly letter, like a conversation with a friend, is a two-way process. Unless you write letters yourself, you are not likely to have the enjoyment of receiving them from your friends. With this thought in mind, master the proper form for a friendly letter. Think, too, about the qualities that an effective friendly letter should have.

There are many acceptable forms for letters. There is, however, one form which is always correct. In the following lessons you will review this form. The parts of a friendly letter are shown below.

1. The letter is centred on the page with margins at top and bottom and on both sides. Even if the letter continues on a second page, there should be a margin at the bottom of the first page.

2. The *heading* is in the upper right-hand corner, but it is not crowded far into the corner. Remember the margins. The first line of the heading is the writer's street address, or the number of the post office box or rural route (for example, *P.O. Box 785 or R.R. 3)*. The second line is the writer's city and province, separated by a comma. The postal code is listed on the third line.

> 17 Montrose Avenue
> Burnaby, British Columbia
> V5G 1W2
> April 23, 1984
>
> Dear Joan,
> _____
> _____
> _____
> _____
> _____
> _____
>
>   Sincerely yours,
>   Helen

A Model Friendly Letter Form

The fourth line is the date, with a comma after the number of the day.

3. The *salutation* is *Dear . . .* followed by a comma. It begins at the left margin.

4. The *closing* begins just to the right of the middle of the page and is followed by a comma. Only the first word is capitalized. The following are commonly used as complimentary closes: *Sincerely yours, Love, As ever, Affectionately yours,* or just *Sincerely,* or *Affectionately.*

Place the address and the return address on the envelope as shown below.

A Model Envelope

EXERCISE   The parts of the following headings are mixed up and out of the proper order. On a sheet of paper write the headings correctly and add omitted punctuation.

1. March 5 1980
   Dalhousie New Brunswick
   Box 835
   E0K 1B0

2. 250 Evergreen Avenue
   January 24 1979
   Montreal Quebec
   H3G 7B5

3. Regina Saskatchewan
   P.O. Box 215
   December 5 1979
   S4S 3E9

4. St. John's Newfoundland
   July 14 1980
   P.O. Box 248
   A0S 0G0

Letter Writing:
The Contents of the Friendly Letter

A friendly letter is very personal. It is like a visit from its writer. What is said and the style in which it is said should sound like the person writing the letter. Above all else, when you write a letter, *be yourself, be natural.* This does not mean that if you are a poor speller, you may misspell several words, or that if you find it hard to be neat, you may send a messy letter. It does mean that you should write as you would talk if you were with the friend to whom you are writing.

Study the following bits of advice on writing a friendly letter.

1. Write what you think will interest your friend. A letter to a friend your age will, of course, differ from a letter to your grandmother.

2. Give a detailed account of one topic rather than a general account of many topics. Details are interesting; generalities are dull.

3. Don't begin with, "How are you? I am well," or "I haven't anything else to do, so I thought I'd write you a letter."

4. Express interest in what your friend has been doing.

Here is a good friendly letter written to a member of the "gang" who has moved away.

125 Greene Avenue
Calgary S.E., Alberta
T2K 3B5
May 14, 1984

Dear Arnold,

Say, do you have any idea how much the editors of our school paper are missing you this year? Now that you're not here to give us your "latest scoops," our paper is really suffering. Honest! In fact, the last issue was only four pages, not six.

Mimo told me yesterday, when we took our driving lesson, that he had a postcard from you last week. He also told me to be sure to bring you up-to-date about our driving experience. Yesterday was an experience all right! After thirty hours of classroom work, we've started work on our six hours of actual driving. Have you ever tried to drive in harness? Well, I've got black and blue marks all over me because of those seat belts in the front seats. Boy, those sudden stops really catch a person off guard!

I hope that you can come over for a weekend soon. Dad and Mom say to insist that you do. What can I say to entice you? Well, the new bowling alley, just six blocks from our house, is finished now. After losing the challenge tennis match at camp last summer, I've decided to take up bowling seriously—and I now boast that I know I can beat you. Want to show me I'm wrong?

Tomorrow night I'm going to a party at Hank's, and I'll tell you all about that in my next letter.

Sincerely,
Nick

WRITING ASSIGNMENT Write a friendly letter that is interesting and in acceptable form. Use regular stationery. Fold and place the letter in a properly addressed envelope to hand in.

Here are some suggestions for this assignment.

1. Write a letter to a friend your own age. Make your letter interesting by giving specific details about the people, places, and activities that you know your friend will want to hear about.
2. Write a letter to an older person, such as a grandparent, an uncle, or a former teacher. Make the content of your letter fit the interests of the receiver. For instance, a grandparent would be especially interested in family news; a former teacher would probably be interested in your activities at school; an uncle might like to hear all about your recent camping trip.
3. Choose one of the following situations calling for a friendly letter and write the letter.

   a. You and one of your friends had been planning for weeks to give a party at your home. The invitations had been sent out; all preparations had been completed. On the morning of the day of the party, your friend developed appendicitis and underwent an operation. You held the party alone. Write a letter to your friend in the hospital, telling him (her) all about the party, which he (she) missed.

   b. Your school has just decided to have co-ed gym classes and teams. Write to your cousin, who lives in another province, and give your reactions.

   c. Imagine that you have been travelling for two weeks in another province or country. Write a letter to a friend at home telling what has impressed you most. You might mention differences and similarities in language, food, amusements, climate, clothing, or industries.

Letter Writing: Social Notes

The Thank-You Note   The thank-you note is a friendly letter written to thank someone for a gift or a favour. The best thing to do about a thank-you note is to write it! Putting it off is bad manners.

Many thank-you notes become long friendly letters. These are probably the best kind. However, a brief, sincere acknowledgment of a gift will do very well. Be sure to write a thank-you note promptly, and always mention specifically the gift or favour.

The form of a thank-you note is the same as the form of a friendly letter.

625 Redwood Street
Charlottetown, P.E.I.
C1A 5X7
March 27, 1984

Dear Aunt Ida,

   Thank you for the sweater you sent for my birthday. Mother says you knitted it yourself. I'm sure she's right, for it's beautifully made. The unusual pattern fascinated my friends when I wore the sweater to school yesterday.

   The whole family celebrated with me on the twenty-fourth. I selected the menu, and my selections were apparently popular. Uncle Arthur ate three helpings of everything. Grandmother and Aunt Edith were here too. There wasn't a cake crumb left!

   Are you coming down for Father's birthday? I hope so.

Love,
Ellen

A Model Thank-You Note

WRITING ASSIGNMENT   Write a thank-you note. Make the receiver of your letter know that you genuinely appreciate the gift or the favour. Be as specific as possible. Below are suggestions for this assignment.

1. Write a thank-you note for a gift you received during the holidays or on your birthday. Be sure to mention the gift by name. Give reasons why you like the gift.
2. Write to someone (the newspaper deliverer, a postal clerk, a neighbour, the driver of the school bus) who habitually goes out of the way to be kind or courteous to you.
3. Write your member of Parliament to thank him or her for voting for or against an important bill.

The Bread-and-Butter Note   A bread-and-butter note is a brief, friendly letter written to your hosts to thank them for their hospitality and for the good time you had during a visit. Write a bread-and-butter note very soon after your return from a stay at someone else's home. If you have been visiting a friend of your own age, you should write your note to his or her parents (or whoever were your hosts). This does not mean, of course, that you need not write a letter to your friend, too. You should write two letters under these circumstances.

Your hosts will appreciate your mentioning particular things that you especially enjoyed about your visit. They will also want to know that you arrived home safely.

The form of a bread-and-butter note is the same as the form of a friendly letter.

> 14 Riverview Avenue
> Brandon, Manitoba
> R7A 4X2
> July 15, 1983

Dear Mr. and Mrs. Perez,

Today I spent most of my time telling my family what a good time I had at Greenacres. I think they're tired of hearing about the things Louise and I did, but I'm enjoying reliving everything as I tell them about it. The trip to Winnipeg Beach on Wednesday and the party Saturday were wonderful.

My train was on time and Dad met me at the station. He hardly knew me, I was so tanned.

> Love,
> Eleanor

WRITING ASSIGNMENT   You have spent a weekend at the home of one of your friends. Following the suggestions above, write a bread-and-butter note to your hosts.

Letter Writing: The Form of the Business Letter

Since a letter represents you, its appearance is very important. A business letter should be written on business stationery, a white sheet 21 x 28 cm in size. The letter should be centred on the page. It should be neat and, if possible, typewritten.

The parts of a business letter are shown below.

1. The letter is centred on the page with equal margins at top and bottom and on both sides.

2. The *heading* is the same as the heading of a friendly letter. On business stationery with a printed heading, write only the date.

3. The *inside address* begins at the left margin a small distance below the

Heading	188 Pembroke Street Weston, Ontario M9A 5M7 May 2, 1984
Inside Address	Consumer Information 555 Yonge Street Toronto, Ontario M5C 3A2
Salutation	Gentlemen:
Body	I understand that you are distributing free of charge a booklet about things to look for when buying a new car. Please send a copy of the booklet to me at the address above. It will be helpful in a report I am making to my high school Industrial Arts class.
Closing	Very truly yours,
Signature	*Arnold Zimmerman* Arnold Zimmerman

A Model Business Letter

heading. In four lines it gives the name of the person or firm to whom the letter is written, the street address, the city and province, and the postal code. City and province are separated by a comma. A letter written to a person in a firm will have a five-line inside address. The person's name will then be the first line.

4. The *salutation* begins at the left margin. In a business letter it is *Dear . . .* followed by a colon (:). If you know the person's name, you will use it: *Dear Mr. White:, Dear Ms. Kennedy:*. If you do not know the specific name but have addressed the letter to Manager, Principal, etc., the salutation will be *Dear Sir:,* although it is understood that the person could be a man or a woman.

If you are writing to a firm, the salutation will be *Gentlemen:* (*Dear Sirs:* is also acceptable).

5. The first line of the letter is indented.

6. The proper complimentary close for a business letter is *Yours truly* or *Very truly yours,* followed by a comma. Only the first word is capitalized.

7. The signature is your full name. You may put (Mr.), (Mrs.), (Ms.), or (Miss) in parentheses before your signature.

EXERCISE A   On a sheet of paper, write the following inside addresses in correct form, adding omitted punctuation. Below each example write the salutation that should be used with it.

1. 16 Fitzroy Street
   Charlottetown, P.E.I.
   C1A 1R1
   Mrs. R. Smyth
   Tourism Parks and Conservation

2. 2313 St. Catherine Street West
   The Forum
   Montreal, H3H 1V2
   Quebec

3. Editor
   233 Main Street
   Vancouver, B.C.
   V6A 2S7
   The Chinese Voice

4. 2026 Hamilton Street
   Regina, Saskatchewan
   League for Human Life
   S4P 2C9

EXERCISE B   Write neatly in ink or type the business letter outlined below, arranging the parts correctly to make an attractive letter-picture. Plan your arrangement on a piece of scrap paper before actually writing the letter.

Home address: your own
Date: today's
Write to: General Foods Ltd.
           2200 Yonge Street
           Toronto, Ontario
           M4S 2C6

Supply the correct salutation.

Body of letter: Our high school Family Studies class has been studying nutrition and consumer buying habits. Will you please send us any literature on this subject which you have for free distribution?

Add the proper closing and your own signature.

Letter Writing:
The Contents of the Business Letter

While business firms are always pleased to receive mail orders for their merchandise, they often are forced to waste time and money because the orders are not clear. Sometimes the articles ordered are not clearly described; sometimes important details like the quantity or size are omitted. When you write an order letter, be sure the company receiving the letter will know exactly what you want.

Study the following order letter:

```
                                        483 rue Dolbeau
                                        Arvida, P.Q.
                                        G7S 4K4
                                        April 3, 1984

    Ace Sporting Goods Company
    245 Cartier Road
    Chicoutimi, P.Q.
    G7G 2X5

    Gentlemen:

        Please send me the following articles as listed
    in your spring catalogue:

    1 dozen Ace tennis balls                        $18.00
    2 prs. Walker tennis shorts, size 30 @ $13.00    26.00
                                          Total     $44.00
                              Taxes and Postage        5.56

        I am enclosing a money order for $49.56.

                              Very truly yours,

                              Robert Mitchell

                              Robert Mitchell
```

A Model Order Letter

WRITING ASSIGNMENT Write to the Murphy Cycle Company, 825 Cook Avenue, Don Mills, Ontario M3C 2A1. Order 2 Roadking tires No. 25B, @ $9.50; 1 Roadking lamp No. 2. price $8.89.

INDEX

Action verbs, 9
Address, inside of business letter, 276–77
Adjective clauses, 71
Adjective phrases, 65
Adjectives, defined, 5
  modified by adverbs, 15
  separated from words modified, 5
Adverb clauses, 73, 131
Adverb phrases, 67
Adverbs, adjectives modified by, 15
  defined, 13
  modified by other adverbs, 15
Agreement, 149–59
  of pronouns and antecedents, 159
  of subjects and verbs, 149, 151, 153, 155–56
  See also Number
-ant and *-ance*, 117
Antecedents of pronouns, 159
Appositive phrases, 85
Appositives, commas with, 123
Apostrophes, in contractions, 137
  for possession, 135, 137
  with pronouns, 137
As, pronouns used after, 199
Assimilation, and prefixes, 145, 165

Be, forms of, 39
Being as, being that, not used for *since* or *because*, 143
Both . . . and construction, and number, 153
Bread-and-butter note, 275
Bring, take, use of, 23
Business letters, 276–78

Capital letters, for geographical names, 105–06
  in quotations, 133
  for special groups and events, 107
  for titles, 109
Case, nominative, 191–92, 193
  objective, 191, 194, 195–96
Clauses, adjective, 71
  adverb, 73, 131
  defined, 69
  independent, 69
  introductory, 131
  noun, 75
  subordinate, 69, 87
Closings, of business letter, 276
  of friendly letter, 271
Collective nouns, 155–56
Colons, after salutation in business letter, 277
Command sentences, 35, 93
Commas, in addresses, 127
  for appositives, 123
  in compound sentences, 129
  in dates, 127
  for direct address, 125
  after introductory phrases and clauses, 131
  after introductory single words, 125
  misuse of, 95, 122
  for parenthetical expressions, 127

inside quotation marks, 133
  in series, 121
Common nouns, 105
Comparisons, use of, 231
Complements, 49
  subject, 49, 193
Composition
  choice of effective nouns and verbs in, 227–28
  comparisons used in, 231
  of letters, *see* Letters
  outline of, 263
  paragraphing, 263
  See also Paragraphs
Compound sentences, 129
Compound subjects, 35, 153
Compound verbs, 35
Conjunctions, adverb clauses introduced by, 73
  defined, 19
  items in series joined by, 122
  independent clauses joined by, 69
  subordinating, 73
Context of words, defined, 27
  total, 189
Contractions, apostrophes for, 137

Definitions of words, techniques of, 147
Direct address, commas for, 125
Direct objects, 51, 194
Direct quotations, 133

Either . . . or construction, and number, 153
End marks, *see* Exclamation points; Periods; Question marks
-ent and *-ence*, 101
Envelope form, for friendly letter, 271
Exclamation points, 93, 133

Fragments, sentence, *see* Sentence fragments
Friendly letters, 270–73

Good, well, use of, 23

Had, misused with *ought*, 143
Had of, misuse of, 205
Heading of letter, 270, 276
Helping verbs, 11, 39

Imperative sentences, *see* Command sentences
Independent clause, 69
Indirect objects, 53, 194
Indirect question, 93
Indirect quotation, 133
Infinitive phrases, 86
Inside address, of business letter, 276–77
Interjections, 19
Introductory phrases and clauses, 131
Irregular verbs, 170, 171, 173, 177, 179
Is when, is where, not used in definitions, 143
It's, its, use of, 137
Lay, lie, use of, 173, 175

Letters, business, 276–78
  friendly, 270–73
Lie, lay, use of, 173, 175
Linking verbs, 10

Model letters, 270, 272, 274, 276, 278

Neither . . . nor construction, and number, 153
Nominative case, 191–92, 193
Noun clauses, 75
Nouns, collective, 155–56
  common, 105
  defined, 1
  plural, 135
  possessives of, 135
  proper, 1
  singular, 135
  vivid, in composition, 227–28
Number, agreement in, of pronouns with antecedents, 159
  agreement in, of verbs with subjects, 149, 151, 155–56
  in *both . . . and, either . . . or*, and *neither . . . nor* constructions, 153

Objective case, 191, 194, 195
Objects, direct, 51, 194
  indirect, 53, 194
  of prepositions, 64, 195
  of verbs, 194
Of, misused with *had, off*, 205
Off of, misused for *from, off*, 205
Or, use of, and number, 153
Order letters, in business, 278
Ought, misused with *had*, 143

Paragraphs
  coherence in, 251–52
  definition of, 235
  descriptive, 257–58
  development of, 245–47
  expository, 259, 261
  narrative, 255–56
  outline of, 240
  topic sentence in, 235, 237, 240, 242, 245–46
  transitional devices in, 253–54
Participial phrases, 85
Participles, past, 85
  present, 39, 85
Parts of speech, determination of by how words are used in sentence, 19–20
Past participles, 85
Periods, inside quotation marks, 133
  sentences followed by, 93
Phrases, 85–86
  adjective, 65
  adverb, 67
  appositive, 85
  defined, 63
  infinitive, 86
  introductory, 131
  participial, 85
  prepositional, 17, 63, 65, 67, 131, 151

subjects followed by, and number, 151
verb, 11
Plural nouns, 135
Plural subjects, 153
Plural verbs, 153
Possessive pronouns, 137
Predicates, of sentences, 29
verbs in, 31, 39
Prefixes, and word meanings, 103
in spelling, 145, 165
Prepositional phrases, 17, 63, 65, 67, 131, 151
Prepositions, defined, 17
list of, 195
objects of, 64, 195
Present participles, 39, 85
Pronouns, agreement of with antecedents, 159
after *as*, 199
case of, 191, 193, 194, 195-96
defined, 3
as objects of verbs, 194
possessive, 137
selection of correct, in sentences, 196
as subject complements, 193
after *than*, 199
Proper nouns, 1
Punctuation, *see* Apostrophes; Colons; Commas; Exclamation points; Periods; Question marks; Quotation marks

Question marks, 93, 133
Quotation marks, 133

Raise, rise, use of, 179
Regular verbs, 169
Request letters, in business, 278
Request sentences, 35, 93
Rise, raise, use of, 179
Run-on sentences, 93, 95

Salutations, of business letter, 277
of friendly letter, 271

Schwa, the, 25, 45, 59, 81, 101, 117, 282
See, principal parts of, 169
Sentence bases, 29, 39, 49
Sentence combining
with adjectives, adverbs, prepositional phrases, 211-12
with adjective clauses, 217
with adverb clauses, 219
with appositives, 215
with compound verbs, nouns, and independent clauses, 213
with noun clauses, 221
with participial phrases, 216
Sentence fragments, 39, 85, 87
correcting, 89-92
Sentences, command, 35, 93
completeness in, 41, 85
compound, 129
defined, 29, 41
end marks for, 93
predicate of, defined, 29
run-on, 93, 95
subject of, defined, 29
topic, *see* Topic sentences of paragraphs
Set, sit, use of, 177
Signature, in business letter, 277
Simple subjects, 33
Singular nouns, 135
Singular subjects, 153
Singular verbs, 153
Sit, set, use of, 177
Social notes, 274-75
Somewheres, misuse of, 205
Spelling, prefixes, 145, 165
the schwa, 25, 45, 59, 81, 101, 117, 281
the sound /-əl/, 81
the sound /-ər/, 59
the sound /k/, 187
the sound /kw/, 207
suffixes, 59, 81, 101, 117
Subject complements, 49, 193
Subjects, compound, 35, 153
as essential part of sentence base, 39
followed by phrase, and number, 151
help in finding, 35, 37
in nominative case, 191-92

plural, 153
of sentence, defined, 29
simple, 33
singular, 153
understood, 35
after verbs, 155
Subordinate clauses, 69,87
Subordinating conjunctions, 73
Suffixes, and word meanings, 103
in spelling, 59, 81, 101, 117
Synonyms, 61

Take, bring, use of, 23
Tense, consistency of, 181
Than, pronouns used after, 199
Thank-you note, 274
That there, misused for *that,* 205
This here, misused for *this,* 205
Topic sentences of paragraphs, 235, 237, 240, 242, 245-46

Verbs, action, 9
agreement of with subject, 149, 151
compound, 35
defined, 9
finding subjects of, 37
helping, 11, 39
irregular, 170, 171, 173, 177
linking, 10
objects of, 194
plural, 153
in predicates, 31
regular, 169
singular, 153
subjects following, 155
tense of, 181
vivid, in composition, 227-28
Vocabulary skills, and context, 27, 189
and prefixes, 103
and suffixes, 103
and synonyms, 61
and word definition, 47, 83, 119, 147, 167, 209

Ways, misuse of, 206
Well, good, use of, 23

INDEX OF VOCABULARY WORDS

(Page numbers refer to definition in text.)

Abject, 209
Administer, 83
Administrator, 83
Adorn, 167
Adornment, 167
Advocate, 148
Agile, 83
Agility, 83
Allege, 62
Allude, 209
Allusion, 209
Anticipate, 209
Anticipation, 209
Arduous, 167
Aspiration, 83
Atrocious, 119
August, 189

Beset, 167
Bicker, 148
Bluster, 148
Bountiful, 189

Cataclysm, 148
Compassion, 62
Compulsory, 209
Condescend, 148
Contagion, 119
Contagious, 119
Contemporary, 27
Contemptuous, 62
Controversial, 103
Cringe, 209
Cultural, 103

Deficiency, 62
Definitive, 209
Degenerate, 47
Deliberate, 27
Delicate, 62
Denounce, 119
Denunciation, 119
Depict, 47
Diminutive, 47
Discreet, 119
Discriminate, 189
Docile, 62

Eccentric, 189
Elocution, 148
Enhance, 62
Ensue, 47

Equilibrium, 27

Faction, 83
Fragile, 47

Gesture, 189
Glamorous, 83
Glamour, 83
Grapple, 27
Grotesque, 83

Heedless, 83

Immaterial, 103
Impact, 119
Imperious, 189-90

(Vocabulary Words, continued)

Inadequate, 103	Managerial, 103	Prudent, 47	Sloth, 167
Incompetent, 103	Mar, 147		Slothful, 167
Inconsistent, 27	Mediocre, 190	Query, 167	Slovenly, 167
Indignant, 190	Migraine, 147		Stamina, 209
Indignation, 190		Radiant, 190	Subsist, 119
Inertia, 28	Notoriety, 61	Radiate, 190	Succumb, 167
Infer, 47		Rational, 62	Sulk, 83
Inference, 47	Omen, 47	Rebate, 47	Sulky, 83
Inflexible, 104		Reconcile, 103	Supersede, 83
Insoluble, 119	Perspective, 190	Rectitude, 148	
Intelligent, 62	Pessimism, 119	Recuperate, 119	Ungovernable, 103
Intercept, 167	Pessimist, 119	Recur, 209	Unintelligible, 104
Invincible, 167	Pessimistic, 119	Refrain, 104	Unpalatable, 104
Isolate, 167	Phenomenal, 209	Renown, 61	
	Piety, 148	Reputation, 61	Valid, 83
	Placid, 62		Validity, 83
Lament, 148	Pretext, 148		Vivacious, 119
Liability, 28	Profound, 47	Seditious, 209	

A NOTE ON SPELLING

Writing may be thought of as a way of recording the sounds of speech by the use of symbols that represent those sounds. The letters in our alphabet are the symbols we use to represent our speech sounds. If we had a different letter for each sound, spelling would be easy; just a matter of knowing which letter to use for each speech sound. Unfortunately, English spelling is not that simple. There are more sounds than there are letters in the alphabet to represent them, and so the task of learning to spell in our language is somewhat complicated.

The complications, however, may be partially overcome by becoming aware of, and learning, the many *spelling patterns* that do exist. These patterns involve the use of various combinations of letters of the alphabet to spell certain sounds.

To show the *sounds* of a word, rather than the letters, a special phonetic alphabet has been developed. Using this phonetic alphabet will help you understand the relationship between sounds and letters, and thereby help you to become a better speller.

On pages 282 and 283 are two charts. The first one, entitled "Consonant Sounds and Their Common Spellings," summarizes 24 main consonant sounds of English, the symbols used to represent these sounds, and common ways of spelling them. The *symbol* for each consonant sound is written between a pair of slanted lines. For example, the symbol /k/ stands for the sound of the first letter in the word *kit,* as you can see by looking at the chart. The sound /k/ may also be spelled by the letters *c* (as in *cold*), *ck* (as in lick), or *ke* (as in *like*).

The second chart, "Vowel Sounds and Their Common Spellings," shows the symbols for 14 main vowel sounds, and the vowel sound called a *schwa.*

If you look at the vowel sound /ī/ on the chart, you will see the several patterns or ways in which this sound may be spelled. For example, in the word *line,* it is spelled with the letter *i* followed by a consonant (*n*), which, in turn, is followed by an *e.* (The letters **VCe,** standing for *vowel, consonant, e,* represent *one* of the ways or patterns in which the sound /ī/ may be written in English.) Other ways include *-igh* as in *high; -y* as in *try; -ie* as in *die.*

The spelling patterns reflected in these two charts should help to balance the irregularities in English spelling. The point is, that *despite* exceptions and seemingly illogical spellings, our spelling system exists as it does for good historical reasons, and is, on the whole, a predictable system.

Consonant Sounds and Their Common Spellings

Sound	At the Beginning	At the End
/p/	**p:** pie	**p:** rip; **pe:** ripe
/t/	**t:** ten	**t:** pet; **te:** date
/k/	**k:** kit; **c:** cold	**ck:** lick; **ke:** like
/ch/	**ch:** chin	**tch:** witch; **ch:** reach
/b/	**b:** bed	**b:** tub; **be:** tube
/d/	**d:** do	**d:** rid; **de:** ride
/g/	**g:** get	**g:** beg; **gue:** league
/j/	**j:** jet; **g:** gentle	**dge:** budge; **ge:** cage
/f/	**f:** fun; **ph:** phrase	**ff:** stuff; **fe:** life; **f:** beef; **ph:** paragraph
/v/	**v:** very	**ve:** save
/s/	**s:** see; **c:** centre	**ss:** glass; **s:** bus; **se:** case; **ce:** rice
/z/	**z:** zoo	**z:** quiz; **zz:** buzz; **se:** rose; **ze:** sneeze
/sh/	**sh:** ship	**sh:** push
/zh/	**j:** Jacques	**ge:** rouge; (in the middle) **s:** treasure
/r/	**r:** run; **wr:** wrist; **rh:** rhyme	**r:** car; **re:** care
/l/	**l:** lose	**ll:** pill; **le:** smile; **l:** fail
/m/	**m:** move	**m:** Sam; **me:** same; **mb:** tomb
/n/	**n:** nose; **gn:** gnaw; **kn:** know	**n:** pin; **ne:** pine
/ng/		**ng:** strong; **n:** trunk
/th/	**th:** thick	**th:** path
/t̶h̶/	**th:** then	**th:** smooth; **the:** bathe
/y/	**y:** you; **u** /yū/: use	
/w/	**w:** will; **o** /wu/: one; **qu** /kw/: quick	
/h/	**h:** hat; **wh:** who	

Vowel Sounds and Their Common Spellings

Fourteen Vowel Sounds

Sounds	/i/	/e/	/a/	/u/	/o/
Spellings and Examples	**i:** hit	**e:** red **ea:** dead	**a:** cat	**u:** but **o:** son	**o:** top **a:** far

Sounds	/ī/	/ē/	/ā/	/ū/	/ō/
Spellings and Examples	**VCe:** line **igh:** high **y:** try **ie:** die	**VCe:** Pete **ee:** deed **ea:** heat **e:** he **ie:** chief **ei:** deceive	**VCe:** lame **ai:** wait **ay:** pay **ei:** weigh	**VCe:** June **oo:** root **ew:** few **ue:** Sue **o:** to	**VCe:** lone **oa:** goat **ow:** slow **oe:** hoe **o:** no

Sounds	/o͞o/	/ou/	/oi/	/au/
Spellings and Examples	**oo:** look **u:** push	**ou:** out **ow:** cow	**oi:** oil **oy:** toy	**au:** haul **aw:** flaw **a:** ball **o:** long **ough:** fought **augh:** caught

The Vowel Sound Schwa /ə/

	i	e	ea	u	o
In Words of One Syllable	stir girl	were her	learn earth	burn spur	world worse

	-er	-or	-ar	
The Sound /ər/	runner maker father	actor orator navigator	beggar liar sugar	

	-al	-le	-el	-ul	-ile	-il
The Sound /əl/	legal moral rural	steeple battle circle	camel satchel travel	beautiful useful helpful	fertile juvenile hostile	April evil council

	-en	-an	-ain	-in
The Sound /ən/	frozen deepen oaken garden	Canadian orphan woman organ	captain curtain mountain certain	robin cabin basin cousin